More Praise for *A People's History of the European Court of Human Rights*

"A passionate work that skillfully combines a passionate narrative with the scientific quality that is necessary for useful comparative thought."

—Dean Spielman, *Revue trimestrielle des droits de l'homme*

"Mr. Goldhaber's unique and fascinating work . . . represents the exercise of a legal journalist's professional skills as an interviewer combined with extensive reading of the academic literature. . . . Overall, those of us who focus on the jurisprudence of the Court will find this book a valuable extension of our understanding of the backgrounds to a number of major cases, and others more generally interested in human rights will gain an intriguing perspective on the ECHR system."

—Alastair Mowbray, *Human Rights Law Review*

"Mr. Goldhaber seizes extremely well the spirit in which human rights were practiced at the early stages of the existence of the European Commission and Court of Human Rights. . . . I had the privilege of living through many of the cases which he describes so well and with the human touch that one can never get in simply reading the judgments and decisions. I recommend the book to all those who are interested in this important part of our law."

—Hans Christian Krueger, Secretary Emeritus,
European Commission of Human Rights

"I love this book. I bought a copy, read it from cover to cover, then lent it to one of my colleagues who has never given it back. A really fascinating piece of research."

—Clare Ovey, legal officer, European Court of Human Rights

"I must admit that I started reading and could hardly stop. I heard the same from some fellow judges. It is a wonderful piece of work. For us judges, it is useful to also every now and then have the possibility to read a narrative story not only of the Court's work, but also about some individual applicants in leading cases, the impact the judgments had, and the aftermath. I hope this will not be the last book Mr. Goldhaber writes on the Court's work."

—Egbert Myjer, Judge of the European Court of Human Rights

"I am very pleased that this book has been written, as there is a real need, in light of U.S. Supreme Court decisions, for greater understanding of the European experience."

—John Dugard, Chair in Public International Law, Universiteit Leiden

"I learned quite a bit from *A People's History of the European Court of Human Rights*, and can't find much to disagree with. The ECHR still does not have its 'insider' exposés as the U.S. Supreme Court has had, and this book comes closest to filling that lacuna. Mr. Goldhaber deserves congratulations for an excellent job."

—Giovanni Bonello, Judge of the European Court of Human Rights

"I finished the book almost in one sitting and greatly enjoyed it. I found it, at different times, funny, poignant and inspiring. Mr. Goldhaber covered an immense amount of ground in a very short period. I certainly recommend the book to anyone wanting an introduction to the ECHR and seeking to understand its importance."

—Matthew Happold, University of Hull

"*A People's History of the European Court of Human Rights* is an extraordinarily gifted and poignant narrative and I will certainly encourage my class to read it."

—Upendra Baxi, University of Warwick

"A wonderfully written and researched book that celebrates Europe's achievements in defending human rights through the stories of the victims who took their complaints to the European Court of Human Rights."

—Kevin Boyle, Human Rights Centre, University of Essex

"A gripping account of the stories behind the cases that have made European human rights jurisprudence the force for moral good that it is today."

—Conor Gearty, director, Centre for the Study of Human Rights,
London School of Economics

*A People's History of the
European Court of Human Rights*

A People's History of the European Court of Human Rights

MICHAEL D. GOLDHABER

Rutgers University Press
New Brunswick, New Jersey, and London

First paperback printing, 2009

Library of Congress Cataloging-in-Publication Data

Goldhaber, Michael D.
 A people's history of the European Court of Human Rights / Michael D. Goldhaber.
   p.   cm.
 Includes bibliographical references and index.
 ISBN-13: 978-0-8135-3983-6 (hardcover : alk. paper)
 ISBN-13: 978-0-8135-4461-8 (pbk. : alk. paper)
   1. European Court of Human Rights—History. 2. Constitutional law—Europe.
3. Courts—Europe. I. Title.
   KJC5138.G64 2007
   341.4'8094—dc22

                                                                2006015373

Manufactured in the United States of America

*To Zeki Aksoy, who gave his life
to establish Europe's ban on torture.*

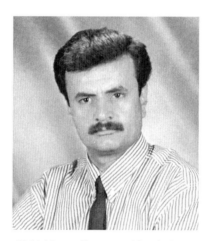

Zeki Aksoy. *Courtesy of Serif Aksoy*

Contents

ACKNOWLEDGMENTS

I would like foremost to thank my wife, Shoshana, and my parents, Sandy and Miriam, for their patience and support. Had I not promised Serif Aksoy that I would honor his son's bravery, this book would be dedicated to them. I'd like to thank my editor, Adi Hovav, my agent, Wendy Weil, and Wendy's colleague, Emma Patterson, for adopting a project that defied category. For helping me keep faith until my book found a home, I'd like to thank my friends in London, Tom Blass, Danny Collins, John Nichols, Tara Pepper, Jeremy Stephenson, and Deepak Vohra; my lifelong friends in the United States, Etan Ayalon, Michael Levitt, Mark McCarren, Rami Levy, David Schizer, Jon Spira-Savett, and Jonathan Springer; and my sister, Aliza Menche, and her family. For their keen insight and institutional memory, I would like to thank Kevin Boyle of Essex University and Michael O'Boyle of the European Court of Human Rights registrar's office. I could not have written this book without my dogged translators, notably Nazmi Gur in Turkey, Malika Magomadova in Ingushetia, and Cenda Ruzieka in the Czech Republic. The British Library, the Royal Courts of Justice Library, and the Middle Temple Library were generous with their access, as was the European Court of Human Rights Library. The Kurdish Human Rights Project sponsored my second reporting trip to Turkey, as part of a fact-finding mission on freedom of expression and the implementation of European Court decisions. Finally, I would like to thank my editors at *The American Lawyer* magazine, Aric Press and Amy Singer, for giving me the flexibility to pursue this independent project while serving as their correspondent in London from 2001 to 2003.

A People's History of the
European Court of Human Rights

Europe's Supreme Court

The exceptionality of the United States Supreme Court has long been conventional wisdom. The dean of American Court watchers, Anthony Lewis of the *New York Times*, once declared, "The Supreme Court of the United States is different from all other courts, past and present. It decides fundamental social and political questions that would never be put to judges in other countries." Lewis was self-consciously echoing the French traveler Alexis de Tocqueville, who was amazed by the reach of America's judges in his own day. The social role of U.S. law was indeed distinctive in the 1830s, when Tocqueville published *Democracy in America*, and even more so in 1964, when Lewis wrote *Gideon's Trumpet*, his classic tale of a simple man fighting for his rights. But the United States has changed since the civil rights era, and so has the world. Memo to Anthony Lewis and Alexis de Tocqueville: the U.S. Supreme Court today has a peer in articulating public rights and values. Arguably, the other court is setting the pace.

Over the past thirty years, the European Court of Human Rights has developed an American-style body of constitutional law, comparable in its level of ambition, and in many ways more progressive. Unheralded by the mass press, this obscure tribunal in Strasbourg, France, has become, in many ways, the Supreme Court of Europe. Interpreting the European Convention on Human Rights, it is the judicial arm of the Council of Europe—a group distinct from the European Union, and much larger. The Council of Europe is the vestige of an early postwar attempt at European unity that largely failed but is quietly succeeding in the realm of human rights. Forty-seven members strong, the Council of Europe stretches from Vladivostok to Reykjavik. It includes Turkey, Russia, and the nations of the Caucasus but excludes the nations of Central Asia. It covers every nation that is at least partly in geographical Europe, except for Belarus, Kazakhstan, Kosovo, and the Vatican. Within this area live some 800 million people, speaking at least 28 languages.

Leading jurists have hailed the Strasbourg court as an embryonic constitutional chamber, or a supreme court in utero. Scholars invariably describe it with superlatives. Among the world's systems of human rights, it has been dubbed "the most advanced and effective"; "pre-eminent"; the "most successful"; "certainly the most fully developed and the best-observed"; "no doubt the most developed and successful." The diplomat and scholar Antonio Cassese proclaims, "[N]o other human rights treaty can claim the level of influence of the European Convention." Another professor calls the Strasbourg tribunal "a sort of world court of human rights." An overeager journalist went so far as to argue that the U.S. Supreme Court "is being upstaged in its traditional role as the world's most powerful and innovative legal body."

The Strasbourg court is a civil court, where individual Europeans sue European nations for violating their human rights. By human rights, Europeans mean what Americans mean by constitutional rights: fundamental norms that are grounded in a basic document. That embraces things like "no torture," which is what Americans think of as a human right. It also embraces what the people in the United States would call civil liberties—equal protection, due process, privacy, and First Amendment freedoms. In short, human rights are about values.

The European court routinely confronts nations over their most culturally sensitive, hot-button issues. And—what is most extraordinary—the nations comply. Strasbourg has, for example, stared down France on the issue of Muslim immigration; Ireland on abortion; Greece on Greek Orthodoxy; Turkey on Kurdish separatism; Austria on Nazism; Britain on gay rights and corporal punishment. On the whole, it is an impressive record of political courage and achievement.

In the public mind, these achievements are lost in the welter of supranational courts. Even the fictional barrister Horace Rumpole, in the short story "Rumpole and the Rights of Man," can't keep his courts straight.

"So we're off to The Hague, are we?"
"*You* may be, Mr. Rumpole, but the Court of Human Rights sits in Strasbourg."
"Of course! That's the one I meant."

In truth, The Hague courts are very different. The international criminal court and tribunals are about holding individuals accountable for genocide. The International Court of Justice (or "World Court") is about states suing other states over boring things like borders. The Strasbourg court, to repeat, is about individuals suing nations for violations of human rights.

What really throws people is the European Court of Justice (ECJ) in Luxembourg. As the high court of the European Union (EU), the ECJ can lay its own claim to the title of Europe's Supreme Court. But the ECJ covers only twenty-seven nations, and it only incidentally touches on human rights. In effect, the two courts divide the functions of the U.S. Supreme Court between them. Because the EU has evolved into something like a federal government, its court must resolve challenges to federal regulation and it must allocate power, both within the EU and between the EU and its member states. (In U.S. parlance, these are questions of separation of powers and federalism.) Preoccupied by these practicalities, Luxembourg has largely left to Strasbourg the debate over rights. Thus, while the EU court is of great economic consequence, the Strasbourg court has taken the lead in defining European values and identity. (For more about the relationship between the two courts, see chapter 16.)

Europe's Conscience

Limiting Strasbourg to human rights began as a British delay tactic. The Council of Europe's Continental founders had ambitious ideas for European unity, which later found expression in Brussels. But during the 1949 debate that gave rise to the Strasbourg system, the British foreign secretary, Ernest Bevin, foiled attempts to give the Council of Europe social, economic, military, or diplomatic powers. He saw judicial rights as a "field where it could do no harm." Less cynically, human rights was seen throughout Western Europe as an idea whose time had come.

The vision for a Council of Europe was laid out by Winston Churchill in a pair of wartime speeches. With such a council's help, Churchill hoped to see the war end with "the enthronement of human rights." Keeping an eye on the eastern front, he specifically envisioned that the Council of Europe would "eventually embrace the whole of Europe, and all the main branches of the European family." Later, Churchill would call for the creation of a court that would bring human rights violations "to the judgment of the civilised world."

The British writer H. G. Wells spelled out the logic behind the human rights response to the war in a best-selling wartime tract called *The Rights of Man, Or What Are We Fighting For?* He described a chat he had about human rights with some draftees who had heard early stories about Nazi concentration camps. "When they realised reluctantly that such things could still be done in the heart of Europe," their reaction was: "These Nazis are *too* bad." To their mind, the war's aim must simply be that "such things must happen no more on earth."

A 1949 pamphlet by the Brussels-based European Movement justified the European court on similar grounds. Nuremberg showed that the world community can and should be concerned with the fate of individuals in another sovereign state. What the European Movement envisioned was "an international code of civilised conduct" and "a system of collective security against tyranny and oppression." If there was even a remote chance that the European court would have prevented Hitler's rise to power, then it was justified. And in the view of the European Movement, those chances were more than remote: if the court had existed in 1932, it would "without doubt" have condemned the acts that cleared the way for Hitler.

In his opening speech at the 1949 convention that created the Council of Europe, France's Pierre-Henri Teitgen called the "sovereignty of justice" the only sovereignty worth dying for. During a debate the next month, Teitgen proclaimed it the role of the court to be the conscience of Europe.

Court Mechanics and Enforcement

The cases in this book revolve around a few basic sets of rights. Article 2 of the European Convention on Human Rights guarantees the sanctity of human life. Article 3 bans torture and inhuman or degrading treatment. Article 5 safeguards the rights of detainees. Article 8 patrols the right to respect for private and family life, broadly conceived. Article 9 bestows freedom of religion, Article 10 freedom of the press, and Article 11 freedom of assembly. Article 14 prohibits discrimination. Intended only as a sampler, this book gives scant attention to the trial rights of Article 6, or the right to property contained in Protocol 1, Article 1.

The Council of Europe's procedures were overhauled in 1998. In the old days, cases were initially heard by the European Commission on Human Rights, which would issue a nonbinding report. Cases could then be referred for judgment to the European Court of Human Rights (ECHR). In 1998 the Commission was eliminated. Cases that are deemed admissible are generally heard in the first instance by a chamber consisting of seven judges. Judgments can then be referred to a grand chamber of seventeen judges.

Although the European Convention authorizes both individual suits and interstate suits, legal battles between nations have been rare and restrained. The reason is that sovereign states don't like establishing precedents that can be used to bite back at them later. By contrast, a legal system founded on individualism taps an inexhaustible fount of grievance and imagination.

Business was slow for thirty years after the European Convention was signed in 1950—so slow that a judge in the 1960s could give a lecture entitled "Has the European Court of Human Rights a Future?" The Convention gathered momentum—at first slowly, and then furiously—as more members ratified the right to individual petition, new members joined, and human rights entered the public consciousness. In 1966, the United Kingdom accepted the principle of individual petition. Italy, Switzerland, France, Spain, and Portugal did the same between 1973 and 1981. Beginning in 1990, the nations of Eastern Europe signed on in full. The cumulative result was exponential growth. Over the past quarter century, the caseload has grown by two orders of magnitude—from 404 applications in 1981 to approximately 45,000 in 2005. Today's court holds seminars on its caseload crisis.

Among the world's international courts, Europe's two "supreme courts" are unique in commanding near-total compliance by nation states. By the reckoning of legal theorist Anne-Marie Slaughter, they are "as effective, for the most part, as national court rulings." This is more amazing as it relates to Strasbourg, because deference to the EU is more clearly about economic self-interest.

The human rights court works by shaming European nations. Technically, the court has two main powers. First, it can order a state to pay compensation to an individual. Generally, this is a piffling amount by American standards, in the tens of thousands of euros. More importantly, it can declare a state to be in violation of the European Convention on Human Rights—and require the state to give an "effective remedy." An effective remedy often means a change in law. But how does the Council of Europe compel a sovereign state to change its law?

The key enforcement role is played by the Council of Europe's executive and legislative arms: the Committee of Ministers and the Parliamentary Assembly. Until it is deemed in compliance, a state in violation must report on its progress to the Committee of Ministers, which is composed of a representative from each nation's foreign ministry. Although a given judgment only applies to the respondent state, it often has implications for law throughout Europe. The Parliamentary Assembly, which includes delegations from each state's legislature, will prod states to bring their laws into conformity. Under proposed Protocol 14 to the European Convention, the Committee of Ministers would have the additional power to sue a non-complying state in a grand chamber of the court. Protocol 14 will take effect if it is ratified by Russia, which was the only state not to embrace it as of late 2006.

In extreme situations, noncomplying members can be booted from the Council of Europe by a two-thirds vote of the Committee of Ministers. The threat of suspension is Strasbourg's most powerful lever, because membership in the Council of Europe is a prerequisite to membership in the European Union. In the 1990s, after the fall of the Berlin Wall, the ex-Communist states rapidly joined the one European club that was eager to admit them. Even today, for much of the former Communist world, Strasbourg remains the public face of Europe. In effect, the Council of Europe is the EU's antechamber.

If a violation persists, individuals can keep filing and winning suits under the principles of the European Convention—either in Strasbourg or in the domestic courts. With the coming into force of the United Kingdom's Human Rights Act in 2000 and the Irish ECHR Act in 2004, the law of European human rights is operative in the domestic courts of every member state. That makes domestic courts a driver of enforcement and uniformity in their own right.

On a case-by-case basis, Strasbourg's record of enforcement is impeccable. For years, *Loizidou v. Turkey* was cited as the great exception, but in December 2003, as part of its push to join the EU, Turkey complied with that judgment and paid $650,000 to honor a Cypriot property claim. The tougher question is the extent to which the European Court of Human Rights can achieve systemic change, like the abolition of torture. We return to that important question in chapter 12.

Court Reform

Despite the mounting importance of the European Court of Human Rights, judicial selection has been a backroom affair. One judge from each nation sits on the court. Each nation nominates a list of three candidates for its seat by a method of its own choosing, generally by executive appointment. The task of choosing among the candidates falls to the Parliamentary

Assembly, where representation is weighted by national population. Under current rules, the judges may be elected for renewable terms of six years, until they retire at age seventy.

However, in 2003, a blue-ribbon panel chaired by Jutta Limbach, former president of Germany's Constitutional Court, criticized the current process harshly. It concluded, generally, that the national selection methods "are politicized and lack transparency." Indeed, it cited instances where a nation seemed to punish its judge for voting his mind, by not renominating him. Reform came swiftly. Under proposed Protocol 14, which opened for signature in 2004, judges would serve for one nonrenewable term of nine years.

The ECHR is rightly preoccupied by its caseload crisis. The court's backlog reached an alarming 82,100 applications by October 2005 and was projected to pass an overwhelming quarter of a million applications by 2010. Perhaps 95 percent will be ruled inadmissible. But even so, Strasbourg's 2005 rate of nearly a thousand judgments per year is more than ten times the pace of the U.S. Supreme Court. The former European Court of Human Rights President, Luzius Wildhaber of Switzerland, has called it a "worrying and frankly excessive amount."

There is an inevitable tension between individual and systemic justice. President Wildhaber has argued that both pragmatism and the nature of the Strasbourg system argue in favor a systemic approach. His ideal is fewer and prompter judgments, "revealing the structural problems which undermine democracy and the rule of law." Leaders of civil society fret that Strasbourg will abandon big new goals, like seeking equality for the Roma of Central Europe (see chapter 15), and resort to shortcuts.

One way of cutting corners is to skimp on fact finding. On-site hearings were crucial to Strasbourg's first Kurdish cases, in the mid- to late 1990s, because Turkish courts failed utterly to create a factual record. Human rights advocates cry that the Court should have held on-site hearings in the Kurdish right-to-life case of *Matyar v. Turkey* (2002). In the future, such a procedure could be essential in Roma and Chechen cases where the facts are disputed and local investigations untrusted.

But the most controversial shortcut is the "strikeout"—a procedure that was created by the reforms of 1998. In *Akman v. Turkey* (2001), the court invoked European Convention on Human Rights Article 37 and, for the first time, "struck out" a right-to-life case against the will of the claimant. One law journal ran an article about the *Akman* case entitled "Letting States Get Away with Murder." Turkey satisfied the court by paying the Akman family compensation, making a unilateral statement of regret, and promising appropriate measures to avoid future incidents. Mr. Akman's lawyers objected that the admission was murky, and Turkey did not undertake a new investigation of the incident. When the court struck out another pair of Kurdish claims, in *T.A. v. Turkey* and *Togcu v. Turkey* (2002), the dissent warned bluntly that—rather than pushing states to make real change—the court was encouraging states that face serious complaints to unilaterally buy them off. Finally, in *Acar v. Turkey* (2003), a grand chamber of the court set limits on the use of strikeouts. *Acar* held that, to obtain the strikeout of a disappearance case, the state must admit to an inadequate investigation, and undertake a new one. The concurrence offered hope to the human rights community—stressing that strikeouts should remain an exceptional, case-by-case procedure.

In the long run, no one maintains that the caseload crisis should be solved by striking out cases and skimping on fact finding. The Council of Europe, in consultation with human rights groups, held a long debate over further reform, culminating in May 2004 with proposed Protocol 14. Under the new system, three-judge committees would hear the "repetitive" cases that form perhaps two thirds of the court's caseload. At the same time, a single judge would have the power to strike out a case or declare it inadmissible. The wording of the new standards of inadmissibility (Article 35) was a matter of keen debate. In the new system, a case may be ruled inadmissible if "the applicant has not suffered a significant disadvantage, unless respect for human rights . . . requires an examination of the application on the merits and provided that no case may be rejected on this ground which has not been duly considered by a domestic tribunal." How this standard is interpreted would of course matter urgently.

But the caseload crisis is so severe that Protocol 14 came to be regarded as a Band-Aid solution even before it could take effect. A Group of Wise Persons was appointed in May 2005, including Lord Harry Woolf, who retired several months later as England's chief justice. A committee led by Lord Woolf issued a review of the court's working methods in December 2005, as a prelude to a new comprehensive reform plan.

"Whatever Human Rights Are"

When I was posted to London by *The American Lawyer* magazine from 2001 to 2003, I scanned the Continent for the best untold stories. I was astounded to find Strasbourg neglected by journalists. The saga of European rights has yet to be popularized because, in Europe, the legal press limits itself to trade gossip, and the general press is blinded by nationalism.

My human rights interest was piqued early in my posting by a quirky personal experience. Under a petty UK law (since repealed), my cocker spaniel/poodle puppy, which I had brought with me from the United States, was locked in a quarantine cell for six months. I sometimes joked with London barristers that I ought to sue. To my surprise, some of them responded by offering to represent me. It turns out that European human rights guarantee the development of a rich personal life, and a fair argument can be made that this includes the right to frolic with one's puppy. After a little research, I decided that this argument wasn't quite strong enough to justify suing. But I was amazed at the strangeness and power of rights in Europe. I kept researching, and started traveling, and soon discovered cruelties that made me embarrassed by the triviality of my entry point.

I've traveled and met with landmark plaintiffs in a dozen far-flung corners of Europe: Belfast and Glasgow, Antwerp and Lyon, Vienna and Ankara, Murcia and Lorca, Athens and Crete. I've interviewed the Kurdish torture victims of Diyarbakir, the Roma slum kids of Moravia, and the Chechen refugees of Ingushetia. This book is the story of how a few ordinary men and women have created the constitutional law for a continent.

I dedicate the book to Zeki Aksoy, who, I believe, was killed for bringing to life the ban on torture under the European Convention. When I interviewed Zeki's father, I expected to find a mild old man who could give me a sense of his son as a person, who could tell me Zeki's favorite color and football player. Instead, I discovered a tough dissident who, unbeknownst to the human rights community, had himself been tortured dozens of times by Turkish authorities, as well as castrated. When I asked Serif Aksoy if he had a message for the European judges, he gave a deceptively simple answer. "Whatever human rights are," he said, as we looked across the Bosphorus from Europe to Asia, "let the judges realize them." Serif's words echoed in my mind as I flew back to London.

This book covers a diverse range of human rights through the personal tales of a few colorful plaintiffs. Among others, it tells the story of the Belgian single mom who fought to make bastardy legitimate. The story of the Ulster activist who made Europe safe for gay sex. Of the Spanish housewife who constitutionalized environmentalism. And of the deaf-mute Muslim rapist whom France couldn't deport. This book shows what happens when an Austrian journalist dares to call Jorg Haider an idiot; and when a Jehovah's Witness witnesses to the wife of a Greek Orthodox cantor in

Crete. It tells the tale of a Kurdish village girl who didn't know the word for rape, and a Kurdish city woman who used the money she recovered for harassment to found a women's shelter. The tale of the Roma school kids who are shunted into Czech schools for the retarded. And the story of a Chechen physics professor, who was first bludgeoned from behind by a Chechen rebel and then shot from behind by Russian soldiers.

Although the villains in this book are European nations, neither Europe nor nations have a monopoly on violence. The horrible stories of Aksoy, Imakayev, or McClean could easily be retold with Latino, African, or Asian names. I focus on Turkey, Russia, and Britain for the simple reason that they volunteered to be held accountable. Of the countless regimes in world history that committed violence against their own citizens, only they acted under the supervision of an effective human rights court. A wholly different book could be written about the atrocities committed by the insurgent Kurds, Chechens, and Irish Republicans. In neglecting these stories, I do not mean to minimize them, or to take a side in those conflicts. Criminal law can hold insurgents accountable. But a human rights treaty protects individuals only against offenses committed by nations.

The vignettes in this book have been selected for their legal significance and personal drama—as well as for the urgency of the social problems they represent. Though each narrative can stand on its own, I have tried to briefly place each in legal and historical context, with special attention to contrasts between Europe and the United States. The chapters are loosely grouped thematically.

The first six essays deal with the astonishing range of rights that Europeans conceptualize under the rubric of privacy or family life. We begin with the more intuitive forms of privacy, pursued by the feminist movement (chapters 1–2) and the gay rights movement (chapters 3–4). From there we progress to the court's creative but halting interpretation of privacy to advance environmentalism (chapter 5) and immigrants' rights (chapter 6).

The next batch of vignettes concern freedom of thought and expression—what Americans call First Amendment liberties. Chapter 7 explores the religious rights pioneered by the Jehovah's Witnesses. Chapter 8 examines press freedom in the sensitive context of Austrian historical memory. Chapter 9 relates the court's debatable refusal to let Islamists associate politically.

A third section delineates the limits of state violence in all its varied forms. Chapter 10 lays out the leading cases on corporal and capital punishment. Chapter 11 tells the story of the Irish "hooded men," who, a generation before Abu Ghraib, exposed the horrors of psychological torture. Chapters 12 and 13 detail the all-too-physical tortures of Turkish Kurdistan, which sorely tested the court's ability to force systemic change.

A final pair of case studies looks at the leading challenges for the future presented by the young states of Eastern Europe. In the case of Chechnya (chapter 14), the court must again find the political courage to confront extreme abuses, and the ingenuity to enforce its judgments against an obdurate member state. In the case of the Roma (chapter 15), the court must innovate, both legally and institutionally, to counter deep and pervasive discrimination in the face of a mounting caseload crisis. While the Council of Europe has been slow to embrace a full right to equality, the court is largely rising to the challenges posed by the Chechens and the Roma. The court's long-delayed ruling on Roma desegregation affirms its ability to perform its core role of protecting unpopular minorities (including Muslims) in the face of a caseload crisis.

In broad perspective, Strasbourg's antifascist origins have left their mark on its jurisprudence. Even as the court has pushed the frontiers of human rights in unimagined directions (chapters 1–6), it has fulfilled its original purpose by striving honorably to halt Europe's later lapses into barbarism (chapters 10–15). But if antifascism has fortified the court in its confrontation with state violence, it has watered down the court's protection of free expression in all its forms (chapters 7–9). This failing, too, has worrying consequences for Europe's Muslim minority.

Although human rights are universal, the European and American versions differ markedly. It is the uncharted space between the two that this book tentatively explores. In that space lie both clues to the European identity (chapter 16), and lessons for American justice (chapter 17). Americans should care about European rights law because, on the whole, it presents a progressive parallel universe. Europeans should care because it shapes their collective sense of self. I have tried to mine this rich, little-known body of law for the human stories that might inspire both constitutive and comparative thought. My hope is that, in the pages that follow, some readers will discover new heroes.

PART I

The Expanding Ambit of Personal Life

CHAPTER 1

Why Bastard?

Wherefore should I
Stand in the plague of custom, and permit
The curiosity of nations to deprive me . . . ?
Why bastard? Wherefore base?
> —Edmund the Bastard
> *King Lear*, act 1, scene 2

*W*hen Paula Marckx discovered she was pregnant at the age of forty-seven, she blessed her luck. A single journalist in Antwerp, Paula joked that her pregnancy might have something to do with her recent visit to a pagan fertility shrine in Greece, but then again the boyfriend with whom she'd visited Corinth wasn't the father. The source of her luck didn't matter to Paula. She knew instantly that she would keep the baby and have nothing to do with the father. She would be a mother.

Or so she thought.

Baby Alexandra was born without mishap on October 16, 1973. A few weeks later, Belgium sent Paula a letter explaining Alexandra's legal status as a child born out of wedlock. The more Paula read the letter, the angrier she got. She was no mother at all, it seemed.

Under Belgian law, an illegitimate baby was not legally recognized as its mother's without a judicial declaration. In earlier times, that had been the rule in France and most of Europe, under the Napoleonic Code. Hence the popular limerick:

A handsome young bastard named Ray
Was conceived on the Rue de la Paix.
According to law,
He can name you his maw,
But as for his pa, je ne sais.

Paula was in the first place insulted by the notion that she didn't automatically qualify as a mother. Then she discovered that—paradoxically—if she took the step of recognizing her baby, that would sharply limit the baby's inheritance rights. Paula hardly expected to die rich—whenever she had any money, she blew it on exotic travel—but she wanted to give Alexandra what she could.

Finally, even if Paula recognized the baby, in Belgian law the baby would be a stranger to the mother's family. That meant Alexandra couldn't inherit from Paula's mother and sister if they died without wills. And when Paula died, Paula's mother or sister couldn't become Alexandra's guardian.

Paula drove to Antwerp's Palace of Justice and stormed through the neo-Renaissance entrance arch flanked by bronzes of Lady Justice. She barged into the office of a justice of the peace and bitterly denounced Napoleon and the King of Belgium. The judge, a middle-aged woman with short blonde hair, mildly agreed from behind her desk: "Yes, this law is revolting." She and her staff had clearly heard from irate single mothers before. The court clerk, who happened to overhear the conversation, mused aloud: "Women always protest but are never prepared to take action."

Paula Marckx took that as a challenge. After all, she'd spent her life defying one man or another's expectations.

Paula's father had always wanted her to join the civil service. Instead, when she was a teenager, Paula became a fashion model and decided to write a French novel. Her father laughed that she didn't know the language, but Paula taught herself French. Her novel, *La Route Sinueuse,* won a prize at the Brussels Expo of 1958, and her interviewers suggested she try journalism. Within a few years she was interviewing Europe's leaders for *Gazet van Antwerpen.* In 1967, she became the first woman pilot trained in Antwerp—so she could earn extra money shuttling diamond dealers around Europe. In 1972, her boyfriend at the time suggested that she start her own business, taunting her, "But I suppose you can't do it—you can't keep still for long enough." Paula's answer was to start an answering service.

So on the day in 1973 when a court clerk dared Paula to do something about the Belgian bastards law, Paula took the dare seriously. It happened to be December 10, which the United Nations (UN) marks each year as Human Rights Day to commemorate the 1948 adoption of the UN Declaration on Human Rights (UNDHR). That evening, on the television news, Belgian Justice Minister Herman Vanderpoorten talked about the human rights of Third World children. Paula thought to herself, "That's all well and good, but what about the human rights of babies in Belgium?"

Thus was born the lawsuit that brought to life the European Convention on Human Rights.

"I Am a Ten-Month-Old Baby . . ."

One of Paula's employees at the answering service was a law student, and Paula got from her a copy of the European Convention. Paula scanned the page, and her eyes lit on Article 8, guaranteeing the right to personal and family life. Well, she thought, a baby is family. In March 1974, Paula wrote a complaining letter to Strasbourg in her own name. The court wrote back that she personally had no standing, because her rights, as a mother, were not violated. Paula didn't know law, but she got the general idea, and she knew how to create publicity. In the summer, she wrote a second letter to the court, this one in Alexandra's name.

"Messieurs," the letter began, "I am a ten-month-old baby." "I hope with all my heart," the letter ended, "that a baby of my age can count on an institution like yours to protect her rights."

Paula leaked the letter to a journalist friend, and it made great headlines ("Je suis un bébé et je porte plainte . . ."). In September, the court deemed the complaint admissible. The legal adviser of the Belgian Justice Ministry later told Paula on the train to Strasbourg, "When we heard that a baby was suing Belgium, we had a big smile. But when we learned that the baby's mother was a journalist we weren't smiling anymore."

Of course, as the court politely reminded her, a journalist alone could take the case only so far. Paula needed a lawyer.

In 1974, Leonora "Moni" Van Look was a twenty-seven-year-old family law research assistant at the Catholic University of Louvain, one of Europe's oldest centers of higher learning. Moni won an essay contest that year in honor of the International Year of the Woman; the essay, entitled "The Pattern of Legal Gender Roles," argued that marriage should be legally irrelevant. At the reception after the prize ceremony, she ran into Tilly Stuckens, an old friend from women's liberation circles at Louvain. Stuckens knew Paula through her sister, who ran the parking garage where Paula parked her car. The two women got to talking about Paula Marckx, Strasbourg, marriage, and feminism.

There's nothing new about the feminist reaction to marriage in Europe. In 1528 an unwed Antwerp teacher named Anna Bijns wrote a paean to singlehood with the tagline, "Marriage would be fine if it weren't plagued with worry." Olympia de Gouges, the French revolutionary feminist who penned the Declaration of the Rights of Woman, was the bastard child of a nobleman. Among the rights she declared was the right of an unmarried female citizen to say to the man who has impregnated her, "I am the mother of your child." Unfortunately, De Gouges was ahead of her time in this as in other respects; she was sent to the guillotine in 1793.

Paula didn't read feminist history or poetry; she was single merely because she was a free spirit. Moni, by contrast, never married on principle. By 1974 she had already been living for six years with her boyfriend, who was a promising lecturer. "We were from the flower power generation," she recalls, "and we saw no point in getting married." She adds with distaste, "The only reason to marry would be for money, to get a pension."

Moni and Paula were at the leading edge of a larger European trend. From 1972 to 1984, marriage in the EU zone went into free fall, declining from about 7.7 to 5.7 per thousand of population. According to the 1990 World Values Survey, 20 percent or more of people in France, Belgium, and the Netherlands believed that "marriage is an outmoded institutions," as opposed to 8 percent in the United States. More than a quarter of EU births are out of wedlock. That's slightly lower than the rate in the United States, but the EU average is brought down by Greece and Italy. In today's Sweden more than half of births take place outside marriage, and in Iceland nearly two thirds. My anecdotal impression is that—in educated circles—single motherhood is far more acceptable in Europe than in the United States. During my posting as a journalist in London, five of my six office mates were helping to raise children out of wedlock. I have known only one American bachelor with a baby—and that baby is being raised by his European mother in Europe.

Moni began to help Paula with her paperwork and soon was designated her lawyer. In July 1976 the two travelled to Strasbourg for their hearing before the European Commission on Human Rights (which, before the institutions were reorganized in 1997, was effectively the court of first instance in Strasbourg). Not only was it Moni's first court case; it was also the first time that a woman lawyer was arguing in Strasbourg.

Paula and Moni bonded at Strasbourg's Grand Hotel on July 12—the night before the hearing—as they fed carbon paper into Moni's Olympia electric typewriter and finished their briefs. Though they each had strong views on marriage, they agreed that their stronger legal argument was on the rights of children. They also discovered that they both identified as Sagitarians—difficult, individualist fighters who loved adventure and hated injustice.

The next morning, they saw a sign in big letters on the courtroom's marquis: "PAULA AND ALEXANDRA MARCKX V. BELGIUM." "It was such a funny feeling," remembers Paula. The two women faced fifteen commission members, all men, and mostly elderly. But the northern European judges asked friendly questions—"Is it really possible you still have such a law in Belgium?"—and Moni's hopes rose. On December 10, 1977, the commission ruled in favor of the Marckxes. It was, perhaps not coincidentally, Human Rights Day, exactly four years after Paula saw the television interview that inspired her.

Moni reargued the case before the European Court of Human Rights itself in October 1978, and the wait for judgment resumed. Paula felt that public opinion was with her, even among her opponents. Belgium's representative to the Council of Europe sat down next to her and whispered, "Never mind my boss; I think you're right." A lawyer who helped draft Belgium's briefs, who knew Moni from the women lawyers' association, admitted, "I hope you win." Leona Detiege, a single mother who was then an alderman and later became Antwerp's mayor, declared her support. Belgian public radio asked Alexandra, by then five years old, to deliver a New Year's greeting to the children of the world to kick off 1979, the International Year of the Child.

Alexandra and Paula Marckx v. Belgium

The judgment fittingly arrived that year, on June 13. The vote varied from issue to issue, but on the broadest basic question, whether, vis-à-vis Alexandra, Belgium violated the Article 8 right to family life, in conjunction with the Article 14 right to equality, the court voted 13 to 2 in favor of Alexandra. The court held incompatible with the European Convention "measures whose object or result is, as in the present case, to prejudice the 'illegitimate' family."

In historical perspective, the court's reasoning was more significant. The court took a strong and lasting stand for interpreting the Convention dynamically, according to the spirit of the day, and not according to some notion of original intent. In particular, the court cited liberal amendments to the laws governing bastards in Germany, Britain, the Netherlands, France, Italy, and Switzerland. The majority wrote:

> It is true that, at the time when the Convention of 4 November 1950 was drafted, it was regarded as permissible and normal in many

European countries to draw a distinction in this area between the 'illegitimate' and the 'legitimate' family. However, the Court recalls that this Convention must be interpreted in the light of present-day conditions [citation omitted]. In the instant case, the Court cannot but be struck by the fact that the domestic law of the great majority of the member States of the Council of Europe has evolved and is continuing to evolve.

With this passage, the court signalled that, in interpreting the Convention, it would rely heavily on the trend in European legislation. In effect, it would force backward states to enact legal reforms embraced by their neighbors. *Marckx v. Belgium* was an unabashed mandate for an assertive European court.

As is often the case, the significance of the majority opinion is made plainer in the dissents. Fighting a losing cause, Sir Gerald Fitzmaurice of Britain wrote a classic critique of judicial activism and dynamic interpretation.

The postwar drafters of European Convention Article 8 didn't care about the minutia of illegitimate inheritance. If that were their concern (Sir Gerald might have noted) they could have adopted a clause from the UNDHR: "All children, whether born in or out of wedlock, shall enjoy the same social protection." Rather, their debates show, Article 8's drafters aimed to prevent Orwellian intrusions into the home. As Sir Gerald wrote:

> [The individual] and his family were no longer to be subjected to the four o'clock in the morning rat-a-tat on the door; to domestic intrusions, searches and questionings; to examinations, delayings, and confiscation of correspondence; to the planting of listening devices; to restrictions on the use of radio and television; to telephone tapping or disconnection; to measures of coercion such as cutting off the electricity or water supply; to such abominations as children being required to report upon the activities of their parents, and even sometimes the same for one spouse against another,—in short, the whole gamut of fascist and communist inquisitorial practices such as had scarcely been known, at least in Western Europe, since the eras of religious intolerance and oppression, until (ideology replacing religion) they became prevalent again in many countries between the two world wars and subsequently. Such, and not the internal, domestic regulation of family relationships, was the object of Article 8.

Be that as it may, Western Europe by 1979 had the luxury of worrying about the inheritance rights of bastards, and Alexandra Marckx became the first beneficiary of Article 8.

By and large, the decision was well received—in the streets and in the courts. The day after the judgment, Paula went to pick Alexandra up from her Catholic kindergarten. The senior nun, who considered single motherhood a statement against abortion, gave Paula a big smile and said, "We prayed for you." *Libelle* magazine, the main Flemish weekly, voted Paula Belgium's Woman of the Year for 1980.

The first legal consequence, unexpectedly, was in the Netherlands. In January 1980 the Dutch Supreme Court, applied the *Marckx* decision directly. It invalidated a Dutch law that, because the child was nonmarital, barred a woman from adopting her four-year-old niece after her sister's death. The Netherlands quickly passed a new law in response—known as the "Little Marckx Law."

While the lower Belgian courts also complied quickly with the *Marckx* ruling, the Cour de Cassation, jealous of Belgian sovereignty, resisted. In May 1985, a Cour de Cassation ruling refused to give *Marckx* direct effect. The European Commission declared this a new violation of the Convention and at last shamed Belgium into action. In 1987, Belgium prospectively amended the parts of the family code attacked by the Marckxes, and, the Commission declared the case closed. The Commission might have added that the old limerick about "the bastard named Ray" was officially obsolete. As she neared her fourteenth birthday, the girl who sued Belgium at ten months had won.

The Rights of Personality

The *Marckx* case established a level of constitutional protection for nonmarital children that the United States has yet to match. In *Labine v. Vincent* (1971), U.S. Supreme Court Justice Hugo Black compared the relationship between a parent and an illegitimate child to the relationship between a man and his concubine: both pairings are "illicit and beyond the recognition of law." In that case, the Court approved a state inheritance law that discriminated against bastards inheriting from their natural fathers. *Labine* has since been contradicted, but it has never overruled. Analyzing the issue in terms of the right to equality, rather than the right to family life, the U.S. Supreme Court has always declined to treat birth status as a "suspect classification," as it treats race or gender. As a result, in American law to this day, it is acceptable to make distinctions partly on the basis of birth status.

More broadly, the *Marckx* decision launched the Strasbourg institutions on a constitutional voyage—pushing the boundaries of family life—that has no parallel in American law. In principle, the European Commission on Human Rights had for many years endorsed a broad concept of family rights whose origins may be traced to the 1949 West German Basic Law. In *X. v. Iceland* (1976), the Commission had recognized that the right of private life may include "the right to establish relationships with other human beings, especially in the emotional field, for the development and fulfilment of one's own personality." Marckx began the process of actualizing that principle, and delimiting it.

Privacy's evolution in Strasbourg tracked the evolution of privacy in Bonn. The human dignity clause in the German basic law too was originally intended to protect against torture. But in the words of former German chief justice Ernst Benda, "modern man's dignity is not endangered by totalitarian tools of suppression but rather by the complexities of modern life." Germany's right to freely develop the personality covers everything from informational privacy to transsexual rights. Landmark rulings extended protection to divorce records (1970), transsexuals (1979), and census records (1983). Self-consciously influenced by Kantian notions of dignity, the German Constitutional Court reasoned that human beings should not be treated as mere "information objects." Interpretive technique places little emphasis on original intent, and much on modern social conditions.

To be sure, Strasbourg's zone of privacy doesn't cover every imaginable domestic right. In the "Icelandic Dog case" (1974), the Commission refused to create a constitutional right to keep a pet. "No doubt the dog has had close relationships with man since time immemorial," the Commission noted. "However, . . . this alone is not sufficient to bring the keeping of a dog into the sphere of the private life of the owner." In a series of later rulings, including *Brock v. United Kingdom* (1996), the Commission rejected challenges to an English law mandating that pit bulls be killed. If I may be forgiven some special pleading, I'd argue that Strasbourg might have reached a dog-friendly result had the test plaintiff been the owner of a twenty-two-pound, buff-colored American cocker spaniel/poodle.

In another restrictive ruling—known as the "Finnish Nickname case"—the Commission refused to create a constitutional right to change a name that's easy to make fun of. "Although the applicant's present name gave rise to an unfortunate nickname and was often misspelt," the Commission concluded in *Stjerna v. Finland* (1994), "this was not sufficient suffering or inconvenience to trigger Article 8." A dog with a dumb nickname is doubly out of luck.

Other limits on Strasbourg's idea of family rights are more serious. Article 8 of the European Convention on Human Rights doesn't guarantee a right to divorce. See *Johnston v. Ireland* (1987). It doesn't provide a right to paternal parental leave. See *Petrovic v. Austria* (1998). And, according to the European Commission on Human Rights, it doesn't protect the right to abortion. See *Paton v. United Kingdom* (1980).

Yet there is no doubt that the dominant theme of Article 8 jurisprudence is expansive. The right to family encompasses polygamy, in the estimation of the the European Commission on Human Rights. See *Alam, Kahn and Singh v. United Kingdom* (1967). "Family" covers the relationship between a woman, her transsexual partner, and a child born to the woman by artificial insemination from an anonymous donor. See *X., Y. and Z. v. United Kingdom* (1997). "Family" also describes the relationship between a man and a woman who had chidren together but were never llinked by marriage or cohabitation. See *Kroon v. Netherlands* (1995).

In Europe, informational privacy is a constitutional right. *Silver v. United Kingdom* (1983) found that Britain's censorship of prison correspondence violated Article 8. A trio of major rulings updated this philosophy by finding police phone wiretap laws too broad. See *Malone v. United Kingdom* (1984); *Kruslin v. France* (1990); and *Huvig v. France* (1990). It's noteworthy that the earliest of these landmarks on informational privacy came in 1983, the year of Germany's landmark census case, and 1984, the year of Orwell's Big Brother prophecy. The EU's Charter on Fundamental Rights, now under debate, would formalize the constitutional status of informational privacy.

As we shall see in the ensuing chapters, the European Court of Human Rights respects the right for women to receive information about abortion; the right of gay people to make love; and the right of gays to serve in the military. The court has used the right of family unity to sharply limit the power of states to deport criminal aliens.

The rights of personality are not confined to the realm of emotional relationships. Most radically—as we shall see in chapter 5—the court has defined personal life to include the right to a healthy environment.

In Europe, privacy even ringfences business premises. *Niemietz v. Germany* (1992) found the search of a lawyer's office in support of a criminal investigation unacceptable. The court reasoned that it is "in the course of their working lives that the majority of people have a significant, if not the greatest, opportunity of developing relations with the outside world." Europe thus took judicial cognizance of the fact that professionals (and especially lawyers) have no life outside work.

The breadth of Strasbourg's family jurisprudence begs a central question of judicial politics: why has the court historically chosen Article 8 as the vehicle for its activism? More particularly, why did it choose *Marckx v. Belgium* as the occasion to begin asserting itself?

The scholar Marc Salzberg has offered two thoughtful answers. First, he says, at the time of the *Marckx* decision, the European Union's European Court of Justice in Luxembourg was starting to come into its own. To be blunt, the European Court of Human Rights in Strasbourg (which, to repeat, is an organ of the Council of Europe and has nothing to do with the EU) felt the need to compete—to prove its relevance.

Second, Belgium's discrimination against bastards was the right kind of issue. The Belgian law's unfairness was blatant. It was an aberration in Europe as a whole. And, at the same time, the law was too trivial for the court's ruling to threaten the respondent state's dignity excessively. Exactly the same may be said for Ulster's antisodomy law, discussed in chapter 2.

Another scholar, Howard Charles Yourow, has suggested that *Marckx* followed soon after the last of the big European nations accepted the full jurisdiction of the European Court of Human Rights. A spate of new memberships to the Council of Europe in the mid-1970s brought new judges to town and created a new consciousness of the Strasbourg option in the legal community.

To these answers, it might be added that the *Marckx* case pressed the right political buttons. The insight behind Paula Marckx's publicity stunt is valid: everyone loves a ten-month-old baby. In Washington, D.C., "children's rights" are a stalking horse for antipoverty legislation. Likewise, in Strasbourg, a cute baby blazed the path for less popular plaintiffs like criminal aliens.

Surely the *Marckx* cause also benefited from a sympathy for women's rights proper, just as the *Dudgeon* cause (see chapter 3) benefited from a vogue for gay rights. In both *Dudgeon* and *Marckx*, the clients met their lawyers thanks to contacts formed in the radical campus movements of the late 1960s. The influences felt by judges are harder to document, but in the 1970s liberation was still in the air.

Finally, it may be ventured that European elites are permissive on sexual issues, certainly by American standards. Look at the historical progression in Article 8 jurisprudence, from the rights of women, children, and gays to the rights of criminal aliens and the victims of pollution. The progression suggests that the court first expanded Article 8 in the context of sexual issues on which there existed a broad consensus. It then used the extraordinarily broad precedents that were established under Article 8 to push the frontiers on more controversial social issues only tangentially connected to the family.

Postscript

Today, Alexandra Marckx is well into her thirties. She bumps into her natural father at the supermarket from time to time, but he is not a part of her life and never has been. After travelling the world as an au pair, Alexandra studied dog grooming and photography. Now, with her mother, she is an Internet entrepreneur—they run a Web site called petsandgo.com that offers advice for traveling with pets.

The octogenarian Paula Marckx holds down two jobs, as a Web entrepreneur and as a public relations executive for Antwerp's airport. The Web site evolved out of a book on traveling with pets that Paula published on a dare. She still occasionally gets behind the controls of an airplane and has recently published her memoir.

Thirty years of practicing divorce law have very much confirmed Moni Van Look's views on marriage. She still lives in unwed bliss with her boyfriend, Josse Van Steenberge, who became the dean of the University of Antwerp. They had three children together—all of whom, obviously, stand to benefit from the *Marckx* ruling. Moni's second son learned about *Marckx* in civics class, but being a cynical teenager, he didn't volunteer that it was his mother's first big win.

Finally, an update on Flemish feminism. In 1995, *Antonia's Line*, a Dutch-Flemish co-production, won the U.S. Academy Award for best foreign film. It tells the story of three generations of women on a Dutch farm, each of whom proudly chooses to have a baby out of wedlock. In one of the film's crucial scenes, the character Danielle tells her mother Antonia that she wants a baby. "How about a husband to go with it?" asks Antonia. "I don't think so," deadpans Danielle. Arguably, Paula Marckx is as much Danielle's forebear as is Antonia. Certainly, Danielle owes Paula a debt of gratitude. Thanks to the changes wrought by *Marckx*, there's no doubt that Danielle can inherit the farm.

CHAPTER 2

When Irish Eyes Are Crying

*T*he American antiabortion movement failed to push through a constitutional amendment in 1982. The next year, it tried the same strategy overseas, and succeeded. In 1983, U.S. and Irish activists collaborated to engineer Ireland's Eighth Amendment, which "acknowledges the right to life of the unborn." The early consequences were grimly antilife.

In 1984, the Irish public was mesmerized by a series of abandoned-baby dramas. In County Longford, fifteen-year-old Ann Lovett was found dead by the body of her infant son in a church grotto beside a statue of the Virgin Mary. In County Kerry, a newborn baby with a battered head and multiple stab wounds was found on the beach. A young Kerry woman named Joanne Hayes, whose pregnancy had ended mysteriously at the same time, was arrested and pressured into a confession. But it turned out that the newborn on the beach wasn't Joanne's. Hers was yet a third baby, found stuffed in a fertilizer bag and abandoned in a muddy field.

Those who favored a right to abortion had seen enough abandoned babies in Eire. They realized that, in order to combat a globally organized antiabortion movement, they too needed to go global. European courts would be their forum of choice.

The Counseling Wars

In the late 1980s, in Ireland as in America, the abortion wars shifted to a new front, from surgical clinics to counseling clinics—and the question of abortion information. In 1985, two activists from Ireland's Society for the Protection of the Unborn Child (SPUC) posed as pregnant women pondering abortion. The undercover pro-lifers got advice from Ireland's only two clinics: Open Door Counselling and Dublin Well Woman Centre. Armed with evidence from these two women, SPUC sued the two clinics in Irish court. In December 1986 a trial court ordered the clinics to stop giving any pregnancy counseling. It would be scandalous, reasoned Justice Liam Hamilton, if the validity of the right to life depended on a flight over St. George's Channel.

Open Door Counselling shut its doors. Well Woman Centre could no longer tell pregnant women their options (although it continued to give counsel on contraception). Libraries hid away their copies of *Our Bodies, Ourselves*. In early 1988 the Irish Supreme Court upheld the trial court, but narrowed the injunction. Now counselors were only barred from telling women where to find an abortion clinic or helping them to travel.

Of course, diehard feminists found ways around the court's diktat. Instead of waving coat hangers, Irish pro-choice marchers chanted the phone number for their favored abortion clinic, in Ealing in West London. They scrawled the number on lady's toilet stalls throughout Dublin—in pubs, in schools, and in medical suites.

Another favorite trick was to subtly refer women to the phonebook, where—thanks to the European Union—English abortion clinics were listed. After SPUC sued Dublin student leaders for listing English clinics in their school manual, the European Court of Justice ruled that a service provider in one EU state has the right to advertise in another. Knowing that English clinics were listed, the Well Woman folks would always keep a phonebook prominently displayed in the lobby and ask their clients suggestively, "Have you looked anywhere?" "It came down to a nod and a wink," remembers one counselor. The phonebook always seemed to fall open to the right page.

But chanting numbers and dog-earring phonebooks were stopgap measures. If abortion activists were ever to end the phenomenon of abandoned babies in the Irish countryside, they needed to challenge the ruling on abortion information in Strasbourg.

The story of *Open Door Counselling v. Ireland* begins with an American Catholic housewife named Bonnie Maher. Bonnie was pregnant and married to a dentist in San Diego in 1973, when the U.S. Supreme Court recognized the right to abortion. *Roe v. Wade* inspired Bonnie to enter the feminist movement. She chose to keep the baby but drop the dentist, and she eventually found her way to Dublin, where she became a founding counselor of the Well Woman Centre. Enraged by what she viewed as entrapment by SPUC, she volunteered to sue Ireland in Strasbourg, alongside her colleague Ann Downes, and the clinics themselves. To add to the list of named plaintiffs, the lawyers felt it was important to find ordinary women who had gone through counseling. Bonnie recruited Maeve Geraghty and Deirdre Dowling. Dublin being a small town, Maeve is Bonnie's niece. Dublin being a very small town, Deirdre was once married to Bonnie's present husband.

Maeve and Deirdre were shrewdly chosen plaintiffs, for they dramatize the range of women's experience. Maeve got pregnant young and opted for abortion. Deirdre got pregnant later and chose to carry the baby to term. Together they illustrate the genuine commitment of the abortion movement to choice.

A Tale of Two Choices

When I met Maeve Geraghty she wore a nose ring. Her head sprouted the scraggly beginnings of dreadlocks. She sported tattoos of a Celtic rope knot on her bicep and a Celtic warrior-woman on her ankle.

While Maeve may be a free spirit, she isn't the type you'd expect to get into trouble. Through her Aunt Bonnie, the counselor at Well Woman, she had been the unofficial condom supplier for her friends from the time she was fifteen. Maeve always made her boyfriend use a condom, but the odds caught up with them. She became pregnant in 1988. She was eighteen, living in a small flat with her nineteen-year-old boyfriend, collecting welfare.

The way Maeve ordinarily dealt with a crisis was to talk about it to anyone who'd listen. But no one would listen. Back then, no one was comfortable talking about abortion in Ireland, not even her best friend in private. If she mentioned the a-word at a party, the room would go silent. For lack of another shoulder to cry on, Maeve went to the Well Woman clinic during her fifth and sixth weeks of pregnancy. The counselors walked her through the consequences of making either decision, to have a baby or to have an abortion. What was the worst thing that could happen? How would everyone react at school? At home? How would that make her feel?

The night after her second session, Maeve dreamt that she awoke at midnight in a hotel and heard a baby crying. She went to the diaper-changing table in the lady's room and saw her baby lying in a bassinet: a chubby-cheeked newborn girl, with Maeve's ruddy complexion. The baby spoke to her, saying, "No, no, it's fine. You can leave me here. Someone else will pick me up." Maeve awoke from her dream and forgave herself. Her decision was made.

Maeve's dad made her boyfriend pay for half the abortion, but, as Maeve saw things, her boyfriend was too much of a screwup to be at her side. At the airport on his way to join her in England, he was caught carrying a switchblade, arrested, and thrown in jail for three days.

After the procedure, Maeve shaved her head bald and tattooed a hemp leaf on her wrist, as a declaration of freedom. When I met her, Maeve was considering having a baby with her new boyfriend. But she felt no regrets about her abortion. In the intervening years, Maeve had traveled around Europe for antiglobalization protests. She had joined a well-known puppetry troupe, the Macnas of Galway Street Theatre, and helped to display a fifty-foot Gulliver on the River Liffey. In short, she says, abortion gave her the gift of youth.

Deirdre Dowling is twenty years older than Maeve and was a decade older when she struggled with the abortion choice. Deirdre boasts of being expelled at fifteen from the Loreto Convent School in Balbriggan for planning an escape, but she comes across as a timid rebel.

Deirdre had two sons with her first husband (who is now married to Bonnie Maher). Deirdre was the one to leave the marriage, and, consequently, didn't qualify under Irish law for single-mother benefits. In early autumn 1979, she marched up and down Main Street in Dunlaoire with her two small boys in a go-cart, looking for her first job. She landed a part-time accounting gig for thirty pounds a week. Pope John Paul II visited Ireland that autumn and Deirdre listened to his pro-life speeches on television with cynicism. Then, suddenly, she discovered she was pregnant, and the choice was no longer abstract.

Deirdre was a twenty-nine-year-old single mother of two with no money. Her boyfriend (who later became her second husband) was six years younger and terrified. Her family was politically progressive for Ireland, but abortion was still off-limits. Deirdre used a psychoanalyst as her counselor. She hated to do something that would please the Pope, but influenced by her analyst's life-affirming philosophy, Deirdre had the baby. She named her Lauren.

Deirdre did not allow her choice to stop her from self-realization, any more than Maeve did. She went back to college at thirty-five, when her Lauren was five, and became an etcher and art historian at University College, Dublin.

Lauren is part of a new generation that must struggle with the eternal question of abortion in a society that remains hostile to the idea. When Lauren was eleven, a male teacher at her state-funded Catholic school asked who in the class of thirty believed in abortion. Lauren was one of only five children who raised their hands. The teacher made Lauren stand up and hounded her with hypotheticals. Lauren stood her ground; she believed in choice.

Lauren's existence underscores that what the clinics advocate is not abortion, but choice. It is impossible to know whether the ban on abortion counseling, when it was in effect, increased or decreased the net number of abortions. Both Maeve and Deirdre believe that, ironically, *more* babies would have been born if all pregnant women had had the benefit of abortion counseling. These, too, may be seen as babies abandoned in consequence of the pro-life crusade.

An Irish Door Reopened

The Open Door Counselling case was ultimately decided less in Strasbourg than in the court of Irish public opinion. It was driven by another of the public pregnancy dramas that periodically roil Ireland.

In December 1991 a fourteen-year-old girl known as X was raped by a friend of the family, and impregnated. The girls' parents asked the Irish police, the Garda, to investigate the rape. Upon learning that the girl's parents planned an abortion, the Garda instead referred them for prosecution. In February 1992 a trial court barred the family from leaving Ireland for nine months. The girl and her parents—already in England, en route to an abortion clinic—flew back as soon as they learned of their legal jeopardy. On the trip back from London, the girl told her parents that she wished to throw herself under a train. The Irish public became obsessed with the desolate girl. In March the Irish Supreme Court reversed the trial court decision on the grounds that the girl was suicidal, and the injunction put her life in danger. X had her abortion, and the Irish public was relieved.

The X case gave the European Court of Human Rights an easy way to resolve *Open Door Counselling v. Ireland*, in its judgment of October 1992. While professing it impossible to find "a uniform European conception of morals," the court held that a state's power to protect morals is limited, and Ireland's policy on abortion counseling went too far. Ireland had perpetually barred the Open Door and Well Woman clinics from offering a woman advice about getting abortions abroad—regardless of the woman's age or mental state, or the circumstances of her pregnancy. Yet when the Strasbourg judges pressed at oral argument, Ireland's attorney conceded that an exception had to be made for a fourteen-year-old girl, like X, who was raped and became suicidal. The X exception in itself justified the court's conclusion that Ireland's policy was overbroad. But the court also found it significant that the Irish counseling was nondirective, and the ban placed pregnant women's health at risk.

The next month, in November 1992, Ireland held a referendum. The people endorsed the rights of an Irish woman to learn about abortion overseas and travel abroad to obtain an abortion. In December 1992 these rights became enshrined in the Thirteenth and Fourteenth Amendments to Ireland's constitution. The victory was formally complete when, in May and June of 1995, the Dail passed a corresponding law, and the High Court lifted the injunction against Dublin Well Woman Centre.

Open Door Counselling v. Ireland represents a sharp contrast with the U.S. Supreme Court case of *Rust v. Sullivan* (1991). Under that ruling, family planning clinics that receive federal funding are barred from helping pregnant women find abortion doctors. Should a woman ask, the clinic must inform her that it does not consider abortion an appropriate method of family planning.

An Irish Door Still Closed

But, before we give Europe another gold star, it needs to be recalled that, in the same 1992 referendum, Ireland rejected a proposed amendment to legalize abortion. There was no recourse in Strasbourg, because Europe has never endorsed the right to choice. At least three cases have presented Strasbourg with the chance to broadly regulate abortion. In *Bruggemann and Scheuten v. Federal Republic of Germany* (1977), two feminists challenged West Germany's less-than-absolute guarantee of abortion. The European Commission on Human Rights declined to hold that the Article 8 right to privacy and personal life encompasses the woman's right to choose abortion. In *Paton v. United Kingdom* (1980), a husband tried to stop his wife from having an abortion. The commission declined to hold that the Article 2 right to human life encompasses a fetus's right to life.

In the more recent case of *Vo v. France* (2004), a doctor had confused Thi-Nho Vo with another Ms. Vo being treated at the same hospital. The doctor made a mistake that led to the abortion of the fetus carried by Thi-Nho Vo. The French Court of Cassation reversed the doctor's conviction for unintentional homicide on the grounds that a fetus is not a human being. The would-be mother wanted the European Court of Human rights to force France to give her a criminal cause of action and recognize the fetal right to life. The court refused, reasoning that Vo was free to sue the doctor for civil damages, and that would be enough to vindicate any rights that might have been violated. On the larger question presented, the Strasbourg judges once again dodged. They found it unnecessary to decide whether there exists either a right to fetal life or a right to abortion.

Finally, in *Tysiac v. Poland* (2007), a grand chamber of the court repudiated Poland's procedures for denying women therapeutic abortion. The court held that, if a nation guarantees a woman the right to abortion under any conditions (even very narrow ones), then a European nation's positive obligations to safeguard privacy entitle a pregnant woman to a due process hearing to determine whether she has met those conditions. This was a wise and efficacious ruling, but it fell far short of imposing a broad right-to-choose on Ireland, Malta, or Poland. As concurring judge Giovanni Bonello of Malta wryly wrote, *Tysiac* did not summon into being a "fundamental human right to abortion lying low somewhere in the penumbral fringes of the Convention." That's judgespeak for: "This ain't *Roe v. Wade*."

The constitutional abortion regime in Strasbourg is thus the mirror opposite of the regime in the United States. In the United States, there is a right to choice pockmarked with numerous exceptions, including a feeble right to health information. In Europe, there is a robust right to health information in the absence of a right to choice. That's of little solace to a poor and ignorant pregnant woman in rural Ireland.

At the start of 1994—a decade after Ireland's "pro-life" amendment and the shocking tragedies of Ann Lovett and the Kerry babies—three more infants were found abandoned in the waterways or ditches of rural Ireland. Ruth Riddick, who was the longtime director of Open Door Counselling, wrote an angry commentary in the *Irish Times*. "We like to think that we've come a long way in 10 years," she wrote. Yet, she noted, even those who get abortion often can't find counseling, especially outside Dublin. Unless abortion counseling became available outside Dublin, she warned, history would repeat itself. Tragically, Riddick proved right. Dead babies continued to be found in the Irish countryside in the second decade after the "pro-life" amendment. In a country where women lack the right to abortion, the right to abortion information is fragile and inadequate.

CHAPTER 3

Gay in a Time of Troubles

A poet in Belfast in 1975 could be excused if he had nothing left to say about violence. John Hewitt would later be honored with that highest of Irish laurels, an eponymous pub. But on Thursday evening, July 3, he was searching for new material. He dropped in at the Belfast Students' Union on the Queens University campus. It was the first open meeting of the Committee for Homosexual Law Reform in Northern Ireland.

Ulster was the last place in Britain, and one of the few in Europe, where gay sex remained illegal. Not just illegal, but punishable by life in prison. "Whosoever shall be convicted of the abominable crime of buggery," said the 1861 law on the books, "shall be liable to be kept in penal servitude for life." Hewitt found inspiration in the blithe students and the workers "with rough-rasped workshop voices" who refused to live under this threat. "They were," he wrote, "lads linking with us against our laggard law which leaves them unpermitted, out of step."

The meeting's minutes show that the lads drew up a wide agenda for action: posters, pickets, letters to the editor. And, almost as an afterthought, "Explore the possibility of approaching the European Court of Human Rights at Strasbourg." This was the first written mention of a lawsuit that would help establish the court in the public imagination, and, ultimately, legalize gay sex in much of the world.

The poet took notice of a "fat lad whose jokes gave light and air." That would be Richard Kennedy. Richard was a twenty-three-year-old working-class rebel from South Belfast, the product of a mixed marriage. "My ma's Catholic, my da's Protestant, and I'm socialist," he liked to say.

Across the table sat the group's chairman, Jeff Dudgeon, age twenty-nine, whose name would forever be linked with the group's landmark lawsuit. Jeff's friends called him Bunny, because of his buck teeth; he impressed the poet as serious and friendly. Jeff was the ideas man.

From civil rights circles, Jeff knew a progressive Queens University law lecturer named Kevin Boyle. The previous autumn, Jeff had been walking down College Gardens Street on his way home from his job as a shipping clerk when he ran into Kevin. The two got to talking about homosexual law reform, as gay rights was then called. Under the influence of American lawyers, Kevin was then bringing one of the first individual petitions in Strasbourg, against British police practices in Ulster. Why not try the same strategy to challenge the sodomy law? "It was all Kevin's idea," says Jeff.

In this city ruled by the tyranny of small differences, Jeff too was the product of a mixed marriage. His father was Irish Protestant and his mother English, the member of a group disliked by all. Maybe that's what made him an outsider.

Jeff stopped going to church at twelve. By sixteen he was reading James Baldwin and knew that he was gay. His mother took him to a shrink, who reassured her that it might be "only a phase." The teenaged Jeff laughed that off and embarked on a gay rights career of notable consistency and staying power. He got a summer job selling bus tickets in London and watched from the gallery as the House of Lords debated legalizing sodomy in England and Wales.

Homophobia has a long tradition in English law, as elsewhere. The Fleta, a late thirteenth-century legal treatise, charmingly held that "[t]hose who have connection with Jews or Jewesses or are guilty of bestiality or sodomy shall be buried alive in the ground." In 1806 more English men were executed for sodomy than for murder, but sodomy executions stopped in 1836. In 1957 England and Wales began a long, intermittent gay rights debate. They would decriminalize gay sex in 1967.

Meanwhile, back in Belfast, both the law and the social scene lagged behind. Jeff had no idea how to meet other gays. In 1965, at nineteen, he clipped an advertisement from the Sunday *Times* of London and sent in thirty shillings for a "Male World" guide. A few weeks later, he gathered his courage and entered what was then Belfast's only gay pub, the Royal Avenue Bar. It was really only half gay, doubling as Belfast's only deaf venue. The front was reserved for the deaf, the back for the gays. After a lifetime of searching for his identity, Jeff opened the door and found himself eyeballed by heterosexuals flirting in sign language.

That began a slow process of discovery. "Here I was this would-be-revolutionary," Jeff recalls, "and I was hiding the key fact about myself." He came out to his innermost circle around 1970 and came out politically in

1974, when he founded the Committee for Homosexual Law Reform in Northern Ireland.

"We were on a high in '74, '75, '76," remembers Jeff. "We were founding groups, having love affairs. There was love and respect, people emerging from mental caves." The Royal Avenue Bar would see thirty-five gay men on a Saturday night when Jeff first went in 1966. By 1976 discos like the Chariot Rooms or the Casanova Club might attract three hundred.

It was the height of the Troubles, and most Ulsterites were just trying to stay alive. The statistics from 1972 to 1976 are astounding for an area of less than two million people. Each year there were thousands of shootings and hundreds of civilian deaths. "The only people walking around Belfast at night were gay people and soldiers," Jeff recalls. "We colonized a section of that city and it became our own."

The city center was gated, and the gate was guarded at night by British soldiers. The soldiers and the gays developed a working rapport. Because the gay pubs were the only ones open, the soldiers would stop by for drinks. If a handsome soldier was guarding the city gate, Richard and his friends would jostle to see who'd be searched first. The highest aspiration of the drag queens was to be convincing enough that they'd be searched by one of the women soldiers.

"We ran the city center," says Jeff. "You could be outrageous. You could walk hand in hand and kiss." Jeff didn't want young people exploring their sexual identities to move in a climate of ignorance, as he had done. So, in 1974, he and his friends founded a second group, a gay counseling service called Cara/Friend, Cara being the Irish Gaelic word for friend. They initially advertised a hotline number at the Queens student union—but the response overwhelmed the switchboard on its first day. None of the young gay activists had phones at home. Instead, they set up a postal service, and within a year received more than two hundred letters.

"Save Ulster from Sodomy"

The year 1976 arrived, and the troubles ground on. On January 4, Loyalist paramilitaries gunned down six Catholics in their homes in counties Down and Armagh. The next day, at Kingsmills, an IRA faction responded by massacring ten Protestant workmen on their way home by van with their lunch pails.

Still, when Jeff turned thirty that week, he was upbeat. Both of his new groups were making progress. The Committee for Homosexual Law

Reform was exchanging letters with the court at Strasbourg, and Richard was in London raising funds for the lawsuit. Cara/Friend got a small grant from the British government. Best of all, Jeff's boyfriend, an ecology lecturer named Douglas Sobey, moved into a flat in a grand brick villa, adorned with all manner of stripes and scrolls and crenellations, on Ulsterville Avenue. On Sunday, January 18, they proudly set up a heavy gray rotary phone in the hall between the kitchen and bathroom. Cara/Friend finally had a hotline.

As fate would have it, the police swooped in two days later on one of Cara/Friend's members, Kevin Merrett. Merrett was dating an eighteen-year-old man whose parents were influential and upset. The cops found Cara/Friend's volunteers' list and began to tick off the names.

The next evening, Jeff was making tea in his own home, around the corner on Dunluce Avenue, when the doorbell rang. The tiny red row house at the bottom of a hill might have fit into a quiet English suburb, except for the concrete wall inlaid with beer bottle shards, which separated its rear from one of those impossibly narrow alleys where Unionist urchins scamper away from cops in movies set in Belfast.

Jeff opened the door and, to his shock, found six officers of the Royal Ulster Constabulary (RUC). The RUC detained him for the evening and took his Strasbourg correspondence. But they were far more excited by Jeff's diary and love letters, where they marked up every passage involving leather or sexually transmitted disease. The RUC also showed considerable interest in Jeff's kitchen cupboard, where they found six ounces of marijuana belonging to Richard.

Richard was arrested as he stepped off the ferry on Thursday, returning from his London fund-raising trip. He was taken to Castlereagh Barracks, used as an interrogation center for IRA men, where he proudly confessed to being a gay chef, famous for his double dope chocolate mousse cake. The RUC, used to gays of an earlier generation begging, "Don't tell me ma and da," didn't know what to say.

Over the next five months, the police detained twenty-one gay men in Belfast. To Jeff it already felt like a purge. But there was one raid left.

Early one Saturday morning in June 1976, Jeff was asleep with Doug at Doug's flat on Ulsterville Avenue, which, thanks to the phone, doubled as Cara/Friend headquarters. They were awakened by a banging at the door. Doug was from rural Canada and had picked a quilt with a maple-leaf pattern. Jeff tossed it aside, drew the purplish pink curtains and saw three men in plainclothes out front, including one he recognized from the raid on his own home. It was Officer Armstrong, whom they code-named "Limpwrist."

"Fuck, it's the cops," Jeff said. "Get your clothes on."

Doug threw on his bell-bottoms and a button-down shirt from the day before and went downstairs. As the police entered the flat, Armstrong gave Jeff a significant look, and Jeff said wryly, "We meet again." Doug was arrested and taken in for questioning, and, under heavy pressure, admitted that, yes, he loved Jeff.

In a way, the police raids were a great stroke of luck. The Strasbourg lawsuit's biggest weakness was the lack of evidence that the antigay law was enforced. After the first raid, Jeff was able to write to Strasbourg, essentially saying, "I'm sorry, we can't respond to your last letter because the Royal Ulster Constabulary raided my home and stole it." Soon after the raid on Doug's home, he formally filed the suit.

The Northern Irish director of public prosecutions approved gross indecency charges against Jeff, Doug, and Richard. Richard was sure he'd be beaten to death by paramilitaries in Long Kesh Prison. But the three waged a letter campaign, and the attorney general's office in London forced Belfast to drop the charges in early 1977. Richard later received a suspended felony conviction for drugs supply, based on sharing slices of his double dope chocolate mousse cake at a disco birthday party.

The RUC roundup not only strengthened the gays' case in Europe but also gave them publicity. It soon attracted a right-wing nemesis nuttier than any caricature a leftist fund-raiser could dream up.

The Save Ulster From Sodomy campaign was started in 1977 by the Reverend Ian Paisley, the godfather of Ulster fundamentalism. Paisley overtly preached Catholic hatred and violence. He would later accost Pope John Paul II at the European Parliament, shouting, "I renounce you as anti-Christ." Sadly, this ideology too had American roots: Paisley was a graduate of South Carolina's Bob Jones University.

While Save Ulster from Sodomy gathered 70,000 signatures, Richard waged a comic countercampaign. He considered a Save Sodomy From Ulster theme but thought better of it. Side by side with Paisley, he set up a table bedecked with glitter and balloons in Belfast's Shaftesbury Square. His slogan? "Save Ulster from Chewing Gum."

Jeffrey Dudgeon v. United Kingdom

For four years, Ulster forgot about buggery and bubble gum and got on with the business of fratricide. Margaret Thatcher was elected prime minister of the United Kingdom. In the spring and summer of 1981, ten IRA men starved themselves to death at Long Kesh Prison outside Belfast.

Finally, on October 22, 1981, came the historic judgment from Strasbourg: twelve to six in favor of Jeff Dudgeon.

The court declined to decide whether Jeff had suffered a violation of his right to equality under Article 14 of the European Convention. Instead, it held that the 1861 antisodomy law violated his right to family and personal life under Article 8. Acknowledging that the law was scarcely enforced, the court opined that "the very existence of this legislation continuously and directly affects his private life."

The core of the court's reasoning was that Europe's mores had evolved, as evidenced by the prevailing legal attitude in Europe as a whole: "As compared with the era when that legislation was enacted, there is a better understanding, and in consequence an increased tolerance, of homosexual behavior. . . . [T]he Court cannot overlook the marked changes which have occurred in this regard in the domestic law of the member states."

The dissent, by Judge Brian Walsh of Ireland, countered that establishing a "Euro-norm" was not a good idea: "[T]he Council of Europe extend[s] geographically from Turkey to Iceland and from the Mediterranean to the Arctic Circle and encompass[es] considerable diversities of culture and moral values. The Court states that it cannot overlook the marked changes which have occurred in the laws regarding homosexual behaviour throughout the member States. It would be unfortunate if this should lead to the erroneous inference that a Euro-norm in the law concerning homosexual practices has been or can be evolved."

Dudgeon v. United Kingdom thus lay bare the debate underlying the court's new activism. On one side were those who saw the court's role as imposing the progressive social trend on laggard states. On the other side were those who refused to recognize a European trend.

Between them, the dissents in the *Marckx* case (see chapter 1) and the *Dudgeon* case articulate the most basic theoretical objections to the court's activism. Judge Fitzmaurice's *Marckx* dissent made the argument from original intent. Judge Walsh's *Dudgeon* dissent made the argument from cultural diversity, what might in the United States be called the state's rights argument. Both, as well, suggested that the court ought not infringe on the sovereignty of its member states. Interestingly, both key dissents were written by judges educated in the Anglo-Saxon rather than the Continental legal tradition. The court's majority, if only by its holdings, made clear that it rejected these arguments. After *Marckx* and *Dudgeon*, the interpretive die was cast—and the way was clear for an activist agenda.

"It's About Time!"

Back in Britain, Rev. Ian Paisley, who was a member of Parliament, geared up for the domestic debate over changing the law. He fulminated to the BBC: "An outside body who is not committed to the moral values the people of Northern Ireland are committed to is prepared to say 'you will legislate perversion and immorality.'" Paisley's rhetoric may have been biblical, but at bottom he was making a point about sovereignty. This was a theme that, with each activist decision, would reliably be sounded by nationalist elements in the press and parties of the respondent nation.

On the evening of October 25, 1982, Jeff Dudgeon and Richard Kennedy took their seats in the gallery to watch the House of Commons debate the legalization of gay sex in Ulster. Half a lifetime earlier, Jeff had sat in the gallery to watch the same debate over gay sex in England and Wales.

Rev. Paisley picked up where he left off in his remarks to the BBC. "Some people," he said, "believe that homosexuality is not only a defiance of human law but a defiance of divine law."

At this, the transcript reflects that the honorable members of the Commons emitted a collective, "Oh!"

A legislator from Pontypool by the name of Leo Abse crafted a more clever comeback. "I do not believe," he said, "that the men of Ulster are so diminished, so lacking in heterosexual drive and desire that ending the criminality of private, adult homosexual conduct will mean that Belfast will become a modern Sodom. I am sure that Ulster men have more robust and confident heterosexual appetites than their representatives in the House."

If Paisley was secretly gay, he wouldn't be the only such member of Parliament. The highlight of the night for Jeff and Richard was a short statement by MP Matthew Parris: "Where I feel as deeply, strongly and personally as I do on this issue, argument altogether fails me." The transcript does not reflect it, but the Commons emitted a collective gasp. With proper British understatement, Parris had just come out of the closet.

The roll was called and the yeas had it. Richard, who was thoroughly enjoying the show, stood up and shouted in his harsh northern brogue, "It's about time!"

Four marshals pounced on him and brought him, for the duration of the debate, to the House of Commons jail, a veritable dungeon buried in the foundations of Big Ben. Released after two in the morning, he returned to his flat (he was now living in London), where Jeff and friends were waiting. They played "Dancing Queen" by Abba, and partied till dawn.

Save America from Sodomy

The radicalism of the 1981 *Dudgeon* decision is underscored by the fact that the U.S. Supreme Court reached the diametrically opposite result five years later, in *Bowers v. Hardwick*. *Bowers* began similarly, when a policeman in Atlanta, Georgia, barged into Michael Hardwick's home during an intimate moment. A dumbfounded Mr. Hardwick asked the policeman, "What are you doing in my bedroom?" That rhetorical question should have decided the case, yet the U.S. Supreme Court ruled against Mr. Hardwick.

Warren Burger, then chief justice of the U.S. Supreme Court, showed no awareness of *Dudgeon* in his concurring opinion. But he placed great store in English legal views on sodomy before the Revolutionary War. He cited Sir William Blackstone for the proposition that " 'the infamous crime against nature' [is] an offense of 'deeper malignity' than rape, a heinous act 'the very mention of which is a disgrace to human nature.' "

The majority opinion in *Bowers* was more subtle, but no less marked in its contrast with *Dudgeon*. Recent research has revealed the thinking of Justice Lewis Powell, who was the swing vote. At heart, Powell was hostile to the notion embraced by the majority in Europe and the dissent in America—that a gay couple could build a family. He scribbled furiously in the margin of the dissent's draft: "what family?" He jotted a note to a clerk: "I find [this] argument repellent. . . . 'Home' is one of the most beautiful words in the English language. It usually connotes family, husband and wife, and children." Finally, he wrote in a draft footnote: "The fundamental reason for the condemnation of sodomy has been its *antithesis* to family."

On June 26, 2003, in *Lawrence v. Texas*, the Supreme Court at last overturned *Bowers* and exposed it for all its ugliness. *Bowers*'s starting mistake, the *Lawrence* Court reasoned, was to define the right in question as the right to engage in sodomy, rather than the right to develop a relationship in the privacy of one's home. In drawing for support on the shared values of Western civilization, *Bowers* exaggerated the American homophobic legal tradition and ignored the *Dudgeon* ruling of the European Court of Human Rights. Finally, the Court noted that, in the years since *Bowers*, the decision had drawn scorn from the academic community, and the rule it embodied had eroded, through changes in state law and nonenforcement. By at last taking their cue from Europe, the American justices achieved a milestone for both gay rights and American legal cosmopolitanism.

Postscript

The effect of the *Dudgeon* judgment eventually was felt around the world. Copycat lawsuits updated gay rights in Ireland in 1988 and Cyprus in 1993. Between 1991 and 1995, eight former Soviet-bloc nations jettisoned sodomy laws as they joined the Council of Europe. Most sweepingly, in the 1994 case of *Toonen v. Australia*, *Dudgeon* was cited by the United Nations Human Rights Committee in its interpretation of the International Covenant on Civil and Political Rights. After a quarter century, the right established by Jeff Dudgeon and Richard Kennedy is secure. What, in the meantime, has become of the Euro-gay-rights fathers?

Richard has maintained his rebellious sense of humor. For several years, he ran an organic bakery in London called Marie Antoinette's, where he continued to sell double chocolate mousse cake. He announced himself a heterosexual in 1988, upon which he lost his life presidency of the Northern Ireland Gay Rights Association. "Before I die," he jokes, "I have to be a dyke."

Jeff has aged with dignity. Indeed, he bears a mesmerizing resemblance to William F. Buckley. His mouth turns downward when he smiles. He hesitates on the first syllable of each thought and speeds up at random intervals. His eyelids half-closed, his eyes bulge with emphasis. Jeff is sipping tea in his home—only a block away from the Ulsterville Avenue villa, and two blocks away from the Dunluce Avenue row house. "I haven't moved far in twenty-five years," he laughs. The windows behind where Jeff sits were smashed six times in the early 1980s by youths armed with bricks and cinderblocks. But that was long ago. And, if Jeff Dudgeon has not moved far, the world around him has.

In late 2001 the Royal Ulster Constabulary accosted Jeff again. It was their "human rights program manager," and he wanted to know if Jeff could give a talk on "Policing a Diverse Society." Jeff assented and addressed the RUC's conference on "policing and human rights." This brand of political correctness is easy to poke fun at, but it sure beats the alternative. "It wasn't long ago," he reminded his audience, "that you were trying to put me in jail."

CHAPTER 4

Dudgeon's Children

*T*he breakthrough victory of European gay rights in *Dudgeon v. United Kingdom* left plenty of unfinished business, starting with the treatment of gays in the military. Indeed, only a few months after *Dudgeon*, the European Commission on Human Rights, in *B. v. United Kingdom* (1982), refused to hear the complaint of a British soldier who was terminated because of his sexual identity. The battle for gay rights in the military would need to wait a generation, until the advent of another charismatic activist, Duncan Lustig-Prean.

The Gay Admiral Nelson

I met Duncan aboard a tugboat in Brighton harbor, where he now works, and sometimes sleeps; the boat was once used to smuggle Jews out of Germany. A complex and fascinating setting for a complex and fascinating man, it is the oldest salvage tug in the world, originally designed in Sweden in 1905 as an icebreaker. The cabin's walls are lined with stacks of Puccini and Mozart CDs, strapped in place by bungee cords, hinting of Duncan's past as an opera student at the Royal College of Music. Duncan bought the tug after he was drummed out of the navy for homosexuality, because he still felt a need to work at sea and the boat's wartime heroics held a special meaning for him. Both of Duncan's parents came to Britain as refugees from Hitler in 1939, his mother as a German Jewish child and his father as an anti-Nazi socialist from a long line of Austrian imperial generals. Duncan named the boat the *St. David*, in honor of a British patron saint, because he felt grateful to Britain for sheltering his parents. It was for that very reason that he gave up opera for the Royal Navy.

It was once whispered in navy circles that Duncan might become the youngest admiral since Nelson. His breast pocket sported one campaign medal for Northern Ireland and another for the Falklands, where he lost nineteen colleagues when his ship, the HMS *Coventry*, was sunk by an Argentine Skyhawk missile. The gold braid on his left shoulder signaled that he'd served on the general staff, where he oversaw half of UK navy personnel. In 1994 he was promoted to lieutenant commander, stationed aboard the HMS *Newcastle* destroyer. According to his 1993 review, he was "a most able, conscientious and industrious officer with outstanding prospects for early promotion to commander."

The timing of Duncan's fall could scarcely have been more dramatic. On Thursday, June 9, 1994, a commander at the Ministry of Defense offered him the position of military adviser to the prime minister (then John Major). This position was traditionally a stepping-stone to an appointment as admiral. Duncan came back to the ship on a high and had a celebratory glass of whiskey with his captain. Just then, the ship's steward came in and told Duncan that his mother had called the ship and needed to speak with him urgently. Apparently, a strange man was repeatedly calling Duncan's mother and demanding that Duncan call him from shore. Duncan called with trepidation. He recalls being told, "It's about an investigation. You want to meet me." Duncan drove the three hours from Portsmouth to London, and at 12:30 that night met the mystery caller underneath the clock at Waterloo Station. They walked along the Victoria Embankment. "I've discovered you're gay," Duncan recalls being told. There was a clear suggestion that the man wanted money. Duncan told the man to take a running jump. In Duncan's account, he did not want to compromise his service and his country by laying himself open to further blackmail. He had often anticipated this moment, and he knew what he had to do.

On Monday morning, Duncan officially informed his colleagues that he was gay. When Duncan told his noncommissioned officers, one laughed and pointed to a photo hanging on the wall, showing Duncan posing with Queen Elizabeth during a royal tour of the dockyards. "I always thought there was more than one queen in that picture," he said.

The navy's head of special investigations was less sympathetic. Duncan was treated as a criminal as soon as he disclosed that he was gay. As was standard when the military discharged a homosexual, the investigators asked pointless and demeaning questions: whether he enjoyed anal intercourse, whether he was abused as a child, whether he played "bitch" or "butch."

In October 1995, *The Guardian* newspaper learned of Duncan's story and asked him to go public. Duncan refused, because he was still hiding from his parents both the fact of his sexual identity and the fact of his military termination. But that autumn a dramatic incident persuaded him that he could make a difference.

A young gay soldier threatened to jump to his death from the Severn Bridge in Wales, and members of the gay military support group "Rank Outsiders" called Duncan in the middle of the night for help. Duncan drove at 120 kilometers (75 miles) per hour to the scene and spent six hours talking the young man down from his perch. Duncan had found his voice.

Dad's Army No Longer

In November, Duncan came out to his parents and gave the green light to a piece in *The Guardian*. Soon he hooked up with a group of lawyers who saw him as the perfect public face for a challenge to Britain's policy on gays in the military.

Ultimately, four test plaintiffs shared the distinction of altering the UK's gays-in-the-military policy. Each had an "outing" story more poignant than the next. John Beckett was a naval weapons engineering mechanic. After being refused time off to collect the results of an AIDS test, he confessed his sexual identity to his naval chaplain and then, under pressure, to his superior officer. Jeanette Smith was a Royal Air Force nurse who found a lover through a lesbian lonely hearts column. She returned from vacation in June 1994 to find the anonymous answering machine message that all closeted gays dread, saying that her secret had been revealed. Graeme Grady was a sergeant in the Royal Air Force who served in a sensitive position in Washington, D.C., as a liaison between U.S. and UK military intelligence. Grady attended a support group for gay married men. It happened that Grady's colonel's nanny, who was herself a member of the gay community, discovered Grady's secret and let it slip to the colonel's wife. The colonel didn't know whether to be more appalled that his deputy was gay or that his nanny was a lesbian. Like all the rest, Grady was fired without ceremony.

The British courts were forced by British law to rule against the plaintiffs, but the trial judge did so with reluctance. "Lawrence of Arabia," he pointedly noted, "would not be welcome in today's armed forces."

On September 27, 1999, the European Court of Human Rights ruled against Britain in the case *of Lustig-Prean and Beckett v. United Kingdom* and the case *of Smith and Grady v. United Kingdom.* The state conceded that all had impeccable service records, unaffected by their sexual orientation. The question, purely framed, was whether soldiers could be fired for being gay. The court ruled that the United Kingdom had violated the Article 8 right to privacy of the four applicants—both in its intrusive investigation and in its policy to terminate. In *Smith and Grady*, where the applicants made broader arguments, the court declined to rule on discrimination grounds but held that the state failed to offer an adequate remedy to its violation of the applicants' rights. This set the stage for the United Kingdom wholly abandoning its policy on gays in the military, in June 2000. In this respect, too, Europe is more progressive than the United States. Without the prodding of a constitutional court, the U.S. military remains mired in the unworkable political compromise of President Clinton's "don't ask, don't tell" policy.

Duncan Lustig-Prean's feelings about the end of his military career are bittersweet, but he knows from his old peers the frustrations of effecting change within a hierarchy. It's likely that Lustig-Prean has made a bigger impact on the UK military as a petitioner to Strasbourg than he would have as the youngest admiral since Nelson. A student of law and history, he is proud to be a successor to Jeff Dudgeon. Now he is waiting to see if his case, like Dudgeon's, can in time influence American law.

An Orgy of Sexual Rights

Military integration is only one of many victories that sexual minorities have won at Strasbourg in recent years. In *Salgueiro da Silva Mouta v. Portugal* (1999), the court recognized the right of a gay parent to receive custody of his child following a divorce. In *A.D.T. v. United Kingdom* (2000), the court recognized the right of gays to engage in private group sex. Gays have also earned the right to an equal age of consent. And, after years of trying, transsexuals have won the right to trumpet their identities.

The line of cases on underage sex shows the evolution of judicial attitudes. It used to be that, in Europe, the age of consent for gay sex could differ from the age of consent for heterosexual sex. In Austria for instance, the age of consent was fourteen for heterosexuals and eighteen for gays. In 1995, in *H.F. v. Austria*, the European Court of Human Rights found this distinction to be acceptable. However, in the 1997 case of *Sutherland v. United Kingdom*, the European Commission on Human Rights found the distinction to be discriminatory. In 2000, the Parliamentary Assembly of the Council of Europe called for the repeal of all remaining European laws that established a discriminatory age of consent. Over the next two years, at least six European nations responded. Meanwhile, new challenges to the Austrian law were percolating in Strasbourg. Anticipating a rebuke by the

European Court of Human Rights, the Austrian constitutional court voided its age-of-consent statute in 2002. Sure enough, in 2003, in *L. and V. v. Austria* and *S.L. v. Austria*, the ECHR held that a differential age of consent violates the European Convention. In other words, the court adopted the position that the commission took in *Sutherland* and overturned its own Austrian precedent.

From an American perspective, what is intriguing is how the Austrian legislature chose to conform its statutory law to the constitutional rulings. It had two choices. It could either raise the age of consent for heterosexuals or lower the age of consent for gays. It chose to lower the age of consent for gays. Thus, in Austria (as in several other European nations), consensual sex between an adult and a fourteen-year-old is legal, including consensual gay sex. This is not the route the U.S. Congress would have taken.

But if there is one case line that captures the slow process of social evolution translating into legal evolution, it is the law on transsexuals. For years, Strasbourg refused to recognize the right of a British citizen to receive a new birth certificate following a sex change. Britain's five thousand transgendered individuals complained that they suffered discrimination, because others could so readily infer from the public records that they had undergone a sex change. An unaltered birth certificate also prevented a transsexual from marrying, because marriage was restricted to individuals who officially had opposite genders. With the passage of time, this situation became more troubling, both to the court and to the European public.

Again and again, Strasbourg was asked to recognize right of transsexuals to change their official gender identity. In 1987, in *Rees v. United Kingdom*, Strasbourg ruled against British transsexuals by twelve votes to three. Its 1990 judgment to the same effect, *Cossey v. United Kingdom*, was decided by a bare majority. The vote was closer because, in the three years between *Rees* and *Cossey*, nine European countries had recognized the rights of transsexuals. In 1992, in *B. v. France*, the court narrowly ruled that France was required to change the gender on transsexuals' identity cards, but it declined to foreswear its harsh decisions on UK transsexuals. Meanwhile, European laws continued to be amended, and in 1996 the European Union in Brussels recognized the rights of transsexuals. See *P. v. S. and Cornwall County Council*. In 1998, yet another British transsexual sued. Strasbourg stuck to its guns, again by a bare majority, but warned Britain to review its policy. See *Sheffield and Horsham v. United Kingdom*. By 2002, Britain was one of only four European nations to disdain the transgender agenda. That year, a retired truck driver named Christine Goodwin at last persuaded the European Court of Human Rights to reverse course—unanimously—and broadly embrace transsexual rights.

To be sure, there have been gay setbacks in Strasbourg. The court has upheld the dismissal of a Belgian school headmistress for being lesbian. See *X. v. Belgium* (1988). It has refused to give a Dutch lesbian shared parental authority over her female partner's child by donor insemination. See *Kerkhoven v. Netherlands* (1992). It has let Britain refuse one partner in a lesbian relationship the right to renew a public housing lease on behalf of the couple. See *S. v. United Kingdom* (2002). It has allowed Britain to deport an alien who was in a long-term same-sex relationship with a British citizen. See *W. J. and D. P. v. United Kingdom* (2002).

On a much broader issue, Strasbourg declined to acknowledge a gay right to adoption. However, on close scrutiny, *Frette v. France* (2002) holds hope for the future. Three judges dissented, and three judges decided on the narrow ground that the Article 14 norm of nondiscrimination was simply not engaged. Only one judge reasoned that discriminating against gays in adoption is justified. It's noteworthy that the three dissenting judges in *Frette* hail from Western Europe and that three of the four judges forming the majority hail from the former Communist zone. This case offers anecdotal support for the theory, to which many in Strasbourg subscribe, that the addition of twenty-five Eastern European judges gives the typical panel more conservative social values. I generally accept the retort that Eastern and Western European judges are equally tolerant. But it's possible that some biases are exceptionally deep and tenacious in Central and Eastern Europe, among them suspicion of gays and gypsies.

For all of Strasbourg's trailblazing, there are several structural flaws in the European Convention from the perspective of gays. First, Article 12 seems to doom any claim to gay marriage, by guaranteeing the right to marry only to "men and women." Second, the Article 14 guarantee of equality does not by its terms cover gays. Third, as *Dudgeon* foreshadowed, the court has been exceedingly timid in its interpretation of Article 14 equality for *any* group. Fourth, the judges from Eastern Europe might, to some extent, put a brake on social progress.

On gay family rights, Strasbourg may well be outpaced in the coming years by the European Court of Justice in Luxembourg. An EU directive, which took effect in summer 2006, extended the EU's excellent law on gender discrimination to sexual orientation. And, although its fate is uncertain, the EU's proposed Charter on Fundamental Rights would expand the "right to marriage" to cover any arrangement for founding a family.

CHAPTER 5

The Greening of Europe?

*I*n their early years, the Strasbourg institutions were uniformly cautious in their approach to the environment. They voiced no objection to the flooding of the Sami people's reindeer habitat for a dam project in *G. and E. v. Norway* (1984). They rejected repeated complaints of noise pollution See, for example, *Powell and Rayner v. United Kingdom* (1990). And they gave no succor to the nuclear protest movement. See, for example, *X. and Y. v. Germany* (1976). Then along came a housewife from a small town in Spain, who refused to take no for an answer. Introducing Europe's answer to Erin Brockovich.

López Ostra and the Greening of Europe

Gregoria López Ostra has never seen *Erin Brockovich*, the 2000 Julia Roberts movie about a paralegal who became an antipollution crusader in Southern California. But Gregoria resembles the real Ms. Brockovich in being a simple woman roused by circumstance to political activism. She and her daughter Cristina identify as environmentalists only in modest ways. Both love the nature documentaries of Felix Rodriguez de la Fuente. And Cristina is known as the green family cop. Woe betide the visitor who puts a beer can in the wrong recycling bin or leaves the tap running in the López Ostra household.

Like many Spaniards, Gregoria's family saved money working in France during the 1960s, in the fields and hotels of the Montpellier area. In 1970, at the age of forty-five, the family patriarch, Jines, fulfilled his life-long dream and built his own home, in the shadow of Lorca's eleventh-century Moorish fortress. The name Lorca is derived from the Latin for "City of the Sun," and the town is famous for its vistas of the sun setting over the fort's two crenellated turrets, the towers of Espolon and Alfonsina. Legend has it that in 1244, during the Christian *reconquista* of Spain,

Lorcan villagers aided the Castilian knights in their nighttime charge on the Moorish stronghold. As a decoy, the Lorcans sent a flock of sheep bedecked with bells and candles careening up the hill, past the spot where Jines would build his home, while the Christian warriors attacked from the other side.

Jines had a son and two daughters. His son, Jose, met Gregoria in 1978, during Lorca's Semana Santa Easter festival, and Jose built a house alongside his father's. Before long, Jose's sisters got married, and the extended family shared the two homes. In their worst dreams they never imagined that the hillside between the fortress and their homes would turn toxic.

Lorca, located in the Murcia province of southern Spain, is an industrial town dominated by a leather consortium called SACURSA. In July 1988, SACURSA opened a plant to treat liquid and solid tannery wastes. The facility was sited all of twelve meters away from the homes of Gregoria and her sisters-in-law.

From day one, the waste treatment plant malfunctioned. It let off rotten-egg fumes and emitted hydrogen sulfide at levels that were clearly unpermitted, and possibly unhealthful. The black liquid waste of the lagoon bred mosquitoes, and the stench made everyone's eyes and throat burn. With the windows shut, and no fans, the heat became oppressive. The family's rose bushes and magnolia and lemon trees wilted away. The children's parakeets opened their beaks to gasp for breath. Some of the parakeets died, as did the pigs that Gregoria's father-in-law raised in his retirement. Racked with worry about her daughters' health, Gregoria had trouble eating and sleeping.

The Lorca town council rehoused the López Ostra family for free in the town center in late 1988 and again from 1992 to 1994. The town ordered a partial closure of the plant in September 1988 and a further closure, under court order, in October 1993.

But Gregoria's family continued to complain of health problems; they regarded the town's actions and compensation as insufficient. Every week without fail, Gregoria would walk the three kilometers to town hall to complain, pushing Cristina before her in an orange and blue baby carriage. It reached the point where the mayor's secretary would say hello to her in the supermarket. Frustrated with the political process, Gregoria hired a young lawyer by the name of Jose Luis Mazón Costa.

Mazón Costa took *López Ostra* as his first case after law school. "We have a saying," he says modestly. "The dolphin breaks the laws of hydrodynamics because he doesn't know them." Mazón Costa is not a physically glamorous man; Gregoria's sisters-in-law, who have seen the movie *A Civil Action*, find it endlessly funny that John Travolta played the role of the environmental lawyer.

Mazón Costa helped Gregoria file an unsuccessful domestic lawsuit in the Murcia Audiencia Territorial. The Spanish Supreme Court dismissed an appeal, and the Spanish Constitutional Court ruled her case inadmissible. Gregoria applied to Strasbourg in 1990, and in 1992 the Commission unanimously ruled in her favor. Spain's representative on the commission, Luis Fernando Martinez, made the opening argument to the European Court of Human Rights on behalf of Gregoria in the broadest possible terms:

> One might say that environmental matters today are fashionable. They give rise to many concerns and worries. Under the flag of environmental preservation, political movements have even been set up. But is enough really done in this field? In deciding the case of López Ostra against Spain an opportunity will be given to the Court to define whether the European Convention on Human Rights can be used by individuals as an arm with which they can defend themselves from environmental aggressions.

On December 9, 1994, the European Court of Human Rights agreed unanimously that Spain had violated Gregoria's Article 8 right to family life. It awarded damages and costs of $31,750, covering the devaluation of her old home and the expense and inconvenience of moving, as well as the distress, anxiety, and nuisance caused by the pollution.

Gregoria was cleaning the apartment when Jose Luis called with the news of her victory. Gregoria rushed to school and caught her daughter Lidia before the beginning of afternoon classes. Lidia started to cry, as television news cameras captured the moment.

The most basic holding in *López Ostra v. Spain* is captured in a single line: "Naturally, severe environmental pollution may affect individuals' well-being and prevent them from enjoying their homes in such a way as to affect their private and family life." From a legal standpoint, of course, the holding was anything but natural.

Until Gregoria López Ostra came along, the European Court of Human Rights treated the environment as none of its business—which is the way constitutional courts virtually always treat the environment. It's true that more than fifty national constitutions and thirty U.S. state constitutions guarantee the right to a clean environment. But by and large these are empty guarantees. The situation in Strasbourg is thus the reverse of the norm. In Strasbourg, the basic document gives no green guarantee, yet the court has created one. Only a handful of other judicial bodies—the supreme courts in Chile, the Philippines, and India, the United Nations Human Rights Committee, and the Inter-American Court of Human Rights—have tackled environmental problems constitutionally.

As if it were not enough to constitutionalize the right to a healthy environment, the *López Ostra* decision sent three signals with radical potential. First, the court clarified that pollution could violate family rights even if it didn't seriously endanger the family's health. By contrast, American pollution suits routinely founder on the difficulty of proving a threat to health. (That's why the environmental lawyer played by John Travolta ends up having his Porsche repossessed at the end of *A Civil Action*.)

Second, the European Court of Human Rights imposed on states *a positive obligation* to protect a family's right to a clean environment. It happens that in *López Ostra* the nuisance could be chalked up to state action. Although the plant was built by a private leather consortium, it was sited on town land and subsidized by Spain. Still, the court went out of its way to note that the outcome didn't depend on Spain's direct involvement. It was enough that Spain failed to take appropriate regulatory steps.

Third, the court expressly left open the possibility that more serious pollution could violate the Article 2 right to live. It is likely, however, that an environmental violation of the right to live would entail a strong scientific showing.

López Ostra was first followed in the similar factual setting of *Guerra v. Italy* (1998). In *Guerra*, a group of mothers complained about air pollution from a nearby factory in the southern Italian region of Foggia. *Guerra* built on *López Ostra* by establishing—again under the rubric of Article 8 family rights—the citizen's right to know about the pollution of her environment. A violation of the Italian mothers' rights was found, regardless of the actual threat to their families' health, because no serious studies of the threat had been undertaken and publicized. What neither *López Ostra* nor *Guerra* did was to lay down criteria that might tell practitioners when the European Court of Human Rights will consider it appropriate to exercise supervision over domestic environmental regulation. It would be easy to characterize *López Ostra* as a unique, exceptional case. After all, how often is a defective toxic plant built twelve meters from a home? The stage was set for retrenchment.

Heathrow Airport and the Browning of Europe

In 1990, neighbors of Heathrow Airport argued at Strasbourg that noise pollution violated their family rights. The court rebuffed them in emphatic terms: "It is certainly not for the . . . Court to substitute for the national authorities any other assessment of what might be best policy in this difficult technical and social sphere." See *Powell and Rayner v. United Kingdom.* This was a sphere, the court added, where national laws deserved a high level of deference. It's unclear whether, by this "sphere," the court meant airplane noise or environmental regulation generally. But it seemed Strasbourg was content to cede the color green to national capitals.

The court's 1990 ruling on Heathrow echoed the standard American argument against constitutionalizing the environment. As an old American court put it, constitutional litigation "is particularly ill-suited to solving problems of environmental control. Because such problems frequently call for the delicate balancing of competing social interests, as well as the application of specialized expertise, it would appear that their resolution is best consigned initially to the legislative and administrative processes." See *Tanner v. Armco Steel Corp.* (S.D. Tex. 1972). It was unclear whether this approach could survive the *López Ostra* ruling. History soon presented a perfect laboratory experiment.

In 2002, a second group of Heathrow neighbors argued that noise pollution violated their family rights, in the case of *Hatton v. United Kingdom.* Citing *López Ostra,* the initial Strasbourg panel held in favor of the sleep-deprived residents by a vote of five to two. The panel pronounced a sweeping environmental standard that got a lot of people excited. The panel held: "States are required to minimize, as far as possible, the interference with [Article 8] rights, by trying to find alternative solutions and by generally seeking to achieve their aims in the least onerous way as regards human rights." Sir Brian Kerr wrote acerbically in dissent that "modern life is beset with inconveniences." The United Kingdom appealed.

At oral argument before a grand chamber of the European Court of Human Rights, Britain underscored the case's importance by sending its attorney general, Lord Peter Goldsmith. He stressed that the rights of the airport's neighbors needed to be balanced against the interests of business travelers, vacationers, the airport, the airlines, their employees, and shareholders. The court would be swamped, argued Goldsmith, if it undertook that kind of minute analysis in every disputed case of environmental regulation.

On July 8, 2003, the grand chamber in *Hatton* ruled for Britain and against the bleary-eyed runway neighbors. It held by twelve votes to five that Heathrow's loud night flights did not violate anyone's family rights.

As is usual when it reaches a timid result, the court recited deferential boilerplate: that the Convention has a "fundamentally subsidiary role"; that "national authorities have direct democratic legitimation and are . . . in principle better placed than an international court to evaluate local needs and conditions." None of this stops Strasbourg when it is in an activist mood. But the court explicitly refused to adopt a less deferential attitude in the context of "environmental human rights." On the contrary, it signaled that it is especially apt to remember its cautious old saws in green cases. The court cited with approval its statement from the 1990 Heathrow case—that special deference is owed in "this difficult social and technical sphere." Whether it should actually defer, the court added not very helpfully, depends on the particular case.

The way the court got around *López Ostra* may give practitioners more concrete guidance for the future. The court explained that it found green violations of human rights only where states failed to comply with domestic law. Read through the lens of the Heathrow cases, the crucial fact in *López Ostra* was that the town had let a waste-treatment plant run without a license. The principle of *López Ostra* was thus narrowed, in both spirit and letter.

A Brownish Green or a Greenish Brown?

The case of *Moreno Gómez v. Spain* (2004) presented almost a perfect laboratory combination of the facts in *López Ostra* and the Heathrow cases. The applicant was a Spanish woman, and she lived next door to bars that blared music at upward of one hundred decibels. The Valencia City Council had failed to enforce zoning laws it had designed to limit noise pollution. Given the lack of a state interest in disco, the court readily found Spain liable for a violation of Article 8. If nothing else, *Moreno Gómez* belied the inference that the court thinks noise a trivial problem.

Fadeyeva v. Russia (2005) presented an extreme version of the facts in *López Ostra*. The air pollution in the Russian steel town of Cherepovets was so severe that 95 percent of children suffered from respiratory ailments, according to a state study funded by the World Bank. Yet residents like Nadeshda Fadeyeva lived at the edge of the town's steel plant, and

Russia had failed to enforce a law to resettle them. The court concluded that, "despite the wide margin of appreciation left to the respondent State, it has failed to strike a fair balance between the interests of the community and the applicant's effective enjoyment of her right to respect for her home and her private life." Given a dirty enough mess—and a government that violates its own commitments—the cautionary standards of Heathrow can be overcome. The good news is that the court is tackling the massive environmental problems of the former Communist zone. The danger is that the complaints of Western Europe will usually seem mild by comparison.

Since the Heathrow affair, the court has persuaded many Cassandras that *López Ostra* was not an aberration. But back in Spain, the López family itself doubts the court's commitment to public health. In September 2003, the European Court of Human Rights dismissed on procedural grounds a complaint based on essentially the same facts as *López Ostra*, brought by Gregoria López Ostra's sisters-in-law, Ana-Maria Gómez López and Maria Gómez López. Perhaps the two Lorcan cases were distinguishable on procedural grounds. But it's as easily argued that the different fate of the sisters-in-law reflects a change in mood at Strasbourg. The court's greenest moment may have passed.

Today, nothing but wastewater flows into the Segura River along the bed of the Guadalentin Creek, where Lorca's children used to swim. Maria Gómez López has become an activist to restore the Segura River system. Together, Maria and Ana-Maria travel to rallies around Spain, carrying a sign, "For a Safe River." They believe, from bitter experience, that the more practical strategy for environmental change is political rather than judicial.

CHAPTER 6

Dumb Immigrants

*I*f a society is judged by the way it treats its most vulnerable, then the treatment of criminals from a despised group is doubly instructive. What happens when a legal immigrant who is not a citizen commits a crime? In many countries, he or she faces deportation after serving time in prison. The French call this phenomenon *la double peine*, because foreigners are made to pay a double penalty for their mistakes: first prison, and then exile. Both France and the Council of Europe have vacillated in their handling of criminal aliens. Perhaps that is because Europe feels ambivalent about its immigrants, and in particular Muslims from North Africa. The tales of Mahamed Nasri and Ali Mehemi, each in their own poignant way, are emblematic of the immigrant experience in France and Europe.

A Kind of Excellent, Dumb Discourse

Mahamed Nasri was born deaf and dumb in Algeria in 1960. He arrived in the *banlieues* of Paris with his family when he was five and ready to start school. One special school rejected him because it lacked space and the boy tested poorly. A second school expelled him for violence. A third school expelled him for missing tuition payments. The rest of Mahamed's story may be told through court reports.

Between 1981 and 1993, Mahamed was arrested thirty times, usually for theft. He was convicted ten times, leading to 108 months behind bars. In 1986 he was convicted of participating in a gang rape, and the following year the French interior minister ordered him deported. The Nasri family appealed to Strasbourg.

Mahamed is said to have the understanding of a kindergartener. Due to his lack of education, he communicates through crude pantomime. The experts retained by the French criminal courts, unable to talk to Mahamed, projected onto him their various social theories. A sympathetic psychiatric report opined:

> The therapy he has received has been unable to equip him with proper and adequate means of communication and he has had to [regress] to his milieu of origin, with which he has to identify in order to have a status and an identity. In his milieu of origin, where he is integrated under the nickname which established his difference, "THE MUTE," it is inevitable that [he] should adopt attitudes of criminality.

But a hostile court report told a very different story about Mahamed:

> His handicap . . . does not prevent him from wandering the streets of Villeneuve-la-Garenne and other villages at all hours of the day and night and from assiduously frequenting the bars where he drinks alcohol, which makes him aggressive. . . . This violent and antisocial individual makes no effort whatsoever to be integrated in our society and takes advantage of his handicap and of the favorable provisions of the administrative and justice systems. He is a real danger to public order, especially since he appears to be the leader of the young delinquents of Villeneuve owing to the fear he inspires.

Two evaluations; two different views of society.

The European Court of Human Rights assumed neither that Nasri was a victim of society nor that he was a predator. It focused on different facts altogether. The court stressed that six of Mahamed's siblings were French citizens and that no member of his immediate family had left France for thirty years. Under these circumstances, the court reasoned, the Article 8 right to family life mandated the preservation of family unity. If separated from his family, Mahamed wouldn't have a prayer of leading a functional life. On July 13, 1995, in *Nasri v. France*, the court blocked his deportation.

Although the facts of *Nasri* are uniquely haunting, Mahamed was only one of dozens of immigrants facing deportation who have brought their cases to Strasbourg. The first French case in this line was *Beldjoudi v. France* (1992). The separate opinions in *Beldjoudi*, both at the level of the European Commission on Human Rights and the European Court of Human Rights, introduced cogent arguments against *la double peine* that would be developed later.

Why should Algeria be held accountable? That's what jurist Henry Schermers demanded to know in his concurrence to the commission's *Beldjoudi* report. "If there is one country responsible for [the applicant's] upbringing and the criminal behavior," he suggested, surely that country is France. It is "morally wrong to send back to Algeria those of the many immigrants who become criminals, while allowing those who contribute to the prosperity of the country to remain in France." In the later case of *Lamguindaz v. United Kingdom* (1993), Schermers made the same point in a British context: "By admitting aliens to their territory States inevitably accept at least some measure of responsibility. This responsibility weighs even more heavily in the case of children educated in their territory."

If national societies abdicate their responsibility for immigrants because of nativism, perhaps the European Court of Human Rights has a special obligation to compensate. In his concurrence to the court's *Beldjoudi* judgment, Judge Siep Martens argued that "[i]n a Europe where a second generation of immigrants is already raising children (and where violent xenophobia is increasing to an alarming extent)," deporting a fully integrated immigrant might never be appropriate. Martens later expanded on this argument in his *Gul v. Switzerland* dissent (1996). It is the court's role, he wrote, "to ensure [that] State interests do not crush those of an individual, especially where political pressure—such as the growing dislike of immigrants in most member States—may inspire State authorities to harsh decisions."

The *Nasri* case is fascinating because it presents the dilemma of the criminal alien in extreme form. On the one hand, Nasri was a convicted rapist who had committed crimes more heinous than any other immigrant in Strasbourg's annals. On the other hand, he belonged to French society, and depended on it. One can blame Mahamed's pathology on his nature or on French social and educational institutions. Either way, he remains France's responsibility. France's political institutions were able to ignore that responsibility because Mahamed is mute—both literally and in the sense that all noncitizens lack a political voice. If the ultimate function of a constitutional court is to protect the voiceless, then in protecting Nasri, the European Court of Human Rights fulfilled it.

Nasri is among the few protagonists in this book with whom I couldn't speak. In his stead, I tracked down another French immigrant, who is mute only metaphorically. Ali Mehemi speaks eloquently for the *musulman français* (French Muslim) who is at home nowhere. A Frenchman but for an accident of birth, he spotlights the arbitrariness of *la double peine.*

An Algerian in France, a Frenchman in Algeria

Ali Mehemi was not even born in North Africa. He was born to Algerian parents in Lyon, France, a few months before Algerian independence. Technically, he was French for the first eight months of his life. But by a quirk of French law, Algeria's declaration of independence stripped Ali of his French status, because his parents did not take French citizenship. They were illiterate, and he says they didn't know that they had the choice.

Ali's anomaly is brought into sharp relief by his friend Miloud Nair. Miloud, too, was born to Algerian parents in Lyon, but he was born a few months after Algerian independence. That made Miloud a French citizen. As young men, Ali and Miloud joined the same hashish ring. They were arrested together in 1989, and each served short sentences in French prison. After they completed their terms and nominally paid their debts to society, Miloud returned to life in Lyon; Ali was deported to Algeria, which was to him a strange and terrible place.

Ali's family came from the village of Biskra in eastern Algeria, at the edge of the Sahara. His father, Ramdane, fought with the French army in Vietnam from 1948 to 1952. He came to Lyon about 1955 and worked long hours as a bricklayer. Ali's mother, Saliah, served as a housekeeper in a Lyonnais home for the elderly. Their kin from Biskra spread out across France, Belgium, and Germany and spent a life of toil in similar thankless jobs. All five of the Mehemi children were born after the family emigrated.

Ali grew up in the Olivier de Serre section of Villeurbanne, named after the founder of Lyon's legendary silk industry. Growing up, he lived an integrated life amid native Catholics, *pied noirs* (the French colonists who returned from Algeria), Jews, Muslims, and other immigrants. "It never occurred to us to ask who was North African and who wasn't," Ali says. His three best friends, with whom he played marbles, were Catholic, Jewish, and Chinese. He worked as an electrician for whoever hired him, and his drug ring, which imported hashish from Morocco, included several Catholics and Europeans. Ali dated a Sicilian girl, whom he eventually married. In the early 1980s Ali and his girlfriend had three children together, who were, of course, French citizens. Ali was no saint, but, in many ways, he was a model of integration.

By the early 1980s the Olivier de Serre section had become a Muslim ghetto, with all the hallmarks of urban pathology. Ali's childhood neighborhood was leveled in a misguided effort at urban renewal. Meanwhile, unemployment for Algerians in France surged to more than 25 percent, and setting cars afire became a favorite pastime in Lyon. In 1990, televised riots in the Lyonnais district of Vaulx-en-Velin linked the city with images of North African street violence. Those images were reinforced in 1995 by the powerful film *La Haine* (*The Hatred*), on the conflict between Muslim youth and police in Lyon. Also that year, a second-generation Algerian immigrant in Lyon was identified as an Islamic bomber and was killed by the police. The newspaper *Le Monde* obsessively analyzed the bomber's milieu. In the French public mind, Lyon had become the equivalent of South Central Los Angeles.

When the police busted Lyon's Moroccan hashish ring in 1989, they seized 142 kilos, including 7 kilos in Ali's brother's bedroom. To my ears, Ali doesn't sound very convincing when he says his involvement was marginal. Still, in affirming Ali's deportation, the Lyon Court of Appeal pushed the bounds of fair argument. It stressed that Ali "voluntarily opted" for Algerian nationality, when in fact he lost his French nationality because his parents did not know they needed to affirmatively declare it. The French court cited "trips to North Africa" as evidence that he maintained a link with his home country when, in fact, Ali had never once visited Algeria. He had visited Morocco, whether for tourism or hashish commerce is not clear.

France put Ali in prison and deported him to Algeria upon his release in August 1993. Ironically, this was a time when France was urgently advising all French citizens to head the other way. Ali found himself in the middle of a civil war between Algeria's fundamentalists, who had won the 1992 elections, and its military, who barred the fundamentalists from taking power. Tens of thousands of Algerians died, and the Islamists singled out foreigners as targets.

Algeria's bloodletting fed French nativist hysteria. During the summer of Ali's deportation, Interior Minister Charles Pasqua, promising "zero immigration," pushed through new laws to facilitate police identity checks and to limit foreigners' entry and residence rights. The next summer, in the so-called Folembray Affair, Pasqua ordered thirteen thousand random identity checks in a week, rounded up twenty suspected Islamic fundamentalists in a barracks in the town of Folembray, and deported them. The French extremist Jean-Marie Le Pen would hit the high point of his popularity in 1995, with 15 percent of the vote, and considerably higher numbers supported his views in polls. As Le Pen's popularity grew, the official list of offenses leading to deportation was expanded.

Ali, as he explained to me, was struggling with his own hysteria. Ali had never been to Algeria in his life and didn't have a single connection there. The French police randomly put him on a flight to the small city of Constantine. When he arrived, the Algerian police saw that he was lost, so they dropped him at a hotel. Ali was able to pay the room rate indefinitely, with money from his family that he'd hidden in his toiletries bag. He could not work, because he was refused Algerian working papers. He could not travel, because he was refused an Algerian passport. He was depressed and rapidly lost weight. (He would ultimately lose fifty pounds). He spent his time listening to the droning of Arabic state television. There was an 11 PM curfew, but he didn't mind it, because there was nowhere to go. The telephone was his lifeline to the outside world. His relatives called so often that the hotel receptionist became friends with everyone in his family. After three months Ali began to hatch escape plans. First he went to Algiers and then to Oran, hoping to stow away on a boat bound for France or Spain. The only thing Ali found in either city was political unrest. In the cafés, all the talk was of God and assassination.

Everyone except the French regarded Ali as French. Fundamentalists set up false roadblocks to extort money from travelers, and Ali feared that they would slit his throat. Ali had no identification except his French deportation papers. He knew a bit of Arabic, but his accent was thick, so he remained quiet, which itself drew attention. In Algiers, Ali was picked up by the military police, who threw him in a jail cell crowded to bursting with Islamists. After release, Ali found another dive hotel and hatched a desperate new plan of escape.

In early 1995, Ali's younger brother pilfered his older brother's identity papers and sent them to Algeria with a friend. Ali bribed an Algerian bureaucrat to alter the photo and tried his luck. He made it to Paris—only to be stopped at Orly Airport and returned to Algiers. There was nothing left to do but wait for Strasbourg.

On September 26, 1997, the European Court of Human Rights found Ali's deportation order to be a disproportionate violation of his right to family life under Article 8 of the European Convention. The court stressed the artificial circumstances of Ali's Algerian citizenship and the fact that the deportation separated him from his wife and children. Highlighting the inconsistency of its case law, Strasbourg on the same day ruled against a Moroccan man who had immigrated to France at the age of seven. See *El Boujaidi v. France* (1997).

Although France complied with the court order and let Ali return in February 1998, his travails were not entirely over. Ali was displeased with the conditions France imposed on his return. He was refused a pardon and given a compulsory residence requirement. He was forbidden to travel outside Lyon or to leave his home at night, and he was required to report to a parole officer. At first he was given renewable work papers that were good only for six months. Beginning in 2001, his work papers were renewable after one year. Ali complained that he couldn't find work because of the questions raised by his work permit. One of his brothers had to create a company to hire him as a taxi driver. Eventually, he was able to find odd jobs as an electrician through a temp agency. Ali brought a second case to the European Court of Human Rights to protest the conditions of his return, but in October 2003 the court ruled that his rights had not been violated.

The Law and Politics of *La Double Peine*

Ali should consider himself lucky, for *Nasri* may have represented the high-water mark of Strasbourg's protection for criminal aliens. Exactly when does the right to family unity bar deportation? Instead of drawing a bright line, Strasbourg follows a fact-specific inquiry. Among the key factors are the applicant's family situation, how long the applicant has lived in the expelling state, the gravity of his crimes, how long ago he committed his last crime, and how he has behaved in the interim. The results of this approach have been notoriously unpredictable. It is hard to square the results in *Moustaquim v. Belgium, Djeroud v. France, Lamguindaz v. United Kingdom, Beldjoudi v. France, Nasri v. France, Ezzhouhdi v. France, Boultif v. Switzerland, Jakupovic v. Austria*, and *Yildiz v. Austria* with the results in *El Maziani v. France, Gul v. Switzerland, Ahmut v. Netherlands, C. v. Belgium, Chorfi v. Belgium, Bensaid v. United Kingdom, Dalia v. France, Boughanemi v. France, Bouchelkia v. France*, and *Boujlifa v. France*.

Many scholars agree with the dissenters in *Boujlifa v. France* (1997), who openly charged the court with casuistry. Others believe, more charitably, that the discrepant results may be explained by the application of neutral principles to different facts. My own belief is that Strasbourg's inconsistency reflects Europe's ambivalence about the Other in its midst.

Meanwhile, French law on *la double peine* has followed its own trajectory. The first spur to change came from Strasbourg. The European Commission on Human Rights' November 1990 report in *Beldjoudi* helped to shape a January 1991 settlement in *Djeroud v. France* (a case that had been consolidated with *Beldjoudi* for a hearing before the European Court of Human Rights). In short order, the French Justice Ministry issued a circular, and the French Conseil d'Etat began to take into account the alien's family rights under European Convention Article 8. *La double peine* persisted in the 1990s, however, and it became a rallying cry for the activist left.

Like Ali Mehemi, many victims of *la double peine* try to sneak back into France. Unlike Ali, many succeed. Lacking identity papers, they find themselves trapped in a secret existence, unable to work. In the spring of 1998, ten of these lost souls went on a fifty-one-day hunger strike, crowding mattresses onto the floor of the Arab youth office in Lyon. Eight of the hunger strikers shared the same lawyer as Ali, Jacques Debray. The hunger strike drew intense media attention and led to a blue-ribbon panel chaired by the French judge and human rights advocate Christine Chanet.

The Chanet Report, submitted to Justice Minister Elisabeth Guigou in November 1998, denounced the "dysfunctionalities" of France's deportation policy. It proposed limiting expulsion to recidivists who committed crimes punishable by life imprisonment and did not attend French schools. The Chanet Report was followed up a year later by another Justice Ministry circular, this one calling on prosecutors to take into account the extent to which the individual to be deported is integrated into French society. It's unclear whether prosecutors have taken this admonition to heart. But the tide of public opinion had turned, and that has been reflected in French court decisions. The French courts take a case-by-case approach similar to that of the European Court of Human Rights. In practice, French courts today tend to be more generous to potential deportees. The phenomenon of *la double peine* is not unknown, but the battleground of xenophobia has mostly shifted to other fronts.

Inconsistent as France and Europe have been, U.S. law makes any legal system look progressive in its treatment of immigrants who commit crimes. In the United States, the deportation of criminal aliens is largely fought on statutory rather than constitutional grounds. Although U.S. courts require a due process hearing before deportation, they consider congressional discrimination against aliens to be constitutional. In 1996, in the wake of the Oklahoma City terrorist bombing, Congress passed a set of restrictive immigration laws. Perhaps the most aberrant result was to mandate deportation of virtually any legal alien convicted of a crime. On its face the law applies only to felonies, but in an Orwellian twist, "aggravated felony" is defined to include many misdemeanors. This certainly aggravates civil libertarians. In 2003, the United States deported more than eight thousand permanent legal residents for criminal violations. Among the acts that trigger deportation are hair-pulling, marijuana possession, calling home on an illegal public telephone, defending oneself against spousal abuse, and—my favorite—turnstile jumping. This debate is strictly about people who have entered a country legally. But in the public mind, at some preconscious level, it's all about turnstile jumping.

Postscript

As Ali Mehemi sits in his lawyer's office, musing on his own experience and the travails of Maghrebi youth, he instinctively adopts the perspective of French society. Ali urges France to do a better job of acculturating North Africans, as he was acculturated in the doubly lost world of Olivier de Serre. "I identify completely as a *musulman français*," he says. "I know about French history, not Algerian history. Islam for me is as important as religion is for a secular Catholic or Jew. I drink alcohol; mosques for me are like cafés. France is the country I love. When I was deported I felt betrayed."

It's hard to know which is sadder: a nation's betrayal of those whom it fails to integrate, or its betrayal of those whom it succeeds in absorbing. France instilled rage in Mahamed Nasri and love in Ali Mehemi, then abdicated responsibility for both. Ironically, the two were equally vulnerable. For all his fluency in French, Ali had no way to voice himself politically short of a hunger strike. Dumb immigrants both, Mahamed and Ali needed a court to speak for them. Strasbourg may not always find the courage to give immigrants refuge, but as Europe struggles with the local legacy of imperialism, it will always have generous precedents like *Nasri* and *Mehemi* available to be retrieved.

PART II

The Rights of Expression

CHAPTER 7

Minos and Jehovah

*I*n 1938 the Greek anti-Communist dictator Ioannis Metaxas passed a strict criminal law against proselytism. Minos Kokkinakis of Crete was the first man arrested under the law and, a half century later, he would be the last. In the intervening years, he would be detained more than sixty times and serve more than six years behind bars. Minos lived an epic life. Despite his name and homeland, it was an epic lived less in the style of Minoan myth than of the catechism.

Minos, like many other Jehovah's Witnesses, loved a verse in the Gospel according to Luke that valorizes legal victimhood. "[P]eople will lay their hands upon you and persecute you," predicted Luke, "delivering you up to the synagogues and prisons, you being haled before kings and governors for the sake of my name. It will turn out to you for a witness." Given a group identity formed on this verse, it should perhaps be no surprise that Witnesses pioneered the constitutional law of religious freedom on two continents. Minos lived to the rhythm of biblical verses, and his life resembled that of a Hebrew prophet—with a strong Oedipal subtext.

"Fifty Years of Persecution"

Minos Kokkinakis was born into a family of cloth merchants. His father and four brothers each had his own shop in Sitia. In 1936, at the age of twenty-seven, Minos branched out to the nearby town of Ierapetra. At first, he was active in the Orthodox church. His father was the Greek Orthodox cantor in Sitia, and Minos became a favorite of the Ierapetra bishop. But soon after he moved, Minos met a traveling Jehovah's Witness minister. Minos converted, and he began to recruit followers, starting with his shop assistant, Elissavet, who became his wife. Minos's father urged the bishop to use every means at his disposal to discipline his son.

Orthodox priests have been allied with the modern Greek state since its beginnings. In 1821, down the road from Sitia, the monks of Toplou monastery helped to lead Crete's rebellion against the Ottomans. To this day, the Greek Orthodox church is a state agency, and the Greek constitution begins with an invocation of the Holy, Consubstantial, and Indivisible Trinity. As the local Witnesses tell the tale, the Ierapetra bishop went to Minos's shop and raised his shepherd's rod against Minos. Minos threw him out, and the police promptly closed the shop. In 1938, the antiproselytism law passed, and Minos found himself in prison.

Elissavet bore her eldest child, Janus, while Minos was behind bars. According to Kokkinakis family lore, one of her Orthodox sisters-in-law took the child for a walk one day. When they returned, Elissavet noticed oil on Janus's face.

"What have you done?" the mother asked her sister-in-law.

"Ask your father-in-law," came the reply.

Beyond baptizing his grandson, the Kokkinakis patriarch was able to change little in Minos's absence. Elissavet was fond of throwing in his face Matthew 10:36: "Indeed, a man's enemies will be persons of his own household."

During the Greek civil war (1943–1949), the Witnesses were shunned by the left because their base was in the United States, and by the right because they were pacifists. In 1949 Minos was confined in the prison camp of Makronisos, an uninhabited Aegean isle with no trees and no water. Minos smuggled in Witness literature (as well as coffee, which he sold at a profit) and circulated among the Communist inmates to preach.

Back in Sitia, Minos's five children were seated separately at school. Every Sunday they skipped church and every Monday they received a public birching at the hand of the principal, who happened to be another Kokkinakis sister-in-law. Minos's son Michael recalls, "When I was in high school, during my first year there I was purposely kept back one grade. The reason? The teacher of theology tauntingly asked me, Hey you! Are you still a 'Jehovah' like your father? I answered him, Yes! And he 'answered' me back in another way." All Witness children were expelled from school by a state decree in 1953, and, although a court overturned the decree, none of the Kokkinakis kids returned to public school.

The eldest brother, Janus, went to Athens at fourteen in an effort to escape the pressure. When he turned nineteen and faced the choice of military service or prison, the pressure became too great. Janus left the Witnesses. Unlike many victims of tyrannical fathers and churches, Minos showed a capacity for tolerance in his own life. Janus later testified, at one of his father's trials, that Minos never rejected him or tried to convert him.

Nothing, meanwhile, deterred Minos. Every Sunday for decades, when he was not in prison, he would don his best brown jacket and saddle up his gray mule. (Later, he graduated to an Opel station wagon, which he would ask one of his children to drive.) When he completed his tour of all sixty-six villages in Lasithi Province, he'd begin again. By the end of his life, Minos claimed to have converted a hundred souls.

In the Greek proselytism cases, Minos was often hauled before the provincial court in Neapolis, a shabby building which stands in the shadow of a grand Metropolitan church. His longtime lawyer, Thanasis Reppas, recalls him as a comically difficult client.

"You serve injustice," Minos would tell the judge.

"What he means, your honor," Reppas interrupted, "is that it's your role to correct the injustice.

"Did you have proselytizing literature with you?" the judge would ask.

"Of course, I have some here with me now," he'd reply. "Come let me show you."

Although persecution of the Witnesses flared up after the military coup of 1968, the end of military rule in 1973 inaugurated a peaceful period for Minos. Only about a tenth as many Greek Jehovah's Witnesses were convicted of proselytism in the 1980s as in the 1950s. Meanwhile, Greece joined the European Union, and Minos grew old.

Then, one Sunday in 1987, Minos and Elissavet were foolish enough to knock on the door of the Kyriakakis, who lived nearby in Sitia. Mr. Kyriakaki was the local Orthodox cantor—the position that Minos's father had once occupied. When Mr. and Mrs. Kokkinakis knocked on the door, Mrs. Kyriakaki invited them into the living room and began to chat. Meanwhile, her husband the cantor eavesdropped in the next room and called the police.

In the European Court dissent, this scene was memorably and ungenerously described:

> On the one hand, we have a militant Jehovah's Witness, a hardbitten adept of prison, a specialist in conversion, a martyr of the criminal courts whose earlier convictions have served only to harden him in his militancy, and, on the other hand, the ideal victim, a naïve woman, the wife of a cantor in the Orthodox Church (if he manages to convert her, what a triumph!). He swoops on her, trumpets that he

has good news for her (the play on words is obvious, but no doubt not to her), manages to get himself let in and, as an experienced commercial traveller and cunning purveyor of a faith he wants to spread, expounds to her his intellectual wares cunningly wrapped up in a mantle of universal peace and radiant happiness. Who, indeed, would not like peace and happiness? But is this the mere exposition of Mr Kokkinakis's belief or is it not rather an attempt to beguile the simple soul of the cantor's wife?

Notwithstanding this vivid depiction of the scene, it is not at all clear who was setting a trap for whom. Though it doesn't appear in Strasbourg's recitation of facts, Minos already had a personal history with this cantor, according to the Witnesses in Sitia. About a year earlier, Mr. Kyriakaki had seen a group of young Witnesses handing out pamphlets in the village square. According to the Witnesses, Mr. Kyriakaki angrily tore up the pamphlets and threw them to the ground. The young Witnesses threatened to sue, until Minos, now an elder statesman, forged a peace between them. While I could not independently verify this account, I readily confirmed that Minos was well known in Sitia.

When I asked my translator in Athens for directions to the Kokkinakis family home, I was told, "Fly to Crete, drive three hours east to the town of Sitia, and ask for Kokkinakis." I followed these instructions exactly, and, sure enough, the first man I asked nodded and pointed the way. Reppas relates a similar story about his first visit to Sitia. He, too, stopped in the town square and asked a stranger for guidance. "Perhaps I might not know Psiloritis," came the reply, referring to Crete's snowy peak, "but Kokkinakis I know." Here, evidently, was a man who made an impression on his neighbors. It seems implausible that either the cantor or his wife were taken unawares.

Whatever the underlying facts, lawyers found that Minos, with his outsize personality, was tough to defend. Panos Bitsaxis advised both Minos and Elissavet to be conciliatory in the Greek appeals court. Mrs. Kokkinakis complied and the court overturned her sentence. Minos delivered an oration that began: "Ladies and gentlemen, I divorced the Orthodox church fifty years ago." Sure enough, the Greek court gave him a sentence of three months.

"Why don't you listen to me next time?" said the lawyer.

"Don't worry, my child, "answered Minos, "Jehovah will win.

Bitsaxis, a young secular intellectual who went on to be a leading Greek lawyer, would have none of it. "I know what that means," said Bitsaxis. "You mean if I win it's Jehovah and if I lose it's my fault."

At the Strasbourg hearing in November 1992, Minos walked into the courtroom with his old lawyer, Reppas, at his side. He reflexively walked to the defendant's table and asked, "Where's my seat?" Reppas laughed and pointed to the other side of the room. "This time," he said, "you're charging Greece."

At the hearing's end, Minos telephoned Elissavet in Crete and was asked how it went. Minos quoted from the Song of Deborah: "Let me sing to Jehovah, for he has become highly exalted. The horse and its rider he has pitched into the sea." Minos was right to sense victory. The Strasbourg court soon voted six to three that Greece had violated Article 9 of the European Convention, guaranteeing freedom of religion. The European Convention clearly safeguarded the right to change one's religion—and this, the court reasoned, necessarily implied the right to ask others to change their religion. It was the first violation of Article 9 ever found.

When the ruling came down, on May 25, 1993, Bitsaxis called Minos with the news of victory. Minos by then was eighty-four years old. To Bitsaxis he responded with a wink, "You see my child, didn't I tell you Jehovah would win?" To the world at large he proclaimed, "The fifty years of persecution was worth going through for this historic moment."

Jehovah's Test Plaintiffs

Kokkinakis v. Greece was the first judgment to recognize the right to religious freedom in Europe. But the judgment was limited both in its scope and its reasoning, leaving plenty of battles to be fought another day. As fate would have it, those battles would largely be waged by the Jehovah's Witnesses of Greece. In Europe, the Witnesses have won some and lost some.

Kokkinakis dealt only with proselytism. And even on the narrow issue of proselytism, it did not invalidate the Greek law outright. Rather, it accepted the Greek law's distinction between "proselytism that is respectable" and "proselytism that is not respectable." Improper witnessing, the court suggested, might entail the use of violence, brainwashing or subtler forms of pressure. In the court's view, Kokkinakis's witnessing did not cross that line. Such reasoning satisfied Bitsaxis, the Witnesses' pragmatic lawyer.

But it was a disappointment to American-style First Amendment purists like Judges Pettiti, De Meyer, and Martens, who wrote separate opinions. Strasbourg's compromise position on proselytism has allowed "anticult" laws and legislative reports to proliferate in the past decade. One critic has gone so far as to dub this trend the "European retreat from religious liberty." A 1999 Jehovah's Witness complaint against the French Assembly's investigation of cults was rejected by the Strasbourg court at its threshold.

From a legal standpoint, a more satisfying victory came in *Manoussakis v. Greece* (1996), which recognized the right to a church of one's own. Titos Manoussakis and three other elders in the city of Heraklion applied for a permit to open a Jehovah's Witness prayer hall in 1983. The storefront they used in the interim was vandalized and shuttered while they endured fourteen years of bureaucratic runarounds. Finally, in 1996, the European Court of Human Rights held unanimously that Greece had used its permit law to curtail religious freedom. *Manoussakis* was far more absolute than *Kokkinakis* in its reasoning: it denied states any discretion "to determine whether religious beliefs or the means used to express such beliefs are legitimate."

The Witnesses struck another blow for religious freedom in *Tsavachidis v. Greece*, which began as a church permit case like *Manoussakis* but grew into a general indictment of the Greek religious right. In 1993 a crude Greek intelligence report on "heretical sects" leaked to the press. It declared that "any Greek who is not Greek Orthodox is a non-genuine Greek," and urged "repressive and preventive measures" against them. Of Jehovah's Witnesses, it stated, "This organization is extremely dangerous, not only religiously, but also (to a greater degree) as far as the nation is concerned. A tremendous problem has been created within Greek society. This must be dealt with quickly and decisively." One way of dealing with the problem was to "be cautious" in licensing non-Orthodox churches. Although Greece attributed this report to a low-ranking functionary, the *Tsavachidis* case made it harder to brush under the rug.

At about the time that the notorious report became public, Greece accused Gabriel Tsavachidis of setting up a Witness's hall without a permit. During discovery in the Greek courts, the defense lawyer, Panos Bitsaxis, stumbled across a surveillance report on Tsavachidis. It was the smoking gun. It seemed to show that the state intelligence agency was tracking the comings and goings of ordinary Witnesses. Tsavachidis filed a petition with Strasbourg, demanding to know: "Who put my private life under surveillance?" Bitsaxis held a press conference and debated the Greek justice minister on radio. In 1997 the European Commission on Human Rights held by a thirteen to four margin that Greece had violated Tsavachidis's Article 8 right to family life. Before the case could go to the next level, Greece settled, and admitted culpability.

If *Mannoussakis* and *Tsavachidis* were their greatest triumphs, the biggest disappointment to Europe's advocates of religious freedom has been Strasbourg's position on neutral laws affecting religion. A law requiring students to salute the flag is the classic example of a generally-applicable law that discriminates against one group. To uphold such a law might be formally neutral—yet effectively tilt against religion. On this thorny question, the United States and Europe have taken different paths.

The dominant figure in the U.S. Jehovah's Witness movement was a lawyer, Joseph Rutherford, who even integrated trial tips into the prayer service. When Rutherford called on Witnesses to stop saluting the U.S. flag in the late 1930s, he precipitated a pair of landmark decisions. The Witnesses initially lost. But in 1943, in the second flag salute case, the U.S. Supreme Court reversed itself, producing one of the classic statements of First Amendment freedom, *West Virginia State Board of Education v. Barnette*. Jehovah's Witness test plaintiffs were off and running. During their Washington heyday, from 1938 to 1955, they won thirty-six cases. In 2002 the Witnesses argued their seventy-second Supreme Court case and won yet again.

In recent years the U.S. has zigzagged on the question of neutral laws affecting religion. At its peak of religious sensitivity, the U.S. Supreme Court exempted Amish children in Wisconsin from compulsory school attendance and exempted an especially touchy group of Jehovah's Witnesses from using New Hampshire license plates bearing the slogan "Live Free or Die." See *Wisconsin v. Yoder* (1972) and *Wooley v. Maynard* (1977). In 1990 the U.S. Supreme Court changed course and approved a New Mexico law banning peyote despite its effect on Native American ritual. This case, *Employment Div. v. Smith*, continues to set the general rule. But the Court voided a Florida ban on animal sacrifice that directly targeted a local cult in *Church of the Lukumi Babalu Aye, Inc. v. Hialeah* (1993). And, in reaction to the peyote case, Congress has, to the extent of its power, mandated strict scrutiny of neutral laws affecting religion. See *City of Boerne v. Flores* (1997).

In Strasbourg, it has been a different story. The European Commission on Human Rights was consistently hostile to religious minorities challenging neutral laws. The commission found it permissible for Sweden to convict a man "shouting out like a trumpet" of disorderly conduct, for the United Kingdom to restrict Druid access to Stonehenge for reasons of public order, and for the United Kingdom to fire a Seventh Day Adventist state employee for refusing to work on the Sabbath. See *Hakansson v. Sweden* (1993), *Chappell v. United Kingdom* (1987), and *Stedman v. United Kingdom* (1997).

But, inevitably, it was those pesky Witnesses who tested the principle of neutral laws affecting religion in the European Court of Human Rights itself. In the early 1990s, two preteen Witness girls, Victoria Valsamis and Sophia Efstratiou, were suspended from school for refusing to participate in school parades held on Greek national holidays. All school children were obliged to march in military step, to the accompaniment of military music, in ceremonies that featured Greek soldiers and Orthodox clergy. In arguing on their behalf to the court, Panos Bitsaxis explicitly cited the second flag salute case. At oral argument, he recited a canonical First Amendment passage penned by U.S. Justice Robert Jackson: "To believe that patriotism will not flourish if patriotic ceremonies are voluntary and spontaneous instead of compulsory routine is to make an unflattering estimate of the appeal of our institutions to free minds. We can have intellectual individualism and its cultural diversities that we owe to exceptional minds only at the price of occasional eccentricity and abnormal attitudes." Nonetheless, the European Court of Human Rights rejected this argument and stuck to a position of formal neutrality—in practice hostile to the demands of the religious claimants. In American terms, the Greek parade case, *Valsamis and Efstratiou v. Greece* (1996), closely tracks the first flag salute case, *Minersville School Dist. v. Gobitis* (1940).

While there has not yet been a "second Greek parade case," the court has sent more subtle signals of a change in tack. A universal military draft is another classic example of a neutral law affecting minority groups. As one might expect, Strasbourg traditionally allowed discrimination against conscientious objectors, while the United States did not. Compare *Grandrath v. Federal Republic of Germany* (1966) with *United States v. Seeger* (1965). However, in the 1997 case of *Tsirlis and Kouloumpas v. Greece*, the European Court of Human Rights held unlawful the principle of imprisonment for conscientious objection. In the follow-up case of *Thlimmenos v. Greece* (2000), the European court found it unacceptable that a Jehovah's Witness, who had already gone to prison as a conscientious objector, should be denied an accountant's license. It remains to be seen whether *Tsirlis* and *Thlimmenos* represent a philosophical turn by the court in the direction of accommodating religion—or a narrow response to a serious grievance. In the Greek Witness community, it had became the norm for young men to enter either exile or prison when they reached draft age. According to Witness records, 1,638 Greek Witness men were imprisoned for pacifism in the 1980s, each for an average of three years. At the very least, the European Court of Human Rights resolved a deep local injustice.

Postscript

For more than half a century, Minos Kokkinakis's home had served as the Witnesses' prayer hall in Sitia. Minos died in 1999, at the age of ninety, but he helped to donate money for a proper "Kingdom's Hall," and lived to see the ground broken. The next year, with the help of the *Manoussakis* precedent and the climate of opinion created by the Tsavachidis scandal, the Witnesses received their religious permit without delay. Thanks to the conscientious objector cases, military-age men can be found among the worshippers.

"You see, my child?" Minos might say. "It's all due to the glory of Jehovah." And so the story will be taught by the Witnesses for generations to come. But in this author's book, the credit must be shared with a few pagan characters: with Oedipus, who helped to motivate Minos; with Bitsaxis, who litigated for Minos; and with the black-robed pantheon at Strasbourg, who ruled in his favor.

CHAPTER 8

Recovered Memories

*T*his is the story of two boys born in Austria under Hitler's rule. Each of the boys spent most of the war in Carinthia, the mountainous province that was a bastion of Austrian Nazism and even today remains a center of neo-Fascism. At very different ages, each dramatically glimpsed the truth of his parents' wartime role. Peter Michael Lingens's earliest memory is of sitting in a car when he was three and admiring the men with shiny guns at the door of his family's fine home. He'd soon learn that the Gestapo had arrested his parents for hiding Jews. They sent his father to the front and threw his mother in Auschwitz. Gerhard Oberschlick was forty-four before he discovered his more prosaic truth. It was then that he ran across a smudged wartime photo of the family. His father, sporting a Hitler-style mustache, flashed a swastika on his left lapel. His mother wore a peasant blouse that, one could see if one looked closely, was clasped by a swastika. The Oberschlicks were members of the Nazi Party.

These two boys who spent the war in Carinthia were inspired in the same direction by their parents' contrasting choices. Each became a journalist who confronted Austrians with unpopular points of historical memory. Lingens faced off against Bruno Kreisky, the self-denying Jew who rose to become the "Sun King of Vienna." Oberschlick took on Jorg Haider, modern Austria's slick and tenacious champion of the right. Each journalist was pilloried by the Austrian establishment, only to be vindicated by Europe. Together, they helped to establish the principle of press freedom in European law.

Bruno Kreisky and Austrian Historical Memory

There are elements of Austria's past that are not very nice to remember. Although Jews flourished in post-Enlightenment Vienna, the city elected as its fin-de-siècle mayor the outspoken anti-Semite Karl Lueger. In general, Austrians welcomed the 1938 *Anschluss* (union) with Nazi Germany and aryanized Jewish business with gusto. Austrians filled the Nazi Party's ranks out of proportion to their numbers, at both the lowest and highest levels. But after the war, Austrians of all political stripes embraced the myth that they were Hitler's first victims. With all the mainstream parties competing for the large ex-Nazi vote, denazification was notably lax. A standard Austrian history textbook written in 1970—the year Bruno Kreisky was elected—states: "The Second World War belongs to world history, but not to Austrian history. It was not an Austrian war. Austria did not participate in it."

Kreisky was the greatest proponent of the postwar myth. Although he lost twenty-odd members of his family in the Holocaust, he emphatically did not identify as a Jew. Kreisky told a Dutch journalist, "I have no Jewish fellow citizens." He told a Palestinian journalist, "There is nothing which binds me to Israel or to what is called the Jewish people." Indeed, Kreisky denounced Zionism as "a posthumous assumption of Nazi ideas in reverse." He negotiated with Palestinian hijackers while publicly embracing Yasir Arafat and Muammar Qaddafi in their more radical days.

One explanation of Kreisky's mind-set is that the Austrian leader merely reflected the attitudes around him. "If you live in an anti-Semitic country," says Peter Michael Lingens," you have two choices. You can separate yourself from the community or you can assimilate. And assimilating means becoming a little anti-Semitic yourself." Another explanation is that, from a young age, Kreisky defined himself in opposition to the Christian right—and, often, that meant making common cause with Nazis. Only an Austrian or a psychologist ought to comment on the first theory, but there is much evidence for the latter.

In the mid-1930s, both socialist and Nazi leaders were jailed by the ruling Christian conservatives. Kreisky formed a bond with his fellow prisoners, which later served him well. He agreed to pass a message from his Nazi roommate, Sepp Weninger, to Weninger's lawyer. Before the message could be delivered, the prison underwent an inspection. Kreisky swallowed the note, which might have incriminated Weninger. In return, when the Nazis came to power, Weninger saved Kreisky from deportation to a concentration camp. Grateful SS officers let Kreisky flee to Sweden in 1938, ten days ahead of Adolf Eichmann's arrival in Vienna. On his return seven years later, Kreisky tried but failed to save Weninger from execution for war crimes.

Kreisky swallowed many memories along with Weninger's note. Although the Austrian Socialist Party initially banned ex-Nazis from holding office, it rescinded the ban in 1947, because the ex-Nazi bloc was too large to disdain. In the hope of splitting the right-wing vote, socialists in 1949 encouraged the creation of a new party led by ex-Nazis, the Association of Independents, which eventually evolved into the Freedom Party, led in recent times by Haider. Many socialist leaders were themselves Nazi-educated, because the Nazis had systematically recruited working-class youngsters for the universities. The result was that the Socialists' first cabinet—when Kreisky at last led the party back to power in 1970—contained four ex-Nazis. Kreisky could boast of many worthy accomplishments over the next thirteen years, as he battled for social justice and reasserted Austria's voice in world affairs. But the first accomplishment of Austria's Jewish premier was to make ex-Nazis respectable.

The Guardian of Austrian Historical Memory

To be honest, Peter Michael Lingens made me nervous when we met. He still has the looks of an Aryan god, blond, tall, and lean, with calf muscles bulging from strenuous hikes in the Alps and Pyrenees. I couldn't suppress the unfair thought that, in the culture of his birth, bulging calf muscles were inspired by Nietzsche rather than Jack LaLanne. Peter Michael was born in 1939 in Vienna into a family from the German-Austrian establishment. His father's father, said to be the richest industrialist in Dusseldorf, served as the Cologne region's police chief through 1936. His mother's family owned Croatian soy farms and factories, and half a Viennese bank.

Politically, however, Kurt and Ella Lingens rebelled against their Christian conservative parents. A brilliant and charismatic woman, Ella became a doctor and a lawyer. She read *Mein Kampf* in 1933 and recognized early the magnitude of the danger it represented. After the war began, Ella and Kurt hid several Jews in their homes, with the hope of smuggling them into Switzerland. Kurt's brother, Klaus, wearing his German army uniform, would bring food to the hidden Jews by bicycle. Other friends of the family illegally transferred food stamps to the hidden Jews. In March 1942 a Jewish policeman informed on them. Kurt was transferred to the Strafkompanie, a dangerous unit on the eastern front. He survived. After the war Kurt separated from Ella and began a new life on his own in America.

Ella too survived the war. She spent two and a half years as a political prisoner, mostly at Auschwitz, where she served as a doctor (not an experimenter) in the hospital supervised by Josef Mengele. She later wrote a memoir about her experience, *Prisoners of Fear*. Tellingly, Ella felt compelled to write her book in English and publish it in England. Like Anton Schmid, Austria's most prominent rescuer of Jews during the war, Ella has been more honored outside Austria than in it.

Even in his absence, Peter Michael is a significant character in his mother's memoir. Ella dedicated the book "TO MY LITTLE SON, ASKING HIM TO FORGIVE ME THOSE YEARS OF MY ABSENCE." At Auschwitz, she could not keep out of her mind the image of Peter Michael at the age of three begging her as she was arrested, "Mummy, stay with me!" But when Ella was given another opportunity in the camp hospital to save a Jew she took it. "I said in my mind to my little boy: 'Child, perhaps you will have to wait still longer for your mummy. But when she comes back to you she wants to be able to look into your eyes—so that you won't have to be ashamed because your mother is German.' "

Without knowing of Peter Michael's personal memory, it is impossible to fully understand his position on national memory. Yet the judicial and legal literature omits the most salient fact in the Lingens family history. It took no great reporting to unearth Ella's past; it came up in the first five minutes of my interview with Peter Michael. I'd like to think that this completion of the Lingens saga is a vindication of journalism's value as an adjunct to law.

After hiding with his family nanny in Carinthia during the war, Peter Michael spent his school years in Vienna with his vivacious mother. He was raised in a salon of anti-Marxist socialist intellectuals, among them the philosopher Karl Popper and the physicist Alexander Weisberg. Peter Michael's first job after his army service, about 1960, was as a researcher for the Austrian-Jewish Nazi-hunter Simon Wiesenthal. He studied philosophy, law, and art—he was even admitted to Vienna's Art Academy, from which Hitler was rejected—but eventually he drifted into journalism. In the very year that Kreisky rose to power, Lingens, at age thirty, became editor-in-chief of a new weekly called *Profil*, which rapidly became Austria's equivalent of *Time* magazine.

In such a small country, a collision was perhaps inevitable between these two men who rose to power in parallel, and whose historical memories so diverged. In 1975, Kreisky's and Lingens's courses did collide, with a dramatic assist from Lingens's first boss, the Nazi-hunter Simon Wiesenthal.

Wiesenthal was tidying his desk after a vacation when he ran across a 1942 list of junior SS leaders nominated for an officers' training course.

Friedrich Peter—the chair of the Freedom Party and a key ally of Kreisky—appeared as a member of the First SS Infantry Brigade, a unit that systematically massacred Jews in the Soviet Union. Wiesenthal gave the smoking-gun document to the Austrian president on the eve of elections. Kreisky, who was running for prime minister, responded by defending Friederich Peter and denouncing Wiesenthal on television for using "mafia methods."

Alone among Austrian journalists, Peter Michael Lingens criticized Kreisky's outburst. The set of articles Lingens wrote on the Kreisky-Peter-Wiesenthal affair was destined to make legal history. The articles form an honorable and auspicious base for the principle of European press freedom. Far from seeming libelous today, they come across as wise and restrained.

In "Reconciliation with the Nazis, but how?" Lingens broadly argued that suppressing the past invites the rebirth of fascism. The "surprise" was not that people still remembered the Holocaust but that people had already forgotten it. The "monstrosity" was not that Wiesenthal had raised the matter but that Kreisky wished to hush it up. The article's concluding passage, poignant in light of Lingens's personal history, invokes the brave Austrians who refused to collaborate. If, instead of protecting Peter, "Kreisky had used his personal reputation . . . to reveal this other and better Austria," he would have helped his country "to come to terms with its past."

The closest Lingens came to a personal attack on the chancellor was to call his behavior "immoral" and "undignified." Had Kreisky's remarks been made by someone else, Lingens wrote, they might be described as "the basest opportunism." But, Lingens hastened to add, Kreisky was sincere.

Restrained as this commentary may seem to an outsider, Kreisky sued Lingens in the Austrian courts for criminal libel and prevailed. On March 26, 1979, the Vienna Regional Court found Lingens guilty of defamation for the expressions "the basest opportunism," "immoral," and "undignified." In an approach that strikes the American observer as absurd, the Austrian court put on journalists the burden of establishing the absolute truth of both their facts and their opinions. It reasoned that, because Kreisky's attitude toward Nazis was ambiguous, it was impossible for the defendant to establish that his understanding of Kreisky was correct. On October 29, 1981, the Vienna Court of Appeal affirmed, although it halved the fine imposed to fifteen thousand schillings, or roughly three thousand dollars. The appeals court seized on a piece of Lingens's own logic and twisted it. The court reasoned that, if Kreisky sincerely believed that Wiesenthal used mafia methods, then his remarks couldn't be "immoral" or "undignified."

On June 24, 1986, the European Court of Human Rights decided eighteen to zero in Lingens's favor, in the court's first interpretation of the European Convention's Article 10 guarantee of free expression. The court affirmed in sweeping language the importance of free speech as a basic condition for social progress and individual self-fulfillment, lying at "the very core of the concept of a democratic society." The court found it unacceptable to place on journalists the burden of proving the truth of their political value judgments.

Free Speech, Over Here and Over There

Lingens is rightly seen as Europe's version of the greatest American victory for press freedom, *New York Times v. Sullivan* (1964). The Mr. Sullivan in *Sullivan* was the Montgomery, Alabama, police commissioner, who sued the *New York Times* for running a full-page ad, inaccurate in some details, criticizing the police handling of civil rights protests in Montgomery. The crux of the analogy is that both cases constitutionalized the law of defamation—placing severe limits on the ability of a public official to use the courts to intimidate critics of his public conduct. One might add that both cases grew out of their society's defining evil: in the case of Europe anti-Semitism and in the case of America racism.

But that is about as far the analogy goes. On almost every issue, the First Amendment to the U.S. Constitution is more protective of free expression than European human rights law.

Even in the exact context of *Lingens*—where a public official retaliates under fire by suing the press for libel—European law is less protective. Under U.S. standards, opinion is always protected, and factual criticism of an official is often protected even when the critics get their facts wrong (as in *Sullivan* itself). In American courts, a public figure needs to show that the journalist made a false statement with "actual malice"; that is, either knowingly or with reckless disregard of the truth. That's tough to prove. By contrast, Strasbourg doesn't protect even opinions absolutely. In theory, a value judgment may be deemed excessive in Europe if it is deliberately careless or gratuitously personal, especially if it has no factual basis.

Europe's record in other areas of defamation is mixed. The *Lingens* rule, protecting journalists who criticize politicians, was extended to the criticism of public policy in *Castells v. Spain* (1993) and the defamation of police in *Thorgeirson v. Iceland* (1994). But the court has been uneven in protecting those who criticize prosecutors and judges. On the defamation of prosecutors, compare *Janowski v. Poland* (1999) with *Nikula v. Finland* (2002). On the prosecution of judges, compare *Barfod v. Denmark* (1991) and *Prager and Oberschlick v. Austria* (1994) with *De Haes and Gijsels v. Belgium* (1997). By contrast, America's hostility to defamation suits has extended to judicial defamation from the moment the field was constitutionalized. See *Garrison v. Louisiana* (1964).

Where public criticism is suppressed before the fact, Europe is again less protective of free speech. In the pathbreaking Strasbourg case, *Sunday Times v. United Kingdom* (1979), a closely divided court found that government policy did not justify a prior restraint on pre-trial publicity. However, the European analysis is fact-specific; Sometimes prior restraints are permitted. In both *Observer and Guardian v. United Kingdom* (1991) and *Vereniging Weekblad Bluf! v. Netherlands* (1995), the European Court of Human Rights approved, on security grounds, the seizure of newspapers publishing dated intelligence information. By contrast, the United States opposes prior restraints on the absolute ground that it is better to punish the few who abuse speech after they abuse it than to silence all beforehand. U.S. courts will not tolerate prior restraints even against "miscreant purveyors of scandal." See *Near v. Minnesota* (1931). And similar strict standards apply in the context of pretrial publicity. See *Nebraska Press Association v. Stuart* (1976). In practice, contempt orders and gag orders are never allowed.

Lingens and *Sullivan* were, in a sense, easy cases, because the journalists were clearly the good guys. After all, the courts were protecting the right of journalists to criticize someone else's hate speech. What happens when an applicant seeks legal protection for his *own* hate speech? To this question, Europe and the United States offer opposite answers.

U.S. courts are content-neutral in regulating expression—no matter how offensive the content. Thus, the Supreme Court allowed a Nazi march to proceed through a Jewish neighborhood in a Chicago suburb. See *National Socialist Party of America v. Village of Skokie* (1977). Likewise, the Supreme Court struck down a Minnesota law that banned public burnings of crosses or swastikas. See *R.A.V. v. City of St. Paul* (1992). Either of these rulings would be unthinkable in Europe.

In Europe after the Holocaust, the taboo on racism trumps free speech. Thus, in *Glimmerveen and Hagenbeek v. Netherlands* (1979), the European Commission on Human Rights upheld the conviction of right-wing Dutch politicians for advocating the return of migrant workers to

Surinam and Turkey. In *X. v. Germany* (1982), the commission permitted a German Jew to sue his neighbor for displaying on his garden fence a pamphlet describing the Holocaust as a Zionist swindle. On at least three occasions, the Strasbourg institutions upheld the German criminal law against group defamation of Holocaust victims, or other penal measures designed to curb neo-Nazi activities. See *Kuhnen v. Germany* (1988), *F.P. v. Germany* (1992); and *Remer v. Germany* (1995). These cases evince a basic philosophical difference on hate speech.

In essence, the United States lets the marketplace of ideas operate freely and hopes that truth prevails. Europeans—who have seen falsehood and hatred prevail—regard this position as naïve. As the French jurist and legal scholar Roger Errera puts it, Europeans "know what they do not want to see, what they refuse, and who and what are their enemies."

However limited European press law may seem by comparison to the First Amendment of the U.S. Constitution, *Lingens* is justly remembered as a landmark. The European Court of Human Rights is highly protective of the press when it critiques politicians, so long as the press itself has not stooped to hate speech.

Certainly, the European Court of Human Rights is inclined to side with the press against a public figure so hateful as Austria's Jorg Haider. Even our old friend Friederich Peter, who preceded Haider as Freedom Party leader, viewed Haider as extreme. In an interview held two days after the court's *Lingens* decision, the man whose SS past started the affair worried that Haider was fostering a Hitler cult. Fittingly, it was Haider who would provoke the next legal controversy on the Austrian past.

Is Jorg Haider Legally an Idiot?

Gerhard Oberschlick was born in 1942 in the Alpine Nazi heartland of Carinthia. It wasn't far from where Lingens was staying as a toddler with his nanny, or where Haider was born eight years later into an ex-Nazi family more prominent than the Oberschlicks. Improbably, this humble provincial boy became a nemesis of Haider and plucked from Lingens the torch of historical truth. Today, rather than honoring his Nazi parents, he hangs above his desk a painting of a bearded rabbi bowed in study.

Though Gerhard didn't learn of his parents' past until he reached middle age, his political awakening came as a teen. Gerhard was a member of a fencing club in Klagenfurt that had been founded after the war by an old man with right-wing leanings. The boys would sing a drinking song:

> Young men are living in the pub all day and night.
> Sitting nearby is a boring fellow,
> Who does not drink and does not laugh.
> Throw him OUT!
>   [Chorus]
>   The Jew . . .
>   The Jew . . .
>   The Jew!

Gerhard sang this song many times without giving it a second thought. But one day he ran across a book on the concentration camps in his father's library and drew the connection to this song. Gerhard brought it up with his friends and suggested that they stop singing the song. Some agreed; others told him not to take himself so seriously. The boys stopped singing the song. For Gerhard, it was the start of a long career in leftist activism.

In 1969, as a young journalist, Oberschlick joined *Forum*, a small, antiestablishment opinion magazine. His avowed goal was to fight Nazism and racism in every issue. The next year, as Kreisky and Lingens both rose to power, Oberschlick mounted a referendum campaign to abolish the Austrian army, which he considered to be irrevocably contaminated by Nazism. His pressure helped inspire the establishment of a civilian service alternative to the draft. But that was only a warm-up.

Twenty years later, in 1989, Haider won his first major public office, when he was elected governor of Carinthia. In an October 1990 speech that helped to form his reputation, he addressed a group that included many Waffen SS veterans, at the peak of Ulrichsberg, a mountain outside Klagenfurt. Haider called Nazi-era soldiers "not villains, but victims" and argued that all deserve gratitude. Attacking an Austrian intellectual who had recently disparaged Nazi soldiers, Haider laid out his own peculiar idea of free speech. "Ladies and gentlemen," he said, "freedom of opinion is taken for granted in a democracy, but it finds its limits where people lay claim to that freedom who never would have got it, if others had not risked their heads for them so that they may now live in democracy and freedom." In an odd sort of symmetry, Austria's second landmark case on press freedom sprang from a critique of Haider's own warped theory of press freedom.

Young *Forum* readers from Carinthia mailed the editor a bootleg cassette tape of Haider's speech. Oberschlick reprinted the speech with his own commentary. Fully aware that the Austrian courts might consider it libelous, Oberschlick noted that—regardless of whether Haider was a Nazi— he was an "idiot." Haider was an idiot, Oberschlick reasoned, because he seemed to think that anyone who hadn't borne arms should be gagged, and that would seem to include himself.

Haider sued for defamation, and the Vienna Criminal Court held, in May 1991, that the word "idiot" (*trottel*) was by definition an insult rather than objective criticism. It ordered that issue of *Forum* to be seized. The appeals court agreed that Oberschlick was guilty, noting that Haider's remarks were at worst "stupid" (*vertrottelt*).

In one of the easier decisions in its history, the European Court of Human Rights in January 1997 found for Oberschlick. Strasbourg came achingly close to judicially declaring Haider an idiot. "It is true that calling a politician a Trottel in public may offend him," the court noted. "In the instant case, however, the word does not seem disproportionate to the indignation knowingly aroused by Mr. Haider."

Postscripts

Bruno Kreisky never abandoned his high opinion of Friedrich Peter, or his low opinion of Simon Wiesenthal. In the late 1980s, Kreisky publicly revived his insinuation that Wiesenthal was a Nazi collaborator. In 1989, an Austrian court found Kreisky guilty of libel and fined him 270,000 schillings, then a record for an Austrian libel suit. Kreisky kept silent, having declared earlier that he was "too old to apologize to anyone for anything." He died within the year.

Austrian governments since Kreisky have shown a far more lucid sense of history. President Thomas Klestil articulated the new official line on a 1994 visit to Israel: "All too often we have spoken only of Austria as the first state to have lost its freedom and independence to National Socialism—and far too seldom of the fact that many of the worst henchmen in the Nazi dictatorship were Austrians." In 2001 the ruling right-wing coalition that included the Freedom Party agreed to pay reparations to victims of the Holocaust to settle class action lawsuits filed in the United States.

Haider has been in the thick of Austrian politics since *Oberschlick* and has continued to use libel suits as a weapon. Haider won 27 percent of the vote in the 1999 legislative elections. When the moderate-right leader Wolfgang Schussel announced the next year that he would form a government including Haider, the other states in the EU imposed sanctions. This move apparently backfired, as nationalism surged in Austria. The EU backed down in July 2000, allowing Haider to attend official ceremonies in neighboring states, starting with a trip to France for Bastille Day. At the same time the EU authorized a report by a three-member panel including two former members of the European Commission on Human Rights, Jochen Frowein and Marcelino Oreja. The report essentially put the Freedom Party on probation as "a right wing party with extremist expressions." Among its most problematic features, the report concluded, were the "systematic use of libel procedures to suppress criticism" and "the attempt to silence or even to criminalize political opponents."

Haider or his allies have brought libel suits against a magazine that pictured Haider with devil's horns on the cover, and against an archivist who described the Freedom Party as extreme and xenophobic. In May 2000 an Austrian court convicted the scholar Anton Pelinka for libeling Haider. Pelinka had criticized Haider for using the term "penal camps" to describe concentration camps, without noting the more conciliatory elements in the same speech by Haider. The lawyer who filed the suit on behalf of Haider, Dieter Boehmdorfer, became minister of justice in Schussel's coalition government.

Austria's compliance with the spirit of *Lingens* and *Oberschlick* has been uneven. The Austrian courts neglected to overturn Oberschlick's conviction for libel, although the government did pay the compensation set by Strasbourg. In *Unabhangige Initiative Informationsvielfalt v. Austria* (2002), the European Court again held Austria in violation of Article 10, because a court convicted the newspaper *TATblatt* for running a piece suggesting that the Freedom Party engaged in "racist agitation."

At the ballot box, Haider's influence has waned in recent years, but he cannot be counted out. He tactically withdrew as leader of the Freedom Party in February 2000 but returned in September 2002 to seize control of the party from its more moderate wing, prompting Chancellor Wolfgang Schussel to dissolve the ruling coalition. In March 2004 Haider was reelected as governor of Carinthia.

Because of his own ethical blunders, Peter Michael Lingens is not covering the latest Austrian drama as an editor. In the early 1990s, while serving as editor of the nation's leading quality daily, *Standard*, Lingens became embroiled in a corruption scandal. He ruefully admits that, through a friend, he lobbied a prosecutor to go easy on a Russian businesswoman under investigation because she had given a job to his son's fiancée. Lingens says he was not aware that his friend tried to bribe the prosecutor. Lingens was ultimately acquitted. Nonetheless, he resigned from *Standard* in disgrace. After two years in the wilderness, he was given a column in his old magazine, Profil.

I spoke with Lingens at his retirement villa in southern Spain. We sat in his living room beneath a framed cartoon of Friedrich Peter, showing Peter taking an army boot off his foot to reveal a claw in the shape of a swastika. When pressed, Lingens will offer opinions on Haider. His chief danger, Lingens believes, lies in the cult of personality that has grown up around him. Like Hitler and Kreisky in their time, Haider inspires supporters to argue, "It's true because he says it's true." As an admirer of Karl Popper's philosophy, Lingens wishes for higher standards of truth in both politics and journalism. That, he believes, is what his mother stood for.

Ella Lingens died in 2002. In her final years she told her son that her memories of Auschwitz were fading, and she was glad. In Peter Michael's view, "Only my mother has a right to say that." For the rest of Europe, forgetting is not an option.

CHAPTER 9

Mohammed Comes to Strasbourg

Sevket Kazan offers me a cup of sugary Turkish tea in his nondescript office, which is distinguished only by its photo of modern Turkey's founder, Mustafa Kemal Ataturk. A portrait of Ataturk is not generally a distinguishing feature in Turkey; indeed it is required by law. But this photo is a collector's item; it shows the militant secularist, who banned Muslim headwear, standing beside a turbaned imam. According to the caption, Ataturk is thanking Allah for Turkey's military successes.

"We are not an Islamist party," Kazan is saying to me, as the call to prayer from the mosque attached to his party headquarters wafts through the corridors. "We are a party struggling against the oppression of Muslim people." Kazan's semantic point is unpersuasive; His party, Saadet, and its powerful predecessor, Refah, were clearly Islamist in the sense that Islam is the organizing principle of its adherents' personal and political lives. But Kazan's affirmative claim is worth considering: that Turkey's Islamists are generally on the side of human rights in the struggle against oppression. Political Islam in Turkey may be imperfect, but it is promising and evolving. To declare it immutably undemocratic, as the European Court of Human Rights has done, is foolish or worse. The shabby reception Strasbourg has given political Islam can only lend credence to the charge, widely heard in Turkey, that official Europe suffers from "Islamophobia."

Europe's tradition of Turk-bashing is long and ugly, although it has occasionally taken eloquent form. "What is a Turk?" asked a Christian cleric while the Ottomans advanced on Vienna. "He is a replica of the Antichrist . . . he is an insatiable tiger . . . he is a vengeful beast; he is a thief of crowns without conscience, he is a murderous falcon . . . he is oriental dragon poison; he is an unchained hellhound; he is an Epicurean piece of excrement; he is a tyrannic monster. He is God's whip." Two centuries later, after the Turks brutally crushed a Bulgarian revolt, William Gladstone declaimed, "Wherever they went, a broad line of blood marked the track behind them, and as far as their dominion reached, civilization vanished from view."

Shakespeare referred to the Turk as "malignant" and "turbaned," and Ataturk tried to change both images. Despite the anomalous photo hanging in Sevket Kazan's office, Ataturk largely succeeded in removing the Turk's turban. What he could not remove was the Turk's malignancy in the eyes of Europe.

Rise and Fall of the Refah Party

In 1973, Sevket Kazan joined with an Islamist populist by the name of Necmettin Erbakan to found the Refah Party. The two never looked back. Kazan served in Parliament from 1973 to 1977 and from 1991 to 1998. (During most of the remaining years, he was barred from running by the military authorities). He served as justice minister in 1974 in a center-left coalition, as labor minister from 1976 to 1977 in a center-right coalition, and again as justice minister from 1996 to 1997, in a coalition formed by Refah and led by Erbakan.

Thirteen years after Kazan entered politics and helped to found the party, Refah held 158 seats out of 450 in Parliament. In June 1996 it formed a coalition government with Erbakan as prime minister, and in November 1996 it won 34 percent of the vote in local elections.

Refah's thirteen months in power saw a steady drizzle of religious controversy, mostly on symbolic matters. Kazan provoked the secularist press by calling fashion models exhibitionists and idly suggesting that sentences be reduced for prisoners who memorized the Koran. The government tried to reorganize public employee hours to allow for fasting during Ramadan, but its policy was annulled by the supreme administrative court. Most controversially, Erbakan floated the ideas that civil servants be allowed to wear headscarves and that a giant mosque be built in Istanbul's Taksim Square. However, he eventually backed down on both points under military pressure. In foreign policy Turkey cozied up to Iran.

Religious tensions broke into a storm on Friday, January 31, 1997, when Refah's Bekir Yildiz, mayor of the Ankara suburb of Sincan, hosted Iran's Turkish ambassador at an al Quds night (al Quds being the Arabic name for Jerusalem). An al Quds night is a ritual occasion for anti-Israel protest inaugurated by Ayatollah Khomeini. Actors reenacted the Palestinian intifada, and, capping a night of hot rhetoric, the Iranian exhorted the crowd, "Do not be afraid to call yoursel[ves] fundamentalists!"

At about 10 AM on Sunday, February 2, Kazan went into his office at party headquarters and learned of the Sincan event in blaring newspaper headlines. In Kazan's account, as the party's vice president for public relations, he was furious at Yildiz for organizing such a provocation without party approval. Kazan says he got Yildiz on the phone straightaway and cursed him—with what curse words he will not specify. He claims to have yelled, "Do you want the party to be banned?!" and slammed down the phone in anger.

Sincan indeed proved to be the last straw for Turkey's secularists. On Tuesday morning the military sent a few dozen tanks and armored carriers rumbling through the suburb. In short order, prosecutors arrested Yildiz and nine others who participated in the rally.

Meanwhile, Kazan says, he was stewing over the conversation he'd had with Mayor Yildiz. Worried that he had been too harsh, Kazan resolved to apologize. He met with Yildiz in prison, in the presence of the prison warden and the public prosecutor. As he recalls the meeting, he reiterated his criticism of Sincan's action but apologized for having used hurtful words.

Over the ensuing months, Turkey's military-dominated National Security Council eased the Islamists out of power. Turks refer to this episode in their history as "the post-modern coup," because the military obtained Erbakan's resignation through legal and political pressure and the implicit threat of force, rather than through actual force. At the end of February 1997, the security council called on the government to resign. Turkey's chief prosecutor opened a court case against Refah on May 21. The government resigned on June 22. On January 16, 1998, the Turkish Constitutional Court dissolved the Refah Party, seized its assets, and imposed a five-year political ban on its three top leaders, Erbakan, Kazan, and Ahmet Tekdal. Kazan's visit with Mayor Yildiz was the principal grounds for his personal ban. The Turkish court attributed to Refah the aim of enacting *sharia*, or Islamic law, and declared, "Democracy is the antithesis of *sharia*." Refah and its leaders challenged Turkey in Strasbourg for violating the rights of free assembly and association, guaranteed by Article 11 of the European Convention on Human Rights.

Militant Democracy

In Strasbourg, the right of political association is limited by the principle of "militant democracy," which originated in postwar West Germany. With the Nazi Party a recent memory, the German constitution called for the vigilant defense of the "free democratic basic order." In the same spirit, European Convention Article 17 stipulates that the Convention not be construed to allow the rise of movements that would crush the freedoms it guarantees. To borrow a phrase coined by U.S. Justice Robert Jackson, the German constitution and the European Convention are emphatically not suicide pacts. On this principle, the West German Constitutional Court upheld bans on the Nazi and Communist parties in 1952 and 1956. The West German Communist Party applied to Strasbourg, and, in 1957, the European Commission on Human Rights found its petition inadmissible. A proletarian dictatorship, the commission reasoned, would ultimately destroy liberty.

This is not to say that the right to political association is a dead letter in Strasbourg. The European Court of Human Rights has upbraided Turkey at least five times for violating the right to assembly in banning parties that advocated Kurdish rights: the Communist Party, the Socialist Party, and a series of overtly Kurdish parties formed under the initials OZDEP, HEP, and DEP. In addition, the leaders of DEP won a separate victory under the right to free elections. The European Court of Human Rights has repeatedly affirmed the general principle that nations are entitled to scant deference when they limit the right to political association.

In each of the Kurdish political cases, Strasbourg rejected Turkey's argument that the party was dangerously antidemocratic. *OZDEP v. Turkey* (1999) explained that a party's platform is the essential starting point in assessing the party's true character. In that case, the court considered whether a banned Kurdish party secretly harbored separatist ambitions, which would be inimical to a democratic state. "[I]t cannot be ruled out that the passages concerned may conceal a different political design from the publicly proclaimed one," the court noted. "However, given the absence of any concrete acts suggesting otherwise, there is no reason to cast doubts on the genuineness of OZDEP's programme."

Mohammed in Strasbourg

The European Court of Human Rights ruled against Refah by a four to three vote of the initial chamber on July 31, 2001 and, after referral, by a unanimous vote of the grand chamber on February 13, 2003. The court concluded that Refah advocated three antidemocratic doctrines: that *sharia* should be the law of the land; alternatively, that the adherents of different religions should obey different legal systems; and that a holy war, or jihad, should be waged to pursue these goals. In short, Refah was said to advocate Islamic law or plural legal systems, and violence in their pursuit.

As evidence, the court relied chiefly on a string of statements made over time by individual members of the party. To prove Refah's commitment to *sharia*, the court cited its leaders' frequent references to "a just order." To prove Refah's commitment to jihad in establishing *sharia*, the court pointed, for instance, to a campaign statement made by Erbakan in April 1994 that could be read as a veiled threat: "How will Refah come to power?" he asked. "Will the transition [to a just social order] be peaceful or violent; will it be achieved harmoniously or by bloodshed?"

Probably the most frightening and explicit statement came from the Refah parliamentarian Ibrahim Halil Celik. In May 1997, when Refah was struggling to hold onto power, he warned that if religious schools were shut down, "blood will flow. It would be worse than Algeria. I too would like blood to flow. That's how democracy will be installed. And it will be a beautiful thing. . . . I will fight to the end to introduce *sharia*." Refah expelled Celik a month after prosecutors initiated proceedings to ban the party. But the grand chamber dismissed this action as a last-ditch effort to dodge the ban. In general, Refah nominated the offending speakers as candidates for important posts and took no disciplinary action until the party was on the verge of dissolution.

While conceding that Refah's platform was harmless and that little was objectionable in its actions to date, the court discerned in the scattered statements of Refah leaders a hidden agenda. Member of Parliament Sevki Yilmaz certainly invited such scrutiny when he declared, in April 1994, that jihad would begin only after Muslims captured state power. "Muslims are intelligent," he said. "They do not reveal how they intend to beat their enemy."

To support its suspicions, the court invoked the history of antidemocratic parties exploiting the political process to take control. As ever, Hitler was the unremarked elephant in Strasbourg's bathtub. But the examples of Iran and Algeria also loomed large. "[F]undamentalism has successfully seized power before," the first panel pointedly noted. "[It's] not at all improbable," mused the grand chamber, "that totalitarian movements, organised in the form of political parties, might do away with democracy, after prospering under the democratic regime, there being examples of this in modern European history." In this light, a party tarred with the antidemocratic brush can do no right. The deeper Refah's democratic support, the greater the threat it poses to democracy. The grand chamber fretted, as if it strengthened the democratic argument against Refah, that Turkish Islamists might be popular enough to form a government on their own, without coalition partners. As a matter of political handicapping, this fear proved to be prescient, but Turkish democracy is doing just fine, which doesn't say much for the court's political wisdom.

In a persuasive dissent to the first ruling, British judge Nicolas Bratza refused to simply assume the existence of a hidden plot. In keeping with the court's *OZDEP* approach, Bratza gave Refah the benefit of the doubt. "There is nothing in its constitution or programme to indicate that Refah was other than democratic," he wrote, and there is no compelling evidence that Refah took "any steps [to] undermine the secular society." In the absence of damning official acts, all the court could point to were a few scattered statements made by individuals in different contexts and at different times— mostly before the party came to power. Moreover, the state had never prosecuted those individuals before resorting to the extreme measure of banning the party.

Refah leaders insist that their isolated references to violence are metaphorical and that, far from being code for *sharia*, "a just order" is shorthand for human rights. Refah lawyer Seref Malkogbeye says the court turned the party's views upside down. "We accept the democratic standards of the West and want to implement them in Turkey," he says. "This is what we mean by a 'just order.'" What's more, says Malkogbeye, "Our movement is a model for other Islamic countries and for Islamic minorities in Europe."

Graham Fuller, a leading American scholar of Turkey, takes at face value the Turkish Islamists' self-image as an authentic democratic movement at odds with a state ideology that oppresses people of faith. He sees Islamism as a force that attracts young and educated voters from the provinces who yearn for social justice and resent entrenched elites associated with patronage, corruption, and Westernization.

Calling such a movement antidemocratic provoked anger and charges of "Islamophobia." On the day the grand chamber ruled, Sevket Kazan told the Associated Press, "We can see from this ruling that the European Court of Human Rights in fact cannot protect human rights in any country and practices double standards." Malkogbeye makes a similar point: "This decision says that Europe is a club for Christians. If there can be Christian Democratic parties, why not an Islamic Democratic Party?"

Those who detect a pattern of "Islamophobia" in Strasbourg can point to a handful of rulings that seem insensitive to American eyes. In *Ahmad v. United Kingdom* (1981), the European Commission on Human Rights rejected the claim of a Muslim teacher who was not allowed to extend his lunch hour by forty-five minutes to pray at a mosque on Friday afternoons. The court reasoned that there is no absolute Muslim requirement that worship take place in a mosque. In *Kalac v. Turkey* (1997), the court held that it was permissible for Turkey to fire its air force's legal director on account of his close ties to a Muslim sect, because Kalac had voluntarily subjected himself to the strictures of the military.

But Strasbourg's support for Turkey's headscarf ban, mind-boggling to most Americans, is by far the most prominent example of perceived Islamophobia. In the 1993 cases of *Karaduman v. Turkey* and *Bulut v. Turkey*, the European Commission on Human Rights rejected applications from a pair of Turkish university students. Each was barred from graduating because she wouldn't pose for the photograph on her diploma without a headscarf. The judges reasoned that the students had chosen a secular (*laïque*) university and were subject to its rules. In October 2005 *Leyla Sahin v. Turkey* reaffirmed this harsh position emphatically. In *Sahin*, a grand chamber of the court ruled by a vote of sixteen to one against a medical student who was refused access to a written exam at Istanbul University because she wore a headscarf. Ostensibly, the court gave precedence to Turkey's right to regulate universities, maintain public order, and protect the rights of secular citizens, bearing in mind the threat of radical Islamist movements.

In fairness, these decisions may not reflect Islamophobia so much as a distinct conception of religious freedom. Under the European Convention on Human Rights, a nation is given wide discretion to limit religious freedom if it clashes with other rights or with the interests of public order and safety. Article 9 doesn't guarantee the right to always behave in public as one's beliefs demand. Indeed, in much of Europe, notably Kemalist Turkey and republican France, the state is expected to patrol a secular public sphere.

Strasbourg's characterization of the school in the Turkish headscarves cases as *laïque* underscores the French origin of this restrictive concept of religious liberty. France itself has struggled with this issue. In October 1989, three Muslim schoolgirls were sent home from a school in Creil, north of Paris, for wearing headscarves. This incident set off a never-ending debate. Five intellectuals wrote an open letter exhorting France not to capitulate to

Islamicism lest Creil become "the Munich of republicanism." Three ministerial circulars and three court rulings struck shifting compromise positions. A September 1994 circular banned "ostentatious" religious symbols from state schools, but a July 1995 Conseil d'Etat ruling held that a headscarf is not ostentatious and does not in itself justify expulsion. Under these ambiguous guidelines, the issue simmered. In early 2004, following the popular recommendations of a commission appointed by President Jacques Chirac, the French legislature voted overwhelmingly to ban the wearing of headscarves and other ostentatious religious ornaments in state schools. To practicing Muslims in France or Turkey, the distinction between Islamophobia and the republican concept of religious liberty is a thin one.

The Mutability of Islam

In concluding that *sharia* is inherently antidemocratic (a conclusion affirmed by the grand chamber), the first *Refah* panel made the astonishing assertion that Islamic law is "stable and invariable," with no place for political pluralism or an evolving concept of freedoms. History may well judge this to be among the stupidest of judicial generalizations, comparable to the U.S. Supreme Court's relegation of African Americans to a "subordinate and inferior class of beings," in the 1856 *Dred Scott* decision.

In the view of many Islamic scholars, while *sharia* itself may be immutable, the human interpretation and application of *sharia*, termed *fiqh*, is infinitely variable. Graham Fuller made the mutability of Muslim law one of the main themes of his book *The Future of Political Islam*. "It is clearly incorrect," he writes, "to think of political Islam as a fixed ideology." And again: "Islam is not a fixed thing, able to be skewered like a butterfly specimen and placed in a box on exhibit for all time." On the contrary, Islamic law, like any other system of law, is shaped by the evolving needs and desires of its adherents.

It is impossible for an outsider to say who is more representative of Refah: the smoothies who charm the venturesome Western journalist or the fire-eating jihadis quoted by the Strasbourg majority. But the analogy to early Christian democracy is worth pondering.

Europe's Christian Democratic parties were first formed in the 1870s, in reaction to a wave of laws that secularized education and other state functions. Christian Democrats gained power in the 1880s, notably in Belgium, the Netherlands, and Austria. Soon the parties cut their organizational ties to the Catholic Church and, beginning about the turn of the century, replaced church doctrine with vague concepts like "Christian values." In his 1996 history, *The Rise of Christian Democracy in Europe*, Stathis Kalyvas concludes that these parties' original goal—the "rechristianization" of society—was quickly abandoned. By eroding party members' church ties and the church's political ties, parties that were formed to bring religion back into politics ended by taking religion out of politics. Whatever else Christian Democracy is, it is surely not, as the court said of *sharia*, stable and invariable. Here's one analogy to remind us that politics often *tames* ideology.

Of course, one needn't venture so far to find an example of an ideological party tamed by power. The newspaper headlines have served up a perfect experiment to prove Strasbourg wrong in its fears of Turkish political Islam.

The European Court of Human Rights was correct in foreseeing that Turkish Islamists were on the verge of winning an absolute majority. But the wing of Sevket Kazan and Necmettin Erbakan, now called Saadet, has been eclipsed by the other, more moderate offshoot of the Refah Party: the AK Party, headed by Recep Tayyip Erdogan.

AK's Erdogan used to be banned from politics too, for, like Erbakan, he could easily be painted as a radical based on a pastiche of old statements. A 1998 court ban cited Erdogan's recitation of a verse that could be interpreted as a call for jihad: "The mosques are our barracks, the minarets our bayonets, the domes our helmets and the believers soldiers." Erdogan proclaimed in 1995, "You cannot be secular and a Muslim at the same time. The world's 1.5 billion Muslims are waiting for the Turkish people to rise up. We will rise up. With Allah's permission, the rebellion will start." The Turkish Supreme Court affirmed Erdogan's ban for life, despite parliamentary changes, in the fall of 2002. But when the AK Party won that fall's elections in a landslide, Erdogan staged what might be called a postmodern countercoup. The AK Party quickly pushed through legislation that succeeded in overturning Erdogan's ban and installing him as prime minister.

In power, Erdogan has shown a capacity for growth not associated with Islam by the European Court of Human Rights, and AK has so far shown its true colors to be democratic. Turkey's implementation of reform has a long way to go. But in terms of legislation, Turkey has made more human rights progress under Erdogan than under all its previous leaders. As Graham Fuller concludes, "Political Islam in Turkey has evolved rapidly out of an initially narrow and nondemocratic understanding of Islam into a relatively responsible force," whether or not it coincides perfectly with Western ideals.

American elites are warming to the notion of democratic Islam. True, in denying the United States military access to Iraq through Turkish territory, the Islamist-controlled Turkish Parliament chose loyalty to its constituents over loyalty to its foreign benefactor. But wiser American voices, such as law professor Noah Feldman, recognized that the entrenchment of Turkey's democracy outweighed any short-term setback to U.S. interests. And in drafting new constitutions for the devout societies of Afghanistan and Iraq, it became obvious to American advisers that some form of democratic Islam was the only option. In that context, the U.S. foreign policy establishment accepts the possibility of Islamic democracy as axiomatic.

Europe can't seem to reconcile the mosque and the polling booth. In caricaturing Islam as immutable, the European Court of Human Rights only revealed its own rigidity of thought. Though Strasbourg is not bound by original intent, it remains haunted by the memory of Hitler's election, even when that analogy is inapt. Regardless of whether the Refah ruling reflected anti-Muslim animus, it felt to Muslims like a slap in the face. That's a big defeat for the European project. Only a constitutional identity capacious enough to include Islam can reflect the diversity of the Council of Europe's 800 million people.

PART III

State Violence

CHAPTER 10

The Death Penalty, Mutilation, and the Whip

Corporal punishment and capital punishment are rarely discussed together, for fear that the one will trivialize the other. But grouping "the death penalty, mutilation and the whip," to borrow a phrase from Tocqueville, is not wholly illogical. Corporal and capital punishment lie on a continuum of state-sanctioned violence against the person. And both are areas where the contrast between European and American practice is especially sharp.

The Cane, the Birch, and the Belt

The tradition of British corporal punishment is well known to devotees of English literature. Remember the sadistic schoolmasters of Charles Dickens novels? Nicholas Nickleby watched with horror as Wackford Squeers whacked his young friends, and Mr. Creakle threatened to give David Copperfield "marks of distinction." The boarding school discipline at Eton certainly left a lasting impression on the poet Charles Swinburne, who later composed a 167-page cycle called *The Flogging Block*, featuring the subtly titled verses "Algernon's Flogging," "Reginald's Flogging," "Percy's Flogging," "Willie's Flogging," "Charlie's Flogging," "Edward's Flogging," "Frank's Flogging," "Frederick's Flogging," "Edgar's Flogging," "Rupert's Flogging," and "Rufus's Flogging." A 1977 survey by the Educational Institute of Scotland showed that 36 percent of Scottish high school boys were belted at least fortnightly. Even Tony Blair, as an overly talkative teenager, was given "six of the best" by his housemaster at Fettes College in Edinburgh.

The American tradition of corporal punishment is no less real for being less storied. In *Ingraham v. Wright* (1977), the U.S. Supreme Court rejected the argument that school corporal punishment is cruel and unusual punishment under the Eighth Amendment to the Constitution. With characteristic reverence for tradition, the American justices relied on the sort of "original intent" logic that the European Court rejects. Noting that the right was designed to protect prisoners, the U.S. Supreme Court declined to "wrench the Eighth Amendment from its historical context and extend it to traditional disciplinary practices in the public schools." The Supreme Court thus turned its back on the alternative approach of dynamic interpretation, embodied in a 1958 landmark. In *Trop v. Dulles*, Chief Justice Earl Warren honored "the evolving standards of decency that mark the progress of a maturing society." While the United States apparently ceased to mature on the issue of corporal punishment, the standards of inhumanity in Europe evolved rapidly.

Soon after the American *Ingraham* ruling, the European Court of Human Rights reached the diametrically opposite conclusion and struck down judicial corporal punishment on the British Isle of Man. In *Tyrer v. United Kingdom* (1978), the court held that it was inhuman and degrading, in violation of European Convention Article 3, for the Manx judicial authority to publicly birch a rowdy holidaymaker.

Strasbourg's ruling provoked a backlash from the start. When *he* was a schoolboy, the British judge Gerald Fitzmaurice wrote in dissent, getting caned was a matter of pride. Even the nominal applicant seemed to agree. Tony Tyrer sought to withdraw his case early on, but the European Commission on Human Rights ruled that the general question merited a hearing. Tyrer declined repeated requests to cooperate with this book. According to family friend Susan Kelly, Tony Tyrer always believed that being birched put him on the straight and narrow. "[H]e felt the sentence was justified," says Kelly, "and was totally mystified and annoyed about the whole matter." For better or for worse, the European Court of Human Rights has shown a willingness to get out ahead of local public opinion on certain issues, perhaps even ahead of the plaintiff's opinion.

With or without Tyrer's approval, the *Tyrer* controversy inspired a generation of parents to bring similar cases. It was just a skip and a hop from judicial corporal punishment to school corporal punishment, whether in the context of state-funded or privately-funded schools. While *Tyrer* was making headlines in the autumn of 1976, the headmaster at a state-funded Scottish school threatened to belt young Jeffrey Cosans for taking a shortcut on his way to classes. Jeffrey's parents objected, and in *Campbell and Cosans v. United Kingdom* (1982), the court stayed the schoolmaster's hand on a new theory. It reasoned that, by subjecting kids in state-funded schools to beatings, the United Kingdom violated the right of the children's parents to choose an education consistent with their own philosophy.

The argument from school choice wouldn't have saved Swinburne from the lash at Eton. But the argument from inhumanity applied at all schools, and soon a new cohort of parents joined the anticaning campaign. *Costello-Roberts v. United Kingdom* (1995) sufficed, barely, to extend the principle. The European judges found that three pats with a slipper didn't amount to degradation. At the same time, they clarified that—if egregious enough—a beating in a privately funded school can also be degrading.

Old traditions die hard. In a painfully slow response to the *Campbell and Cosans* ruling, Parliament finally banned corporal punishment in state-funded schools, effective August 15, 1997. Light caning in privately funded British schools persists, although it is declining, and its abolition has been debated. The tradition's decline has been definitively documented in badly punning headlines. According to the *Sunday Standard* of Glasgow ("Rise and Fall of the Belt," February 28, 1982), the production of leather tawses in Scotland came to a quick halt after the *Cosans* ruling. In 1994, in anticipation of the ban on corporal punishment, the *Sunday Observer* of London ran a similar story about English manufacturers of canes, under the headline, "Cane-makers See Bottom Fall Out of Their Market" (May 1, 1994).

The next step beyond banning beatings in the judicial and school systems is to ban beatings in the home. In the case that came to be known as *A. v. United Kingdom*, a man had severely beaten his stepson with a garden cane. The English jury found the stepfather not guilty of assault under the English principle that a parent is allowed to "reasonably chastise" his child. The European Court of Human Rights, in September 1998, held that England's "reasonable chastisement" rule did not adequately protect the boy from inhuman and degrading treatment. The upshot is that the European Convention places limits on parental beatings.

In recognizing that an individual has a right to affirmative government protection, the court made a conceptual leap that the U.S. Supreme Court will not. In the infamous case of *DeShaney v. Winnebago County Dept. of Social Services* (1989), four-year-old Joshua was beaten by his father into a coma. Wisconsin's child welfare authorities had ignored overwhelming evidence, from hospital visits and social worker reports, that Joshua was in danger. Chief Justice William Rehnquist concluded—over the dissent's anguished cry of "Poor Joshua!"—that "a State's failure to protect an individual against private violence" is constitutional. Shocking as it may sound, the United States admits "no affirmative right to governmental aid, even where such aid may be necessary to secure life."

As the contrast between *DeShaney* and *A. v. United Kingdom* dramatizes, individual rights come in two philosophical flavors. The American tradition, flowing from Locke, lays more of a stress on liberty and sees the court's role strictly as limiting government. The European tradition, which is also favored internationally, flows from Rousseau. As elaborated by Francesca Klug in *Values for a Godless Age*, the European approach sees more of a role for equality and community and lets the court put affirmative obligations on the state.

Perhaps the neatest contrasts with *DeShaney* are presented by *Z. v. United Kingdom* (2001) and *E. v. United Kingdom* (2002). In each of these cases, British child welfare authorities allowed children to remain in the custody of abusive adults despite repeated warning signs, and the children suffered abuse. The European Court of Human Rights held that British authorities failed to manage the situation acceptably. Under Article 3, the state has positive obligations to take reasonably available measures (better investigation, better communication) to minimize the risk of private violence to those who are vulnerable. In addition, under the Article 13 obligation to provide an effective remedy, domestic law must give the victims a practical cause of action for negligence. Given the different constitutional streams that flow on either side of the Atlantic, it's hard to avoid the conclusion that the poor Joshuas of the future would be better off living in Europe.

Death and Death Row

No issue divides the chattering classes in Europe and the U.S. more sharply than the death penalty. A telling cartoon in *The Economist* has depicted the Statue of Liberty holding a hypodermic needle, primed for lethal injection, instead of a torch. In December 2005, officials in Arnold Schwarzenegger's hometown of Graz, Austria, removed his name from the local football stadium to protest the muscular governor's approval of an execution in California. Many European lawyers regard judicial executions in the United States as a human rights violation on a par with extrajudicial executions in Latin America.

Even in Europe, the death penalty's legitimacy was unquestioned when the human rights convention was drafted in 1949. Article 2 of the European Convention bars only *extrajudicial* execution. But European opinion has evolved. Protocol 6 of the Convention, accepted by every nation except Russia, abolishes the death penalty in peacetime. Protocol 13 abolishes the death penalty in all circumstances. The absolute ban entered force in July 2003 and was accepted by thirty-three nations in short order.

In 1995 and 1996, the Council of Europe made Albania, Ukraine, Macedonia, Moldova, Bosnia, and Russia undertake to abolish the death penalty as a condition of membership. In 1999 the Parliamentary Assembly of the Council of Europe expressly resolved to make Europe "a death penalty–free continent." When Ukraine and Albania wavered, the Parliamentary Assembly began the process of suspending Ukraine from the Council of Europe and warned Albania that it faced a similar fate. The constitutional courts of Ukraine and Albania renounced capital punishment at the end of 1999. Turkey abolished its death penalty in 2003 as part of a larger effort to harmonize its laws with the EU. With the exception of Russian executions under emergency rule in Chechnya, Europe is indeed a death penalty–free zone. Having folded up the electric chair in Europe, Strasbourg is openly campaigning against the U.S. death penalty. The Parliamentary Assembly has called for a moratorium on U.S. capital punishment, and the European Court is exerting pressure through its judgments.

The unlikely standard-bearer of the anti–death penalty crusade in Strasbourg is Jens Soering. The son of a German diplomat, Soering was a nineteen-year-old freshman at the University of Virginia, on a full-merit scholarship, when he was accused of slaying the parents of his girlfriend in a bizarre folie à deux. Elizabeth Haysom's parents, who incidentally disapproved of the match, were found dead of knife wounds in their Virginia home on April 3, 1985; her father was stabbed thirty-seven times. The disturbed young couple toured Europe for the next fourteen months, playing with disguises and kiting checks, until they were caught by Scotland Yard. Soering confessed to the murders, and the United States requested extradition from Britain. Fearing execution, Soering turned to the European Court of Human Rights to halt his extradition.

Soering v. U.K. (1989) gave the court an opportunity to outlaw the death penalty once and for all. Amnesty International, in an amicus brief, pushed the most direct point, arguing that the death penalty itself was inhuman and degrading under Article 3 of the European Convention. It was hard for the court to accept this argument when the text of Article 2 so clearly contemplates capital punishment. But the judges seemed determined to obstruct the death penalty. Their trick was to find it significant that a convict might await execution in Virginia for eight years. In that light, the court held that the *wait* on death row was inhuman and degrading. In May 2005, in *Ocalan v. Turkey*, the court was again pressed to outlaw the death penalty, and it again compromised with a creative position as to death row. In *Ocalan*, a grand chamber of the court suggested that, when a defendant is convicted after an *unfair* trial, waiting on death row is inhuman and degrading. In both cases, the reasoning of the court recalls the proverb of the enlightenment advocate of prison reform, Cesare Beccaria, that uncertainty is "the cruelest tormentor of the miserable."

With considerably less eloquence, New York Senator Alfonse D'Amato led a chorus of American critics, denouncing the *Soering* ruling as "indefensible." As Soering later put it, "D'Amato bitterly condemned those interfering liberal Europeans for daring to lecture the U.S. on human rights, and for depriving law-abiding Virginians of the pleasure of watching an animal like me fry."

Be that as it may, U.S. diplomats promised not to seek the death penalty, and Britain extradited Soering to face a jury in Lynchburg, Virginia, that was understandably hostile. Televised in full, this German baroque trial became the American South's answer to the O. J. Simpson show. Suffice it to say that Soering's mockery of the local police as "yokels" didn't endear him the jury in Lynchburg. He was convicted on two counts of first degree murder and sentenced to consecutive life terms in prison. Elizabeth Haysom pleaded guilty as an accessory before the fact and received a sentence of ninety years.

In his prison memoirs, Soering constructs a not-wholly-implausible tale that Elizabeth Haysom committed the murders. He gave a false confession, he says, in the mistaken belief that he'd be shielded by his father's diplomatic immunity. All he wanted to do was save his girlfriend from the electric chair. Striking a heroic pose, à la Sidney Carton in *A Tale of Two Cities*, Soering says he doesn't regret lying on behalf of Haysom: "I am glad I did not become part of the judicial process that would have sent Elizabeth to her death."

Notwithstanding Soering's new claims, the U.S. Court of Appeals for the Fourth Circuit affirmed the denial of a writ of habeas corpus in 2000. The circuit court noted that Soering's confessions matched the murders in details. It also stressed that his blood type, unlike Elizabeth's, matched the blood found at the scene. Known to be tough on crime, the circuit court didn't stress that Soering's confessions contained some discrepancies, and that he shares a blood type with 45 percent of the general population.

Regardless of whether he was the murderer or the accessory, Jens Soering is the least heroic of this book's "heroes." Then again, Clarence Gideon, whose case enshrined the indigent right to counsel in America, was called a "maniac" in his time. As one lawyer in the Gideon case commented, "Upon the shoulders of such persons are our great rights carried." One hardly needs to accept Soering's tale to deplore the fact that he was nearly executed, nor to admire the anti–death penalty campaign that his case advanced.

CHAPTER 11

The Original Hooded Men

The tension between state antiterror policies and individual rights was not invented on September 11, 2001. Thirty years earlier, the world was shocked by reports of British soldiers rounding up Northern Irish terror suspects, throwing hoods over their heads, and using bizarre methods of interrogation, including sensory deprivation. The parallels to the American scandals at Guantánamo Bay and Abu Ghraib are lost on no one in Europe with a sense of law and history. But, sometimes, the United States seems to suffer from its own form of sensory deprivation, being blind and deaf to the experience of the world. The European Court of Human Rights has long grappled with issues of detention and torture. Although Strasbourg's track record on detention is imperfect, its record on torture is instructive. In 1976, the European Commission on Human Rights spotlighted the problem of psychologically abusive interrogation, using stress and duress, and called it "a modern system of torture." European law has evolved to handle this contemporary form of punitive mistreatment, while American law has not.

A Short History of Torture

Torture developed in Europe to fill a highly specific need. As the historian John Langbein has shown, it emerged in the thirteenth century with the Roman canon law of proof. Canon law replaced the superstitious system of the medieval ordeals, which, for instance, deemed a man innocent if he drowned when thrown into a pool of water. But the new system had its own built-in perversity. Under canon law, the only possible bases for convicting a man of a serious crime were two testimonials, or a confession. One witness and strong circumstantial evidence weren't enough. Given these rules, a prosecutor who lacked two witnesses and wanted a conviction would be sorely tempted to compel a confession. Torture became routine in Europe and stayed that way for five hundred years.

Images of torture abound in European art and documents of the early modern period. Consider the torture technique that paralyzed Zeki Aksoy (see chapter 12). Suspending a man by his arms with his hands bound behind his back has a long European tradition under the name "strappado." (Mysteriously, this method is commonly called "Palestinian hanging" today, although torture monitors say it used by neither Israel nor the Palestinian Authority.) One man hung in the strappado position may be seen in a 1560 print by Bruegel entitled *Justice*, the detail of which is reproduced on the cover of this book. Another may be seen in a 1633 etching from the series *The Miseries and Misfortunes of War* by Jacques Callot, based on the practices of French troops who invaded Lorraine (only a few miles from Strasbourg). Yet a third illustration of strappado may be found in an appendix to the Austrian criminal code of 1769.

By that time, however, thinkers like Cesare Beccaria were persuading Europe's princes that torture offended something called human rights. Beccaria's *Treatise on Crimes and Punishments* (1766) exerted a major influence on Bentham, Jefferson, and, especially, Voltaire. In language that appealed to a stirring public conscience, Beccaria deplored "the moans of the weak, sacrificed to cruel ignorance and opulent laziness; the barbarous torments, multiplied with lavish and useless severity, for crimes either not proved or imaginary; the squalor and horrors of a prison, increased by that cruellest of tormentor of the miserable, uncertainty." Pragmatically, he argued that torture is a poor test of truth, calling it "a sure route for the acquittal of robust ruffians and the conviction of weak innocents." Under the influence of the *philosophes*, torture was abolished between 1734 and 1788 in Sweden, Prussia, Saxony, Tuscany, Denmark, France, and the Habsburg possessions. In Russia and Spain it was abolished early in the nineteenth century.

While torture did not disappear in the nineteenth century, it did go into remission. Even Napoleon's police and gendarmerie, who perfected many modern methods of surveillance and detention, shied away from torture. Torture returned with a vengeance under the totalitarian regimes of World War II and has not disappeared since. The historian Eric Hobsbawm has called this reversal of enlightenment trends the "barbarization" of the West.

Jean-Paul Sartre, during the French debate over torture in Algeria, eloquently captured the irony of the West's postwar barbarity. During the darkest days of World War II, he recalls, "Frenchmen were screaming in agony" at the Gestapo's Paris headquarters, and "all France could hear them." In those days, he continued, "we did not want to think about the future. Only one thing seemed impossible in any circumstances; that one day men should be made to scream by those acting in our name." Sadly, Sartre's impossibility has repeatedly come to pass.

The Hooded Men of 1971

In 1971 Britain conducted a gruesome experiment on fourteen suspected terrorists in Belfast, who came to be known as the "hooded men." The British army adapted five techniques used by Stalin's KGB—hooding, noise bombardment, food deprivation, sleep deprivation, and forced wall-standing in a painful position. Applied simultaneously over the course of several days, these five methods induced psychosis and lasting trauma. But to merely state the techniques does no justice to the horrors of the men's lived experience. Two of the hooded men would ultimately try to communicate those horrors to the European Court of Human Rights.

At the time of detention, Patrick Shivers was a forty-year-old plasterer with five children at home. Convinced that he was dying while under torture, Shivers saw a vision of his son Finbar, who had died in infancy. After his release from the torture center to the Crumlin Road Jail, a cellmate found him standing against the cell wall, reliving his torture in a hallucination. Shivers remained nervous and disoriented for the rest of his life—he would jump at the sound of a car engine idling. One of three hooded men to die at a young age, Shivers succumbed to stomach cancer at age fifty-four, in 1985.

Shivers' experience inspired a powerful work by the poet Vincent Buckley, collected in *The Pattern* (Dolmen Press, 1979):

Internment

> They have him squeezed into the square room
> Patrick Shivers   stripped naked
>   a tight bag
> Covering his head feet splayed rope round his neck
> All day   for fourteen hours
> Fingers tight against the wall   blood hammered back
> Into his hands   his brain screaming with a noise
> As of compressed air   his mouth without water
> Scum filling his lips

. . .

Patrick Shivers
A mouthful of water after five days.

I was unable to speak with Pat Shivers because of his untimely death, and the poet had already told his story more powerfully than could a mere journalist. So I set out for County Tyrone, to speak with the only surviving "hooded man" who had testified at Strasbourg: Paddy Joe McClean.

P. J. McClean was born in 1933, the eldest of eight children in the village of Altamuskin. In an intriguing parallel to Jeff Dudgeon, the Ulsterman who pioneered European gay rights, Paddy Joe came from a "mixed" family. His full given name was Patrick John: Patrick after his Catholic grandda and John after his Protestant grandda. This background predisposed Paddy Joe to the politics of tolerance. For all his suffering at the hands of the British, the first thing he said when we met was that the IRA were worse than the British in their use of torture.

Paddy Joe flirted with militant politics as a young man. He was detained in 1956 for being a member of a nationalist group called the Warriors of Ulster, which was retroactively declared illegal after his arrest. But over the next four years at Crumlin Road Jail, he distinguished himself chiefly by organizing games of Gaelic football. After release, P. J. married his childhood sweetheart, Annie, and became a remedial schoolteacher. In 1963 he played forward on the all-Ireland Gaelic football championship club. Disapproving of the conflict's militarization, he joined the Wolfe Tone Society and the proto–civil rights movement, documenting housing and electoral discrimination by the Unionist government.

On August 9, 1971, the British government in Ulster announced that it was exercising special antiterrorism powers, dating to 1922, that authorized indefinite detention. Based on old and faulty intelligence, hundreds of suspects were rounded up that day and placed in internment camps. Within this group, Paddy Joe was among a dozen unlucky men initially set aside for the Brits' grisly experiment with the "five techniques" of psychological torture. Two days later, hooded and handcuffed, they were transferred by helicopter to a place believed to be Shackleton Army Barracks in Ballykelly, County Derry.

Like Pat Shivers, P. J. saw visions of death during his torture sessions. He imagined that he stood before a firing squad, that he was drowning at sea. He heard hymns and watched as a hearse picked up his casket from home, with Annie and their seven children leading the funeral procession.

Alone among the hooded men, Paddy Joe realized in lucid moments that the torturers were trying to shatter him. P. J. told them so, and he refused to cooperate even by standing against the wall. For twenty-nine hours he repeatedly let himself go limp, each time only to be beaten and lifted back up against the wall. At one point P. J. heard a voice say, "This boy is trying to break the system." He found strength in the conviction that he'd die. P. J. figured that no civilized state could treat an individual so and let him tell the tale. Alternatively, he figured an Irishman would kill him, because he'd been fitted with a UK army-issue boiler suit.

Paddy Joe was brought to the hospital at Crumlin Road Jail on August 17. He'd lost more than forty pounds. A friendly Presbyterian prison guard recognized P. J. from his time there in the 1950s and asked if there was anything he could do to help. Paddy Joe asked for pen and paper and wrote a list of twenty-four distinct tortures that he'd endured. "Take this list to William Cardinal Conway in Armagh," he whispered. P. J. believes that the cardinal conveyed the message personally to British Prime Minister Ted Heath, and this influenced the British decision not to use the five techniques on a second set of twelve men who had been set aside for the purpose.

McClean's account of his message to Heath and its consequences was reported with fanfare in Ireland's *Sunday World* newspaper in 2001. I could not fully corroborate the account, but papers that became available in 2003, under Britain's "thirty-years rule," do show that Cardinal Conway relayed messages from the hooded men to Sir Edmund Compton, who was asked by the British government to conduct an inquiry. The new archival materials also reveal that the prime minister personally amended the guidelines for security interrogation in Northern Ireland on August 4, 1972. Specifically, Heath deleted the statement: "[P]sychological attack is called for. The interrogator has the advantage that from the moment of arrest the subject may be under mental stress."

The "hooded men" affair predictably evoked public grandstanding on terrorism. High British officials referred to the detainees as "thugs and murderers" on television and stated in the House of Commons, "The basic fact is that there was no brutality, no torture, no brainwashing, no physical injury, no mental injury." Sir Edmund Compton, who issued his report in November, drew mainly on state testimony; he heard evidence from at most two detainees, and from none of the hooded men. The results were comical. Hooding, Compton concluded, "provides security both for the detainee and for his guards." Noise too was a security measure, to prevent the detainees from hearing each other. Those who complained of hunger and thirst had simply refused food and drink. Compton concluded that the injuries to P. J. must have occurred by accident during transit. The Compton Report was reminiscent of the Italian police's cover story in Dario Fo's 1970 play, *Accidental Death of an Anarchist*, and anticipated the South African police's testimony about Steve Biko. In both cases the basic excuse was: "He fell out the window."

In response to popular pressure, the state convened a second committee, composed of three senior judges, which in March 1972 yielded the Parker Report. Lord Parker, speaking for the majority, found the five techniques morally acceptable in combating serious terror. He revealed that similar techniques had been used throughout the British Empire, in Palestine, Malaya, Kenya, Cyprus, the Cameroons, Brunei, Guyana, Aden, Borneo, and the Persian Gulf and had "produced very valuable results." Lord Gardiner in dissent opposed any use of torture, for he could see no moral or logical stopping point. In a very different version of history, he stressed that the methods of sensory deprivation were pioneered by the Soviet secret police. While the British may often have followed in this shameful tradition, in prouder moments they helped form new world standards of legal restraint. Approving the five techniques, he said, would "gravely damage our own reputation and deal a severe blow to the whole world movement to improve Human Rights." Apparently influenced by Lord Gardiner's dissent, Prime Minister Heath announced that month that Britain would cease using the five techniques. In 1974 and 1975, the Northern Ireland High Court awarded the hooded men compensation for false imprisonment, assault and torture. P. J. McClean received fourteen thousand pounds and Patrick Shivers fifteen thousand pounds.

But this did not satisfy the Republic of Ireland. Determined to bring Britain before the bar of world opinion, it pursued a rare interstate complaint at Strasbourg.

Article 3 of the European Convention on Human Rights bans torture and inhuman or degrading treatment. And the European Commission on Human Rights had already established, in a case brought by Cyprus against the military regime that seized control of Greece in 1967, that "inhuman treatment" can cover the deliberate infliction of mental distress. In the "hooded men case," the commission went a step further. It discerned in Britain's five techniques "a modern system of *torture*" (my emphasis), with a "clear resemblance to those methods of systematic torture which have been known over the ages."

In its arguments to the European Court of Human Rights, Britain did not even protest the commission's finding of torture. In an act of dubious wisdom, the court reached out to proclaim that the techniques merely constituted "inhuman or degrading treatment"—and not torture. This makes no practical difference under Article 3 of the European Convention. But, to the dismay of human rights advocates, the British press seized upon this aspect of the opinion to declare vindication for the five techniques. "Can a state threatened by anarchy be properly and realistically expected not to employ such methods?" asked London's *Daily Telegraph*.

It took another twenty years before the court at last recognized the existence of outright torture in Western Europe. Interestingly, that case dealt not with antiterrorism—which might have been too politically sensitive—but, rather, police brutality. In *Selmouni v. France* (1998), Strasbourg called out the French police for beating and sodomizing an ordinary criminal. Nothing subtle there.

While the "hooded men" court got caught up in the semantics of "torture," it got one big thing right. It recognized that even subtle methods of making detainees confess can violate human rights. In this respect, Europe was more than thirty years ahead of the United States, which is still coming to terms with its own "hooded men" affair at Abu Ghraib. Within Europe, *Ireland v. United Kingdom* left important battles on detention to be fought another day.

The Law of Terrorist Detention

European Convention Article 15 permits a state, in emergency, to excuse itself (or "derogate") from most of its treaty obligations to the extent strictly necessary. There is never an excuse for killings, torture, slavery, or ex post facto laws. But a state can evade the limits on detention that flow from an individual's right to liberty.

Inauspiciously, the very first judgment of the European Court of Human Rights cut a state slack on detaining terrorists. In *Lawless v. Ireland* (1966), the court upheld Ireland's five-month detention of an Irish Republican Army terrorist under a state of emergency. The *Lawless* court stressed that a state in such straits is entitled to heavy deference. More precisely, the court respected the state's "margin of appreciation," an awkward term of French origin that the court has used ever since as a magic formula of deference.

The *Lawless* case set a permissive tone. In the "hooded men" judgment of 1978, the court placed no limits on the British policy of prolonged detention under a state of emergency, even though the rules permitted detention without a hearing for up to six months. The court rolled out for the occasion its most deferential language:

> It is certainly not the Court's function to substitute for the British Government's assessment of what might be the most prudent or most expedient policy to combat terrorism. . . . Adopting, as it must, this approach, the Court accepts that the limits of the margin of appreciation left to the Contracting States . . . were not overstepped by the United Kingdom when it formed the opinion that extrajudicial deprivation of liberty was necessary.

Later, in *Brogan v. United Kingdom* (1998), the court set a standard (non-emergency) limit of four days of detention before a detainee must be charged. But rather than abide by this limit, the United Kingdom responded to *Brogan* by citing terror in Northern Ireland and invoking its Article 15 right to derogate from the European Convention. The UK's evasion of the *Brogan* limit on detention was approved by the court in *Brannigan v. United Kingdom* (1993). Disappointingly, the court missed an opportunity in *Brannigan* to narrow the power of derogation. For instance, it might have forbidden the use of a derogation to evade a particular judgment. It might have questioned the genuine nature of the emergency, or the degree to which Britain's detention policy was strictly necessary. At a stretch, the court might have argued that limits on detention are not avoidable, because they are designed to prevent Article 3 torture. It remained for national courts to take a tougher stand on terrorist detention under human rights law.

The Terror Debate in Britain Today

Britain has responded to the Islamist terror crisis, as it responded to the IRA terror crisis, with a strict detention policy. Only this time, Britain was slapped down by the courts. Under the Anti-Terrorism, Crime and Security Act of 2001, Parliament again derogated from the European Convention and authorized the indefinite detention of alien terror suspects without charge. However, the United Kingdom Human Rights Act of 1998 gives British courts the power to interpret European human rights law. In *A and others v. Home Secretary*, [2004] UKHL 56, the House of Lords ruled that Britain's policy was incompatible with human rights because derogation is allowed only to the extent "strictly necessary." (Judges sitting in the House of Lords, known as Law Lords, have traditionally functioned as the English court of last resort.) Several judges reasoned that the restriction of the measure to aliens indicated that it was not strictly necessary. Lord Hoffman argued more sweepingly, "The real threat to the life of the nation comes not from terrorism but from laws such as these." The upshot was that Britain had to free its detainees at Belmarsh Prison, commonly known as the British Guantánamo.

The Law Lords' reasoning left wiggle room for nations to evade human rights limits on terror detention—subject, as always, to the political mood of the moment. In March 2005—on the very day that Britain released the remaining eight detainees from Belmarsh Prison—Parliament passed a new law permitting British authorities to place terror suspects under house arrest without trial. However, the House of Commons dealt Prime Minister Tony Blair an embarrassing legislative defeat in November 2005, when it voted down his proposal to enact a ninety-day detention law for terrorists.

Why doesn't Britain just deport terror suspects to a nation that observes no limits on detention? This option is currently closed to European nations. It's well established that deporting a detainee to a place where he faces a serious risk of torture is tantamount to torture under the European Convention. See *Chahal v. United Kingdom* (1997). However, the ban on sending a detainee to a place of persecution—known as the principle of non-refoulement—is under challenge. The UK has intervened to argue that the torture ban should be balanced against national security interests, and that refoulement is permitted so long as the receiving country gives diplomatic assurances of humane treatment. Human rights groups dismiss such assurances as worthless. In *Saadi v. Italy* (2008), a grand chamber unanimously rejected the UK's argument and reaffirmed the absolute ban on refoulement established in *Chahal*.

Both the European Court of Human Rights and the House of Lords have sent signals that they take refoulement seriously. In *Mamatkulov v. Turkey* (2005), a grand chamber of the court ruled that a nation violates an individual's right to free petition when it ignores an interim measure by the court urging it not to deport him or her until the risk of torture can be assessed. In December 2005 the Law Lords ruled that information obtained through torture in a second country is inadmissible as evidence. See *A and others v. Secretary of State*, [2005] UKHL 71.

Paula and Alexandra Marckx. Paula Marckx (left) was infuriated when Belgium refused to legally recognize her out-of-wedlock baby, Alexandra (right), born in 1973. Their application to the European Court of Human Rights helped to bring the court to life and changed family law throughout the world. *Courtesy of Paula Marckx*

Jeff Dudgeon. Jeff Dudgeon, pictured in front of the home on Ulsterville Avenue, Belfast, where the constabulary disturbed him and his boyfriend in June 1976. Dudgeon's court victory in Strasbourg effectively legalized gay sex in Europe, two decades ahead of its legalization in the United States. *Courtesy of Michael D. Goldhaber*

Maria and Ana-Maria Gómez López. Maria (left) and Ana-Maria Gómez López stand atop their clan's home in Lorca, flanked by a Moorish fortress and a treatment plant for tannery waste; the latter is only twelve meters away. Their sister-in-law, Gregoria López Ostra, effectively constitutionalized environmental law when she persuaded the European Court of Human Rights that the siting of the plant violated her right to family life. *Courtesy of Michael D. Goldhaber*

Minos Kokkinakis. From 1938 to 1987, the Greek state arrested Minos Kokkinakis sixty times for the crime of bearing witness to his faith. Minos, pictured here with his wife Elissavet, finally prevailed at the age of eighty-four. He told his lawyer with a wink: "[D]idn't I tell you Jehovah would win?" *Reprinted with permission of Watch Tower, 25 Columbia Heights, Brooklyn, New York, 11201*

Paddy Joe McClean. Paddy Joe McClean was one of the original "hooded men." Rounded up as a terror suspect by the British authorities in Ulster, he was subjected to torture strikingly similar to that suffered by U.S. detainees at Guantánamo Bay. The parallel is not lost on Paddy Joe, who became a human rights activist. He is pictured here in 1975, shortly before vindication by the European Commission on Human Rights. *Courtesy of Paddy Joe McClean*

Serif Aksoy. Serif Aksoy pressed the torture complaint initiated by son Zeki (pictured on the dedication page) after Zeki was seized by Turkish agents and murdered. The Aksoy case went on to affirm the banning of torture by the European Convention on Human Rights. But Serif himself was later tortured numerous times—raising questions about the capacity of a regional court to effect systemic change. *Courtesy of Michael D. Goldhaber*

Nazmi Gur. A Kurdish human rights activist, Nazmi Gur strikes a symbolic pose atop the old city walls of Diyarbakir. When the plaintiff Sukran Aydin went missing, the Turkish state accused her of terrorism. Nazmi tracked her down in a migrant farmers' camp, and faxed her thumbprint to London. *Courtesy of Michael D. Goldhaber*

Nebahat Akkoc. The modern face of Kurdish feminism, Nebahat Akkoc founded a center for abused women, and used her European Court winnings to fund it. She told the Turkish Daily News: "We are working to make human rights valid for women." *Courtesy of Kurdish Human Rights Project*

Sukran Aydin. Sukran Aydin (left) was a seventeen-year-old villager when she was abducted and raped by Turkish paramilitary agents. The state's efforts to paint her as a terrorist fell flat as soon as the judges laid eyes on her. Sukran named her eldest child Eziyet, or Torture, because she "lived very difficult days." *Courtesy of Kurdish Human Rights Project*

Zara Isayeva. Zara Isayeva lost a son and three nieces when the family minivan was strafed by Russian fire, during an attempt to escape the Chechen village of Katyr-Yurt. *Courtesy of Michael D. Goldhaber*

Roza Akayeva. Roza Akayeva mourns for her brother Adlan, a Chechen physics professor, who was hit from behind by a Chechen rebel and shot from behind by Russian troops. *Courtesy of Michael D. Goldhaber*

J. M. and family. Eighteen Roma families accuse the Czech Republic of segregating its schools. In February 2006 the families met with disappointment. Unless a Grand Chamber of the European Court of Human Rights reaches a different result, theirs will be remembered only as the case that could have been Europe's *Brown v. Board of Education. Courtesy of Michael D. Goldhaber*

Britain would love to deport detainees to countries that incidentally use torture. But until Strasbourg says otherwise, the torture ban is an absolute bar to refoulement. And unlike the United States, European nations are unwilling to defy international norms. In a 2003 television interview, in discussing deportation, Tony Blair floated the idea of "reconsidering" Britain's obligations under the European Convention. This remark promptly led to speculation that Britain might withdraw from the European Convention altogether. Just as quickly, the British government climbed down from Blair's untenable position. "The option of pulling out [of the Convention], said then-Home Secretary David Blunkett, "is one which none of us would want to contemplate lightly, not least because of the acrimony, the disdain that we would be held in the international community."

Tony Blair is no softy when it comes to terror. But European human rights law, interpreted abroad or at home, has restrained him in significant ways. Out of respect for *Ireland v. United Kingdom*, he has made no attempt to revive torture in any form, including psychological torture. He has not attempted to deport detainees to nations that disrespect human rights, although he has claimed the right to do so with diplomatic assurances, and he is pressing the argument in Strasbourg. Meanwhile, the Law Lords have made clear that Blair can not use evidence obtained by torture elsewhere as evidence. And the Law Lords have placed limits on his detention policy. Although he may occasionally champ at the bit, Blair does not see defiance of international law as an option. A certain head of state across the way has no such qualms.

The Terror Debate in the United States Today

The *Washington Post* reported on December 26, 2002, that American interrogators at overseas detention centers have been using some highly familiar techniques of duress. Among them: beating, hooding, forced stand–sleep deprivation, and withholding medical care. A U.S. official overseeing the capture of suspected terrorists told the *Washington Post*, "If you don't violate someone's human rights some of the time, you probably aren't doing your job." It soon came to light that American practices at the Abu Ghraib prison in Baghdad overlapped almost completely with the "five techniques" condemned by the European Court of Human Rights. According to the October 2003 Interrogation Rules of Engagement, interrogators resorted, on approval, to "sensory deprivation" (hooding), "dietary manipulation" (food deprivation), "sleep management" (sleep deprivation), and "stress positions" (forced wall-standing). The fifth technique, noise bombardment, was on the list of "enhanced interrogation techniques" that the White House approved for CIA use after 9/11, along with stress positions and sleep deprivation.

These rules have been renounced in response to bad publicity, but it is far from established that the United States considers them unlawful. When the U.S. Senate consented to the U.N. Convention against Torture in 1990, it emphasized that the United States feels bound by international norms on torture only to the extent that those norms are consistent with U.S. constitutional law. Likewise, when President Bush yielded to political pressure and signed the legislation known as the McCain amendment in 2005— ostensibly banning all "cruel, inhuman and degrading" treatment of military detainees—the president issued an ominous signing statement, emphasizing his broad view of executive power.

Like Britain, the United States tried to evade legal limits on detention, and it overreached. The United States brazenly argued that Guantánamo Bay in Cuba is a legal no-man's land, subject to neither international nor U.S. law. In *Rasul v. Bush* (2004), the U.S. Supreme Court held that federal habeas corpus law does apply to Guantánamo and in *Hamdan v. Rumsfeld* it held that Gitmo detainees are protected by the Geneva Conventions. The Military Commissions Act of 2006 is a nervy attempt to roll back the civil liberty gains embodied in the McCain Amendment and the *Rasul* and *Hamdan* rulings. That law will doubtless provoke further debate in Congress and the courts.

If the U.S. Supreme Court continues to place limits on executive policies of torture and detention, the temptation will grow for the president to continue evading them by rendering suspects to countries with less respect for law. According to press reports, the CIA since 9/11, has secretly rendered dozens of terror suspects into the custody of states that it knows to use torture. The American policy of "rendition" plainly violates the human rights taboo on "refoulement."

The U.S. torture scandals have yet to be fully processed by the courts. They were utterly ignored in the 2004 presidential debate, and they have not been assessed by an independent commission. By default, torture has been left to popular discourse.

The Fallacies of Torture

There are two standard rhetorical maneuvers used to condone torture. Call them the "ticking bomb" fallacy and the "torture lite" fallacy. The first draws a distinction between the torture of innocent victims and the torture of a terrorist who knows how to stop a ticking bomb. The second fallacy draws a distinction between real (severe, physical) torture and "torture lite," which covers mental or modest physical pain. Real torture of innocents is of course reprehensible; that's what the other guy does. Psychologically torturing dangerous terrorists is the brave moral stand taken by tough-minded liberals only after the most rigorous soul-searching.

Mark Bowden, best known for his impressive reporting of the U.S. Somalian debacle in the book *Black Hawk Down*, invoked both pro-torture fallacies in his cover story, "The Dark Art of Interrogation," in the October 2003 *Atlantic Monthly*. "One cannot help sympathizing," he wrote, "with the innocent, powerless victims showcased in the literature [of Amnesty International and Human Rights Watch]. But professional terrorists pose a harder question. They are lockboxes containing potentially life-saving information." Clearly agonized by this dilemma, Bowden moved on to the next fallacy: "All manner of innovative cruelty is still commonplace, particularly in Central and South America, Africa, and the Middle East. . . . Then there are methods that, some people argue, fall short of torture. . . . [T]hese tactics generally leave no permanent marks and do no lasting physical harm. . . . I will use 'torture' to mean the more severe traditional outrages, and 'coercion' to refer to torture lite, or moderate physical pressure." Though Bowden thus far maintained a distance from those who would make these brave distinctions, he finally let slip his conclusion: "A method that produces life-saving information without doing lasting harm . . . appears to be morally sound." By my reading, Bowden supports torture. For this brave position, "The Dark Art of Interrogation" was nominated for a National Magazine Award in the "public interest" category.

For an inglorious moment, between September 2001 and the Abu Ghraib revelations of March 2004, torture was positively in vogue. In a November 2001 *Newsweek* column entitled "Time to Think About Torture," the ordinarily sensible Jonathan Alter fell for both the "ticking bomb" and the "torture lite" fallacies. "In this autumn of anger," he wrote, "even a liberal can find his thoughts turning to . . . torture. OK, not cattle prods or rubber hoses, at least not here in the United States, but something to jump-start the stalled investigation of the greatest crime in American history. Right now, four key hijacking suspects aren't talking at all. Couldn't we at least subject them to psychological torture, like tapes of dying rabbits or high-decibel rap?" Alter's breezy tone almost makes one long for Bowden's equivocations.

Psychological torture emerges in any culture when physical torture comes under attack. After a 1931 report commissioned by President Herbert Hoover found physical assault to be routine in American police interrogations, the U.S. Supreme Court, in *Brown v. Mississippi* (1936), clarified that police violence to coerce confessions violated due process. By 1966, *Miranda v. Arizona* could observe that the physical "third degree" had evolved into the psychological "third-degree." But no constitutional limits were set on emotional pressure, and, as Bowden's piece explains, it remains the keystone to a state-of-the-art interrogation.

"Torture lite" is easily rationalized by a society struggling against terrorism. The 1955 Wuillaume Report by Algiers inspector general Roger Wuillaume characterized the French practices in North Africa as "not quite torture." In the 1971 Compton Report on British policing in Ulster, Sir Edmund Compton drew a (not very artful) line between "ill-treatment" and "brutality." In a separate opinion on the hooded men, British judge Sir Gerald Fitzmaurice of the European Court of Human Rights called the same practices "rigorous, searching and quasi-hostile." By contrast, the judge's idea of torture was feeding a suspect to "a bevy of starving rats." George W. Bush betrayed a similarly narrow mindset in his 2003 State of the Union address, when he cataloged the methods of physical mutilation used by Saddam Hussein and observed, "If this is not evil, then evil has no meaning."

The problem with the idea of "torture lite" is that there is no stopping point, and there are many ways to traduce the human spirit without wielding a hot poker. From the torturer's standpoint, psychological methods have the advantage of leaving no marks. The problem with the "ticking bomb" scenario is that it exists only in philosophy textbooks. Even the law professor Alan Dershowitz, who has mooted the idea of permitting torture under a judicial warrant, admits that the "ticking bomb" has never materialized in American history. At best, the argument is invoked to round up suspects, based only on limited intelligence, to give the impression that a state is combating terror. At worst, it is used as a cover for political repression. As the scholar and journalist Michael Ignatieff has written, "Torture is fundamentally a political strategy. Generally, it is not used, as the thought experiment supposes, to save lives, but to break the will of political opponents."

Ultimately, there are two arguments against torture. Kantians simply believe that it is wrong, uncivilized, and debasing. This point is hard to argue, because it is either accepted instinctively or it is not. It's to be hoped that the story of a Pat Shivers or a P. J. McClean will prick our humane instincts.

The pragmatic point is that torture doesn't work, which is to say that it produces false or unreliable information. In the most stunning example, reported in the *New York Times* on December 9, 2005, the forcible interrogation of a detainee handed off by the United States to Egypt in January 2001 yielded false information linking Iraq with al Qaeda, which helped to justify the U.S. invasion of Iraq.

Even when torture may yield helpful information in the short run, it creates a backlash in the long run. Looking back on the Battle of Algiers, Ignatieff concludes that torture "only creates more terrorists and lends their movement popular support. . . . Any temporary advantage gained in Algiers in 1957 dissipated by the time the French retreated five years later." A 2001 cover of the French humor magazine *Charlie Hebdo* caricatured the French general Paul Aussaresses, who defended torture in his memoirs. "Yes, torture was necessary!" he declares gravely. "Without it, we would have lost Algeria."

In Ulster, torture was counterproductive in both the short and long runs. Even the hardheaded *Economist* concludes, "Tough anti-terrorism laws, including internment without trial, caused huge ill-feeling, and did little to put real terrorists behind bars." The same argument can be made about U.S. antiterror practices after September 11. And no one is better positioned to make it than Paddy Joe McClean, who survived the "hooded men" experiment of 1971.

The Voice of Moral Authority

Today Paddy Joe lives in the town of Beragh, in a house that served from 1850 to 1936 as a station for the Royal Constabulary. One of his windows is still covered with prison bars. But Paddy Joe refuses to see any bad symbolism. He loves to tell of an exchange he had with the warden of Long Kesh Prison during his internment.

"Where am I?" asked Paddy Joe.

"You're in jail," replied the warden, perhaps worrying that the poor man was hallucinating again.

"Who told you that?"

The warden pointed to the bars.

"Now wait a minute," replied P. J. "My body may be behind bars, but no one can imprison my mind, and you're not about to do it."

After his release from Long Kesh in 1973, P. J. went on to chair the Northern Ireland Civil Rights Association. From 1998 to 2001 he served on the Police Authority, overseeing police discipline in Northern Ireland, and the proper treatment of detainees. Perhaps history can't be escaped in Ulster. But it can be transcended and learned from.

When Paddy Joe McClean sees the photos from Guantánamo of hooded men in orange jumpsuits, the parallels to 1971 are not lost on him. When he hears the refrain that the detainees are murderers and terrorists, he laughs. "We too were declared murderers and ruthless terrorists," he says. Ultimately, the suspicions proved so baseless that none of the hooded men at Long Kesh were even charged. P. J. felt an obligation to speak out about Guantánamo. In January 2002, he published a column in the *Belfast Telegraph* entitled, "Degrading detention didn't work here and it won't work in Cuba."

"Who can deny," he asked, that the British excesses of 1971 "left us with the bitter legacy still burning itself out in the bitter sectarian clashes of North Belfast?" Paddy Joe continued, "[W]hen governments adopt the methods of the terrorist and sink to their barbaric level of depravity, the dragon's teeth they sow take years to reap." Alas that the United States did not heed the warning of the original hooded men.

CHAPTER 12

The Tortures of Aksoy

*T*urkey's Kurds receive less attention than Iraq's Kurds, although they are perhaps three times as numerous. They receive less attention than the Northern Irish, although their conflict was ten times bloodier. And they receive less attention than the Bosnians or Kosovars, although their suffering posed a similar test for Europe's democratic self-image. An armed conflict raged between Kurdish separatists and Turkish state forces in southeastern Turkey from 1984 to 1998. At its height in the early 1990s, the conflict rose to the level of a full-scale war. Thirty thousand people were killed, and more than a million dislocated, with well-documented atrocities on both sides. In dozens of cases, stretching from the mid-1990s to the present, the European Court of Human rights has held Turkey liable for torture, disappearances, extrajudicial executions, and village destruction, as well as for mishandling the trial of the Kurdish insurgent leader Abdullah Ocalan. Strasbourg's sustained engagement with Turkey has shown the real if limited ability of a regional court to transform a national society and blazed new law on gross human rights abuses, beginning with torture.

The Kurdish chapter in Strasbourg began in 1990, when Turkey accepted the individual's right to petition under Europe's human rights convention. Soon Prime Minister Hikmet Cetlin was boasting that there were obviously no human rights violations in Turkey, because no one was petitioning. This enraged human rights advocates in both Turkey and the United Kingdom. The boldest among them took the prime minister's boast as a dare. In 1992 a lawyer from the Diyarbakir Human Rights Association, Fevzi Veznendaroglu, ran into Kevin Boyle, a professor at Essex University who was active in the European court's early Northern Irish cases. They began to discuss a Strasbourg strategy for the Kurds. That strategy was embraced by a young activist in London named Kerim Yildiz, who at the end of 1992 founded the Kurdish Human Rights Project. At about the same time, deep in Anatolia, tragic events were unfolding that would give the Kurdish advocates their first cause célèbre.

Serif Aksoy was the eldest of six brothers; he was born in 1930 to a family from the Surgucu tribe, in the village of Tizyan. Serif as a young man moved to the nearest big town, Kiziltepe, on the edge of the ancient city of Mardin, at the northwest tip of the Fertile Crescent. There he raised six sons of his own and, with their help, ran a carpentry shop. Serif's son Zeki Aksoy, born in 1963, preferred metalwork. Anticipating a boom in oil smuggling during the first Gulf War, Zeki opened a shop on the E5 highway, along the old Silk Road, to make and repair truck-mounted oil tanks. The metal shop thrived, and the rest of the Aksoy men soon joined in. Zeki also did an occasional turn as the Kiziltepe correspondent for the Kurdish *Ozgur Gundem* newspaper. This was a frontline job. In 1992 and 1993, the paper's newsstands were firebombed and its newsboys knifed. Seven adult staffers were gunned down, not counting Zeki.

On November 24, 1992, near midnight, twenty policemen burst into the Aksoy home on a tip that Zeki had joined the separatist fighters of the Kurdish Worker's Party, or PKK. According to the accounts related by the European Commission and Court, of Human Rights, Zeki was brought to Kiziltepe security headquarters and transferred the next day to Mardin antiterror headquarters. On the second day, he was hung upside down by his arms for thirty-five minutes, with his hands tied behind his back. The police hooked electrodes to Zeki's genitals while he was hanging, then ran the current and doused him with water. Nerve damage partially paralyzed both of Zeki's arms, but when he asked for medical care he was mocked. Finally, on December 8, an officer brought him to the facility's doctor, asserting that he'd been hurt in an accident. According to court testimony, the doctor remarked sarcastically, "Everyone who comes here has had an accident." On December 10, Zeki was taken to a prosecutor and asked to sign a statement that he was a Kurdish terrorist. He objected that the statement was false and, anyway, he couldn't sign because his hands were paralyzed. According to court testimony, the prosecutor bowed his head and said, "You are free." Charges were never brought.

Zeki returned to his metal shop, but all he could do was supervise. He resolved to recover use of his hands in any way that he could. Going to the European Court of Human Rights was not the obvious thing to do; Zeki only knew of the option through his friends at the Kurdish newspaper. Serif Aksoy says that Zeki believed in justice, but he also hoped fervently that applying to Strasbourg would get him health care in Western Europe. In May 1993, Zeki applied.

During the next eleven months, Zeki's lawyers recall, he often called them in a fright. He was constantly trailed by the secret police. Anonymous callers rang the metal shop, threatening to kill him if he didn't drop the case. Police would visit the shop and ask menacingly, "Why are you applying to the Human Rights Association?" On April 13, as these threats mounted, he spoke by phone with Kerim Yildiz in London.

"You must withdraw," Yildiz told him.

As Yildiz recalls, Zeki answered, "If I withdraw my case, and he withdraws his case, and they withdraw their cases, who is going to bring the brutality to light?"

The next afternoon Zeki had a similar conversation with the attorney Mahmut Sakar in Diyarbakir, who, at twenty-six, was three years younger than his client.

As your lawyer I ask you, "Do you want to withdraw or continue?"

"I want to continue," Sakar remembers Zeki saying. "But how can I protect myself?" Sakar could do nothing but advise him to change his hours and routes. Yildiz and Sakar would forever be haunted by these phone calls.

Two days later, at 4 PM on April 16, a white Peugeot pulled up across the street from the Aksoys' metal shop, and two plainclothes policemen from the local station called for Zeki to get in. Zeki assented, and his brothers were too afraid to protest. The car drove three hundred meters downhill, out of earshot. Zeki's father and lawyers believe that the police shot Zeki dead on the street in broad daylight. A woman who was baking bread nearby witnessed the shooting, says Serif Aksoy, but she refused to testify.

Although it violated Muslim custom, the local prosecutor ordered the funeral to be held that night, to avoid rioting. Even on a few hours' notice, two thousand guests attended the funeral, with representatives from each of the thirty-three villages peopled by Serif's tribe. Security forces ringed the crowd with water cannons. Serif buried Zeki in an unmarked dirt grave. He would later plant an olive tree there, only to see it uprooted by the authorities.

As their tribe dispersed, Serif lingered at the grave to keep Zeki company. By Muslim tradition this was the time for the deceased to be approached for questioning by angels. Instead, a policeman accosted Serif.

"This is what you get because you are Kurds," Serif recalls the policeman saying.

"I am ready to have this," replied Serif, "but I am still Kurdish."

The next day, Serif told Kerim Yildiz that he wished his son's case to proceed. He explains his thinking: "When my son was killed, I became an open enemy of the state. If there is any chance for me to somehow defeat the state, then I will do it."

Serif was detained three times in the next three months, for a total of nineteen days. According to a report by human rights monitors, the police openly threatened him. "If you don't drop the case we will kill you," they said. "We will kill your whole family and bomb your house." Finally, the state security chief ordered him to abandon his shop and home in Kiziltepe. Serif fled to Diyarbakir, secretly sending friends later to gather his possessions.

The case of *Aksoy v. Turkey* went on to be a legal landmark. In tandem with *Akdivar v. Turkey*, it was the first Kurdish case to be admitted (October 1994), heard by the European Commission on Human Rights (March 1995), and heard by the European Court of Human Rights (April 1996). Put simply, it was where Europe drew the line with Turkey over its war on the Kurds.

In broader perspective, *Aksoy* was the first European Court of Human Rights judgment to confirm a torture incident anywhere in Europe, and the first individual lawsuit to occasion a finding of torture by a Strasbourg institution. (The commission had previously recognized torture in three inter-state cases.) Equally important, *Aksoy* helped to persuade Strasbourg that—in places where local justice is utterly ineffective—it could not rely on local courts for fact finding. Instead, the European Commission on Human Rights sent three of its delegates to personally hold evidentiary hearings in Diyarbakir. Local hearings have proved to be a vital part of Strasbourg's procedural toolkit.

Aksoy's first doctrinal innovation was to put the burden of proof for torture on the state. It should come as no surprise that torture is rarely proved affirmatively through official testimony. Zeki's interrogator and prosecutor from Mardin told the commission that ill-treatment was unknown in Turkey and that they did not even know Zeki. This was so implausible that the commission professed itself "astonished." As the commission well knew, the Committee for the Prevention of Torture, which does spot inspections on behalf of the Council of Europe, had repeatedly found electric shock gear in the police headquarters of Ankara, Istanbul, and Diyarbakir.

The European judges needed a way to establish the incidence of torture without relying on official testimony. Inspired by the Inter-American

Court of Human Rights, *Aksoy* set forth the following rule: if a European is taken into police custody healthy but is found to be hurt when released, it is up to the state to give a plausible explanation. Otherwise, the state will be held liable for torture under European Convention Article 3.

Aksoy's other key holding was to shorten the time of incommunicado detention. Routine as this may sound, no rule is more crucial to preventing torture. Torture almost always occurs between the time that a suspect is arrested and the time that the suspect is brought before a judge. Shortening that time minimizes the opportunity for torture. What *Aksoy* did was to deem fourteen days of incommunicado detention intolerable—even in an emergency situation, as in southeastern Turkey—under the European Convention's Article 5 right to liberty. The results were instant. On November 27, 1996, the day after *Aksoy* was announced, Turkey introduced a bill to shorten incommunicado detention. Passed in March, the bill reduced the limit from thirty to ten days in emergency areas, and from fifteen to seven days elsewhere. The time limits in both Strasbourg case law and Turkish legislation have since grown considerably tighter, but this was a crucial step in the right direction.

The *Aksoy* ruling was disappointing in two respects. First, the court refused to recognize that state agents had killed Zeki in retaliation for blowing the whistle on their brutality. In legal terms, Zeki's lawyers argued that Turkey had violated Zeki's right, guaranteed by the European Convention, to freely petition Strasbourg. Zeki's murder would seem to be the ultimate interference with the right of free petition. But Turkey insisted that Zeki had been murdered in an intra-PKK feud, and it succeeded in muddying the waters.

The court ruled ineffectually that—while Zeki's death was tragic, and that applicants ought not be "pressured"—there was "no evidence" of a link between Zeki's death and his application to Strasbourg. In truth there was considerable proof of a link, starting with the death threats documented by Zeki's lawyers and the testimony that Zeki was in the company of police officers minutes before his death. The European Court of Human Rights has found that Turkey harassed an applicant in at least six cases; see *Akdivar v. Turkey* (1996), *Kurt v. Turkey* (1998), *Tanrikulu v. Turkey* (1999), *Akkoc v. Turkey* (2000), *Sarli v. Turkey* (2001), and *Orhan v. Turkey* (2002). The evidence of retaliation seems no stronger in these cases than in *Aksoy*, but the forms of retaliation were much milder. Perhaps state gangsterism is so grave a charge that, in practice, it demands a higher standard of evidence.

The other disappointing aspect of *Aksoy* was its enforcement. European Convention Article 13 requires states to give an "effective remedy" for any rights violation. Human rights advocates wanted the European Court of Human Rights to formally recognize that the problem of torture in Turkey was systemic and to expressly demand systemic reforms. What *Aksoy* held is that, in the torture context, an "effective remedy" means an investigation capable of leading to punishment of the torturers. Strasbourg could only hope that this reading of Article 13 would be broad enough to inspire systemic reform.

For six years there were few signs of it. *Aksoy* was among thirty-eight cases of violence cited by the Parliamentary Assembly of the Council of Europe when, in autumn 2002, it called on Turkey to improve the training and accountability of its security forces. Ironically, the Parliamentary Assembly had first passed such a resolution in autumn 1996, about the time of *Aksoy*. Serif Aksoy told me that he regards the case as a failure because his son's killers are still at large. "I don't know law," Serif said, through an interpreter, "but it seems to me that universal law must require the value of a human being to be superior to everything."

The marks on Serif Aksoy's body are the ultimate proof that his son's case had little immediate impact. In July 2003, Serif Aksoy told me that he had been tortured twenty-four times since late 1994, when his case was last monitored by a human rights group. Serif could remember only the most extreme incidents, and even those imperfectly. "I have had many adventures," he joked grimly.

In 1998, according to Serif's account, he was tortured so severely that he was left unconscious in a ditch. He was carried home by several women who were released with him. In the most gruesome episode, in 2000, Serif was lifted up by a string tied around his penis, and thus castrated. Serif went for medical care to the Turkish Human Rights Foundation. He considered an application to Strasbourg, but he was embarrassed and did not want to jeopardize his five sons who remained alive.

In January 2001 Serif was detained and tortured for fifteen days, which was his longest stint. At various times, he was electrified, hung in a crucifix position, and (like Zeki before him) hung upside down by his hands. Serif says that this bout of torture nearly "finished" him and again forced him to visit the Human Rights Foundation for medical care.

In late 2001 Serif began to serve a prison sentence on the charge of assisting terrorists. He was released after three months, in January 2002, due to a lung ailment that he attributes to being doused with icy water.

On April 17 he was ordered to sign a statement that his injuries were accidental, or else the authorities would kill his son who was then serving in the military. He signed, although it went against his nature. Serif says he was often told by his torturers that his troubles would end if he agreed to become an informer for the state. By way of answer, he would tell them to their faces, "I don't like you. You are my enemy. You are bad people."

In late 2002 Serif received a call from the gendarmerie secret police at his sons' photo shop in Diyarbakir and told that they would be visiting. He was detained for three days, stripped, and sprayed with cold water. "Not so bad," Serif noted with a laugh. He was seventy-three at the time of our interview, with a chronic lung condition that he attributes to a regular regimen of such treatment. The full story of Serif Aksoy suggests that, six years after the 1996 *Aksoy* decision, Strasbourg was still struggling to complete its first victory in Turkey.

Turkish Reform

Serious change in Turkey began belatedly in 2003 and 2004, when the Islamist government of Prime Minister Recep Tayyip Erdogan took most every legislative step it could to earn the approval of the European Union in the run-up to the EU's decision on opening membership negotiations with Turkey. Reform reached a crescendo on June 9, 2004, when a Turkish court ordered the release of four Kurdish members of parliament who had been imprisoned for a decade, and Turkish state television broadcast its first program in the Kurdish language, "Our Cultural Riches." In August 2004, Turkey appointed the first civilian to head the National Security Council, a body that has traditionally been used by the Turkish military to dominate the state. These are steps that were unimaginable to Turkey's critics a few short years ago.

To prevent torture, Turkey has improved the rules on detention of suspects. Most fundamentally, under the state security code in January 2003 and under the penal code in June 2003, it abolished incommunicado detention. In addition, beginning in October 1998, police have been required to keep careful custody records, conforming to ECHR case law. Police must tell the detainees why they are detained, tell them they have a right to remain silent and see a relative, and give the detainees a copy of their medical report. In May 2002 blindfolds were banned. In September 2002 the detainee was given the right (with exceptions) to be examined by a doctor with no one else present, and a stronger right to notify relatives of arrest.

What about the punishment of torturers? In August 1999 the maximum penalty for torture was increased from five to eight years. At the same time, the statutory definitions of torture and ill-treatment were clarified. In March 2002, a law was passed requiring individual torturers to reimburse the state for any money Strasbourg makes the state pay as a result of their conduct. In January 2003, the five-year time limit on bringing suits against torturers was eliminated, and judges were denied the discretion to suspend torturers' sentences or reduce prison to fines.

Finally, there have been educational efforts. For instance, in October 2001, police training was extended from nine months to two years, with a unit on human rights law. Later, the Turkish police academy translated a collection of ECHR judgments, and Turkey launched seminars to train nine thousand judges and prosecutors in European human rights.

These changes are impressive on paper—indeed, the right to immediate counsel for all detainees is more than the United States or the United Kingdom can boast—but in practice change is slow. A chorus of human rights monitors have reported that the detention rules have been routinely evaded by falsifying police custody logs and medical records. The ban on blindfolds has been ignored. Detainees have been pressured to "waive" their rights to see a lawyer, contact a relative, and consult with a doctor in private. Detainees have been pressured to withdraw complaints.

Torture in Turkey persists, with the Turkish Human Rights Foundation still reporting hundreds of torture incidents each year. The U.S. State Department, in its 2003 report, observed "a gradual decrease." Amnesty International, which used to call torture in Turkey "widespread and systematic," concluded grudgingly in its 2004 report that "the use of some torture methods appeared to diminish," although Turkish torture continued to be a matter of grave concern. Human Rights Watch, while noting that progress was patchy, concluded more generously in a September 2004 briefing that reform had "significantly reduced the frequency and severity of torture to the extent that . . . deaths in custody may be thing of the past."

What mainly seemed to decline was physical torture. Monitors no longer found electric rods lying around police stations. Amnesty International cited a decrease in "suspension by the arms," which is the technique that paralyzed Zeki Aksoy. At the same time, Amnesty continued to report the regular use of beatings, strippings, and sexual harassment, as well as the manipulation of sleep, food, drink, and toilet access. To this list, the International Federation for Human Rights (FIDH) would add blindfolding, hosing with pressurized cold water, prolonged standing in the cold, hooding, isolation, loud music, forcing the detainee to witness the torture of others, threats to relatives, and mock executions. The FIDH concluded that detention reform has led torturers to favor psychological methods, and other techniques that leave no marks. Whether these techniques amount to torture or whether they amount to ill-treatment is legally irrelevant. Either way, they clearly violate Article 3 of the European Convention on Human Rights (see chapter 11).

Impunity for torturers is a principle that dies hard. In 2002, only sixteen police or gendarmes were convicted for torture, and the U.S. State Department still perceived "a climate of official impunity." But, in fairness, Turkey has shown progress. In April 2003, a Turkish court gave serious prison time to the ten police officers responsible for torturing a group of leftist teenagers in the city of Manisa in western Turkey. Then, in September 2003, a former head of the Istanbul Organized Crime Branch was discharged from the police for allegedly committing and condoning torture. Even Turkey's harshest critics applauded.

Human Rights Watch continued to document incidents of torture in Turkey through the end of 2005. However, Human Rights Watch notes with approval the spread of a new form of monitoring. In many Turkish provinces, local government human rights boards are carrying out spot inspections of police and gendarmerie stations, often led by representatives of the local bar or medical association. Provincial governors have been required to inspect places of detention in 1999, but only recently has this obligation become meaningful. Transforming a culture of violence is a long and tricky process.

Strasbourg and Systemic Change

The 1996 case of *Aksoy v. Turkey* is studied in human rights courses throughout the world as the definitive European triumph over torture. The full story is more complicated. An update of the case highlights the persistence of torture and underscores the difficulty of implementing change. Still, *Aksoy* broke new legal ground, and it educated the European public about southeastern Turkey. With Prime Minister Erdogan moving in the right direction on so many fronts, Turkey must be adjudged a success for the Strasbourg system.

Of course, Strasbourg shares credit with Brussels. The timing of serious reform in Turkey suggests that the carrot of EU membership was crucial. Turkey felt pressure to comply with Court of Human Rights judgments because it knew that a suspension from the Council of Europe would bar entry into the EU, and that every Strasbourg demerit would hurt its chances. Unfortunately, that extra layer of incentive is absent in other regional human rights systems. Even within Europe, the precedent of Turkish reform may not be transferable to Russia, where EU membership is not in the cards.

If Turkey is the gauge of Strasbourg's past success, Russia will measure its future. Certainly, Russia is poised to overtake Turkey as Strasbourg's primary whipping boy. Just look at the docket. Turkey accounted for the lion's share of ECHR judgments in 2005 (26 percent, as compared with 7.5 percent for Russia), but Russia accounted for the lion's share of applications (17 percent, as compared with 13 percent for Turkey). Those numbers encapsulate a lot of grief and will translate into hundreds of reprimands. If Strasbourg wishes Russia to respond, it will need to use every lever at its disposal.

The Council of Europe offers two ways to hold a state accountable other than through an individual suit. Nations may bring state-to-state suits in the European Court of Human Rights, and the Committee of Ministers, which consists of each state's foreign minister, may suspend member nations. However, political timidity has sharply limited the effectiveness of these tools.

Strasbourg has seen only a few interstate cases. Despite the success of *Ireland v. United Kingdom* (see chapter 11), most were ineffectual. In complaints brought in the late 1950s by Greece against the United Kingdom over British treatment of detainees in colonial Cyprus, the commission recognized a state's discretion to depart from the Convention in a "public emergency." During the three years following Turkey's 1974 invasion of Northern Cyprus, the Republic of Cyprus filed three suits against Turkey. The commission found violations based on the first two applications, but the report was kept under seal and no action ensued. Two years after Turkey's 1980 military coup, Turkey was accused of systematic torture by Denmark, Norway, Sweden, the Netherlands, and France. But the application was withdrawn in December 1985, possibly as the result of U.S. diplomatic pressure. Denmark sued Turkey again in 1997, to protest Turkey's torture of a naturalized Danish citizen of Kurdish origin. Turkey settled the case in May 2000 by making a general admission of guilt and promising new measures aimed at reducing torture.

The Committee of Ministers came close to suspending a member nation only twice. In "the Greek colonels case," which represented the most effective instance of interstate action, Denmark, Norway, Sweden, and the Netherlands spotlighted the atrocities ushered in by Greece's April 1967 military coup. Greece withdrew from the Council of Europe in December 1969 to preempt its suspension and remained outside the system until civilian rule was restored in 1974. In April 2000, the Committee of Ministers suspended Russia's voting rights to protest its policies in Chechnya, only to restore them after nine months, based on flimsy assurances (see chapter 14).

A promising new way for states to exert pressure on other states is through Protocol 14 to the European Convention. Protocol 14 would allow the Committee of Ministers, by a two-thirds vote, to sue a state for noncompliance in a grand chamber of the court. Human rights advocates hope that the Council of Europe will be more apt to discipline its members once it has a non-nuclear option. But as history shows, diplomats can't be counted on to be bold.

Individual lawsuits are the court's lifeblood—and, somehow, they must be the agents of systemic change. Happily, the judges are growing more creative in making individual judgments meaningful.

For starters, the court has strengthened the requirement, laid out by Article 13 of the European Convention, that a state give an "effective remedy" for rights violations. The court has clarified that a "remedy" must be reasonably speedy and effective in both law and practice and must not permit improper steps that are potentially irreversible. See *Conka v. Belgium* (2002) and *Kudla v. Poland* (2000).

In practice, today's Court of Human Rights is willing to hold a nation in systematic violation of a norm—and to give specific orders to rectify the situation. The court has long chided Italy for a pattern of unduly lengthy judicial proceedings, and it has recently sent a similar message to Slovenia. See *Bottazzi v. Italy* (1999) and *Lukenda v. Slovenia* (2006). Although the court is formally restricted to making declarations, it came awfully close to giving orders in *Assanidze v. Georgia* (2004). The *Assanidze* court found that Georgia had wrongfully detained a man for twelve years. It refreshingly concluded that—while the state could choose how to comply with the judgment—Georgia didn't have "any real choice" but to free him.

Most significantly, where there is evidence of a systemic problem affecting a large class of people, the court has adopted the practice of selecting one case for a "pilot judgment." Thus, in *Broniowski v. Poland* (2005), the court laid the groundwork for solving thousands of Polish land claims in the Ukraine, dating back to World War II. The court held that the individual violation of property rights "originated in a systemic problem connected with the malfunctioning of domestic legislation" and directed Poland to fix it. Wisely used, pilot judgments are a way to tame the docket while advancing the cause of social justice.

Of course, pilot judgments offer little in the way of catharsis, but few Strasbourg cases do. The celebrated *Aksoy* case delivered neither catharsis nor, in the short term, reform. What Serif Aksoy craves—even more than an end to torture—is the outing of his son's killers. I didn't tell Serif, but catharsis is best achieved by criminal prosecution or a truth commission. When societies are torn apart by bloodshed, human rights law may be inadequate to repair the damage.

CHAPTER 13

Two Faces of Kurdish Feminism

*T*he Kurdish cases gave the mature European Court of Human Rights its first extended chance to grapple with political violence in all its forms. Among them were rape, as in the case of Sukran Aydin, and sexual harassment, as in the case of Nebahat Akkoc. Although Aydin and Akkoc will forever be linked in the histories of European human rights and of Turkish feminism, they came from opposite ends of the Kurdish social spectrum. "Rape" was not part of Sukran's mental or verbal vocabulary. Nebahat not only knew the word, she could write a dissertation on it. In every way possible, she would use her pain to educate the men of Turkey and Europe.

A Baby Named "Torture"

A month after Zeki Aksoy first applied to Strasbourg, Sukran Aydin still lived a simple life. She had never used electricity, for she had never ventured outside her mountain village of Tasit. She was a seventeen-year-old in a tribal, Muslim world. At dawn on June 29, 1993, while her father was tending to his animals, ten or fifteen Village Guards burst into her home and abducted her. The Village Guards were state-supported paramilitaries, recruited from the local population, waging a war in Turkey's southeast against the Kurdish separatist guerillas, known as the PKK. Sukran and her family were paraded through the village square as the Guards shouted: "PKK supporters have been to these people's house, helping the PKK; see how we'll show them." No charges, however, were ever brought against the Aydins. The trauma that followed is documented in the opinions of the European Court of Human Rights and Commission on Human Rights.

Sukran was led blindfolded to gendarme headquarters in the town of Derik. She was beaten, stripped, rolled inside a truck tire, and hosed with pressurized water. Then she was brought to the mountains and, while her interrogators fired shots into the air, asked to reveal the terrorists' hideout. Sukran was again blindfolded, and led back to the station. Now she was placed in a separate room, where someone ripped off her dress and laid her on her back. She thought the man was wearing a military uniform because the fabric was rough, and she made sure by peeking out from under her blindfold. She remembers that he spoke Kurdish. The man held her mouth to stop her from shouting, and, as Sukran recalls it, "did dirty things to her." The same was done to her the next day. On the evening of the second day, an officer with a beard beat her and said that if she went public, they would kill her and her family. On the third day, Sukran was abandoned alone in the mountains. If she spoke of the "dirty things," she was warned, more bad things would happen. Sukran found her way home.

Sukran seemed to have trouble comprehending what had happened. According to a lawyer who befriended the family, Mahmut Sakar, Sukran only understood fully after she stumbled home, and her sister-in-law asked if she'd been raped. The women in the family told Sukran's father what had happened, and he set in motion the slow wheels of justice.

Life after rape is difficult in a culture where honor killings persist and it's a custom for the mother of the groom to wait outside the newlyweds' door for proof of the bride's virginity. Luckily, Sukran had already been promised in marriage to a cousin named Abidin (Abit) Aydin. Abit's family wanted out, but, according to Mahmut Sakar, Abit insisted. The wedding plans were accelerated to late July and, in a simultaneous "marriage by exchange," Sukran's younger brother married Abit's younger sister.

Soon Sukran's stomach began to protrude. The villagers knew her story, and she couldn't look anyone in the eye. She visited a big-city doctor to establish that Abit was the child's father, but the villagers' doubts would not go away. The Aydins moved to Derik.

In town, Sukran had a baby daughter and named her Eziyet—or "Torture." In testimony to the European Commission on Human Rights, Sakar recalled Sukran explaining her predicament: "I have no more relations with people. I cannot speak to my family, not even to my spouse whom I married later. . . . I sit always on the side, think about what was done to me and feel unhappy. . . . Because I have become so bad, there are those who think that my child is not from my spouse." When a local newspaper asked

Sukran why she had named her daughter Torture, she answered: "Because I lived very difficult days."

In the autumn of 1994, the police in Derik raided the Aydin home three times, according to testimony accepted by the commission. Family members were repeatedly summoned to the police station and questioned about Sukran's application to Strasbourg. The family home was stoned, and Sukran's father received a death threat. Not long after Sukran's application was accepted in Strasbourg, Abit and Sukran fled town.

When three Strasbourg judges flew to Ankara in July 1995 to find the facts, Sukran was still nowhere to be found. Strasbourg was losing patience. Turkey was suggesting that the whole tale was a propaganda ploy; that the girl had never been raped; that she was again with the PKK, perhaps reunited with her lover. The commission demanded a letter affirming that Sukran still wanted to bring the case. The Kurdish lawyers in London told their Ankara liaison, Nazmi Gur, that he needed to drop everything and find Sukran.

Nazmi Gur was an affable young man who later became secretary-general of the Turkish Human Rights Association and also served as my interpreter in Turkey. Nazmi himself has been tortured and imprisoned, and as we strolled atop the ancient walls of Diyarbakir, he showed me the courthouse where he'd been convicted. It sounds too corny to be true, but moments later, he spotted a wounded dove on the city walls and cradled it with his hands. While Nazmi voices no bitterness about his personal experience, his stomach is too nervous to take more than a half glass of raki. I strive to keep an open mind, but I have fonder memories of Nazmi than of the clumsy secret police who trailed me around the clock in eastern Turkey.

Nazmi tells an epic tale about his search for Sukran. Starting in the Kurdish city of Mardin, he was told to follow the path of migrant labor seven hundred miles west, to the Mediterranean port of Izmir. In Izmir he found Sukran's father, who told him to check Bursa. Nazmi asked for migrants from Mardin on the crowded streets of Bursa and was told to search villages near Mustafakemalpasa. The trail was warm, but time was short. On August 3, Nazmi faxed London that he could find Sukran if Strasbourg gave him four more days.

Feverishly, Nazmi worked the outskirts of Mustafakemalpasa. By the fourth village, a despairing Nazmi had been searching for two weeks. In the next village he hit pay dirt: the local fruit farmers were using migrants from Mardin. Nazmi was directed to a camp of fifty families living in nylon tents.

There was no water and no toilet. When he approached the clearing at the camp's center, the women scurried away. Three older men came to greet him, and Nazmi began speaking in Kurdish. One of the men had heard of Nazmi's human rights work and declared him a visiting dignitary. They insisted that he sit on their one pillow, while they sat on the ground. After several minutes of small talk, Nazmi quietly told the man who knew of him that he was looking for Abit Aydin. As Nazmi recalls, the stranger looked at the ground and said, "I don't know." Nazmi was given a meal of Black Sea tea, flat bread, yogurt, and crude white cheese. After a few more hours of chat, the man who had heard of Nazmi admitted that Abit was among them and would soon return from the fields.

That evening over a campfire, a dusty, barefoot young man approached Nazmi, without volunteering his name. He said he was a friend of Abit Aydin and asked why Nazmi needed to see him. Nazmi explained that Abit was involved in a case of historical importance but had disappeared. The young man said that perhaps Abit was sorry to have fled, but his family had been continually threatened by the Mardin gendarmes. Nazmi said that thousands of later cases might depend on Abit's case. The farm hand mumbled that others in Abit's position had been killed. Nazmi said that if the young man were a true friend of Abit he would help Nazmi to find him. The young man walked away. After fifteen feet, he wheeled around and said, "I am Abit Aydin." Nazmi had been sitting beside his tent all afternoon.

"Forgive me," Nazmi remembers Abit saying, "but I have a daughter to think of." Nazmi understood but he wished to speak with Sukran alone. Abit agreed only to speak together. They approached Sukran, who was holding her baby, and Nazmi asked if she wanted to continue pressing the case. Sukran answered yes without hesitation. Nazmi warned that bad things might happen, and Sukran's answer did not change. Nazmi said to Abit, "Look, she wants to continue." The young couple had a long side discussion. At last, Abit sighed and said, "Soon they will find us and kill us." Sukran said that she agreed to press the case for the sake of her daughter's future. Nazmi took out a letter addressed to Strasbourg, written in Turkish, that he had brought for her to sign. But Sukran did not understand Turkish and could not sign her name in any language. Before she could change her mind, Nazmi hurriedly scribbled a Kurdish version of the letter. It read:

"I would like to maintain my case which is already before the European Commission of Human Rights. . . .

"This statement has been read to me. It has been written of my own free will. I confirm that it is true and I have signed it."

Nazmi furiously scribbled on Sukran's thumb with his ballpoint pen, and she pressed her thumb on the page to sign. It was by now the night of August 5. The next morning, Nazmi bought rice, sugar, and beans for the struggling couple. Then he caught a taxi and ordered the driver to speed to Bursa. He found the local human rights office and faxed the letter to the lawyers in London, just in time for Strasbourg's deadline.

On October 18, Sukran was due to testify at Strasbourg. Nazmi, who is a born storyteller, can tell another biblical epic about getting her a last-minute visa. Suffice it to say that it doesn't reflect well on French bureaucracy. When Nazmi finally cleared the red tape, he phoned Sukran's London lawyers and, fearing a wiretap, told them in code: "Your parcel is on its way."

Kerim Yildiz, who heads the Kurdish Human Rights Project, recalls that the lawyers and jurists were shocked by the simple nineteen-year-old village girl who walked off the airplane in Strasbourg. Abit and Sukran were the last to exit. Sukran was crying, and both were confused. They had no luggage and no coats, nothing with them but slippers on their feet and thin dusty cotton on their backs. Sukran's nose was running and she didn't know how to use a tissue. Her breasts were leaking (for her baby had stayed behind) and she didn't know how to use a breast pump. When a lawyer extended his hand to shake, she didn't know what to do. She spoke no English, no French, and no Turkish, and had a limited vocabulary even in Kurdish.

Turkey's insinuations about Sukran had planted doubts even in the mind of Kerim Yildiz. "After all their allegations, I was expecting some kind of sophisticated militant," he recalls. Yildiz took one look at the lost girl who stepped off the plane and said to himself, "Fucking hell."

Both the jurists and the lawyers felt an urge to take care of the youngsters. A woman in the registrar's office procured a breast pump for Sukran. She and Abit were treated to their first meal of steak and chips. And the young couple was given a suite at the Hotel de Prince. Sukran called Yildiz "big brother" and confided that, because of the rape, her husband wasn't "treating her like a wife." Yildiz promptly had a brotherly talk with Abit.

At the hearing, Sukran never used the word "rape"—whether because she could not bring herself to say it, or because she never properly learned the word. She spoke only of men "doing dirty things to her." The commission delegates instinctively took her cue and referred back in their questions to the "dirty things." The government oafishly argued that this phrase was not specific enough. Turkey insisted that Sukran had to be lying, because Kurdish culture would not allow her to wed after being raped. But now the commission delegates were sure that the simple girl before their eyes was genuine.

Sukran later could recall little of Strasbourg. "Because I traveled during the night," she told a newspaper, "I saw nothing while going to Europe. I am sorry for this. The excitement of the Court suppressed the joy of seeing those places." Still, her lawyers could tell that she enjoyed being asked her opinion for a change.

In September 1997 the European Court of Human Rights ruled that Turkey had violated the European Convention's Article 3 ban on torture. Although the court granted that the cumulative treatment of Sukran clearly amounted to torture, it reached out to hold that the rape alone also constituted torture. "Rape of a detainee by an official of the State must be considered to be an especially grave and abhorrent form of ill-treatment," noted the court. While the European Commission had cited rape as an Article 3 violation in the old case of *Cyprus v. Turkey*, *Aydin* represented the first acceptance of this principle by the court. This breakthrough in Strasbourg came just as the UN's International Criminal Tribunals were ruling that rape can be a crime against humanity. Rape had not even been on the rap sheet against the Nazis at Nuremberg. Together, the rulings of the late 1990s revolutionized the status of rape under international law.

But in the back rooms of Turkish police stations, women's troubles are far from over. In late 2000 a group of victims of sexual abuse in state custody held a conference in Istanbul to condemn the practice. The following year Turkey banned a book collecting their speeches and indicted nineteen of the speakers for insulting the security forces. Five were indicted for promoting separatism (by pointing out that Kurdish women suffer disproportionately). The most prominent speaker—Eren Keskin, then the Istanbul chair of the Turkish Human Rights Association—has been prosecuted at least seven times for her campaigns against sexual harassment. By some strange logic, she was charged with "insulting the state security forces" based on the statement: "The peace mothers were blindfolded, stripped naked and sexually ill-treated by soldiers young enough to be their grandchildren. They were harassed and insulted using names such as 'whore' and 'bitch.'"

In a statistic cited by the U.S. State Department in its 2003 report on Turkey, an NGO called The Legal Aid Project Against Sexual Assault and

Rape in Custody estimated that three-fourths of Turkish women detainees experience sexual harassment, although only a fraction lodge complaints. Of 157 documented cases of custodial rape, 119 involved Kurdish women. Five of the women miscarried and five others died: two in suicides, two as the result of torture, and one (a fourteen-year-old) in an honor killing. Twenty-eight of these incidents led to filings in the European Court of Human Rights.

Sukran's City Soul Mate

Nebahat Akkoc was born in 1953 in Diyarbakir, the unofficial capital of Turkish Kurdistan. Located near the headwaters of the Tigris River, Diyarbakir is among the world's oldest cities. But it has only recently become a teeming metropolis. By some estimates, Turkey's assault on the countryside in the 1990s quintupled the city's population to a million.

As an urban Kurdish postal worker, Nebahat's father belonged solidly to the intellectual vanguard of his generation. Unusually, he encouraged all of his six daughters to pursue higher education. Nebahat left home at age ten for a women's boarding school in Mardin, which is the region's other ancient city. Although teaching is traditionally a man's role in Turkey, Nebahat had a woman teacher in Mardin and took her as a model. After attending a training seminary in western Turkey, Nebahat returned to teach at a school in the east. There she fell in love with another teacher, Zubeyir Akkoc. They married, and together they rose to become leaders of the teachers' union in Diyarbakir. Unfortunately, as avatars of Kurdish ethnic identity, teachers were perceived as a threat to the state.

When I visited Nebahat in 2002, she sat on the porch of her women's center and restaurant, the Ka-Mer Kitchen, framed by two large arches painted in yellow and light blue. She looked much like a woman professional in Istanbul, with short, henna-colored hair and an addiction to Marlboros. We looked out on an outdoor produce market, where boys scurried with wheelbarrows and hawked oversized gourds and eggplants. Nebahat's eyes and mouth were fixed in a smile, even as the conversation turned grim. Her son, now a pharmacologist, was about to leave home and get married, and in preparation, Nebahat was resolved to normalize her life. For years, she could not bear to hear her doorbell ring; only the night before, she had reconnected it. I felt guilty drawing Nebahat back to her trauma, which is well documented in the opinions of the European Court of Human Rights and Commission on Human Rights. But she felt a duty to tell her story again, no matter how painful to her or to those in the world who care to listen.

In autumn 1992, the local teacher's union was outlawed, forty of its members exiled, and one of its members slain. Part of Nebahat's job was to go to the morgue to identify the body. Her own trouble began after a group of teachers, including Nebahat, arranged to meet with the national education director. Only the police showed up at the appointed time and place. Eleven teachers were detained, and some were assaulted. Nebahat was rebuffed when she complained to the mayor. "You don't raise your voices when the state's soldiers or police die," she recalls the mayor telling her. "Why do you want to see me when teachers die?" The next day, Nebahat received an anonymous telephone threat: "You are going to die. It is now your turn. We are going to kill you off." Nebahat shrugged it off. At the end of October she wrote an article in the *Diyarbakir Soz* newspaper about the police targeting teachers. On Turkey's national Teacher's Day, in late November, she wrote in the same paper that teachers had nothing to celebrate.

A few weeks later, Nebahat's husband, Zubeyir, was killed with two bullets to the head on his morning walk to the elementary school where he taught. After mourning, Nebahat filed a complaint in Strasbourg, charging that Turkey had violated her husband's right to live. Her own ordeal was only beginning.

Over the course of 1993, Nebahat was pressured to leave her job and her union position. Education Ministry panels ruled against Nebahat in a series of disciplinary hearings. The practical result was that she was denied severance pay and widow benefits. Before midnight on February 12, 1994, Nebahat heard a knock at the door. Seven officers entered, planted PKK pamphlets in the house, and made her sign a statement that they were hers. They then threw an anorak over her head and hauled her away, while taunting her two children: "Your father's dead. They killed your father and now we're going to take your mother."

At the police station, interrogators confronted Nebahat with the letters she had sent Strasbourg and the faxes she had sent Kurdish lawyers in London. Complaining to Europe, they said, was tantamount to terrorism: she might as well join the PKK in the mountains. "It was us who killed your husband," they told her. "You speak to Kerim Yildiz on the phone. Stop this or your end will be bad."

For nine nights, Nebahat tested the ingenuity of her torturers. On a typical night she would first be blindfolded, stripped, beaten, bombarded with loud music, and shouted at under hot lights. Then the officers would soak her, alternating between hot and icy water. Finally, they would hook electrodes to her toes or nipple and jolt her. Nebahat's tortures often had an element of sexual harassment. One night she collapsed and was dragged to her cell half-naked. For most of forty-eight hours, she was handcuffed naked to her cell door and forced to listen to the sound of women and youths tortured. Once she was stripped and made to run a gauntlet of police officers, who pawed her and threatened her with worse. "We'll provide our special guest with a special service," they said. On another occasion, the officers snapped nude photos and promised to publish them. Of all the tortures, this one bothered Nebahat most.

On the seventh night, during the water routine, Nebahat felt a burning in her ears and put her hands up to her head. The officer, perhaps thinking she was going to remove her blindfold, threw a roundhouse punch to her jaw. Nebahat spun to the floor. A man claiming to be a doctor prodded her stomach with his foot and forced her to say she was okay. Nebahat was breathless. Blood ran down her head and her jaw throbbed with pain.

Too wrecked to be physically tortured further, Nebahat was forced to listen to the screams of others on her last two nights. The officers swore that she heard the voices of her own two children. This was too much. At last Nebahat banged on the door and agreed to sign a confession to terrorism. After confessing, she was lined up with a group of other detainees and filmed in front of a stash of weapons. The detainees were told that when the doctor came they were to say that nothing was wrong, or they would be detained again. Nebahat alone insisted on seeing a doctor. She showed the doctor her injuries and asked him for a medical report, but she could later find no record of one; on her way out, she was smacked a few times for having dared request a doctor. Finally, Nebahat was brought before a prosecutor and released.

Outside the courthouse, Nebahat collapsed into the arms of her two sisters and a brother who all lived nearby. They brought her to their mother's home, where Nebahat's own teenaged son and daughter were waiting. The family watched the official television channel in disbelief that Thursday night. The video of Nebahat and the weapons cache was aired as the newscaster nattered on about terrorists.

Nebahat's most severe injuries were a broken upper jaw and a broken psyche. At first she sought treatment only for her jaw. The outside doctor prescribed painkillers, but when he learned that she had been injured during detention, he tore up the prescription and refused to have anything to do with her. Nebahat saved her X rays, but could not find a doctor courageous enough to write a medical report. Meanwhile, her psychological symptoms persisted. Her hands trembled. She felt pain and numbness in parts of her body. She was inattentive, underconfident, and indecisive. She couldn't sleep. She crossed the street when she saw uniformed men. She disconnected her doorbell and replaced her lights with low-watt bulbs. She avoided listening to music and answering the phone.

Nebahat and her family received new phone threats in March and October 1994. "Your relatives will suffer," the voice said. "If you're taken into custody again," the voice said, "you won't get out again." In September 1995, on her daughter's sixteenth birthday, Nebahat was taken into custody again. Nebahat left her daughter decorating the house for a party, while she ran off to buy a birthday gift for her (a wristwatch), along with a going-away gift for a friend who was leaving school. When she went to drop off the gift at school, her car was cut off by a police minivan. She was kept overnight in a cold cell in the antiterror department and interrogated about "complaining to Europe." Nebahat's daughter waited and waited on the balcony of their home, fearing the worst. Nebahat at last came home and delivered her gift. But Nebahat's daughter could not bring herself to wear the wrist watch. She would go on to study human rights law.

A month after that horrible birthday, Nebahat sought help for her psyche at an Ankara clinic run by Turkey's Human Rights Foundation. It did not take the doctors long to diagnose post-traumatic stress disorder. For a few months they prescribed Fluoxetine, also known as Prozac, which it is safe to assume Sukran Aydin has never tried. They also advised Nebahat to move to western Turkey—but she knew where her duties lay.

As she slowly gathered her strength, Nebahat came to the realization that Turkey's human rights groups did nothing for women—and its only women's groups were in the west. Looking back on her life, Nebahat saw that even the most liberal institutions were male dominated, and that her traumatic harassment fit into a larger pattern of discrimination. She hatched a plan for what to do with the money she hoped to win in Strasbourg.

In August 1997 Nebahat founded eastern Turkey's first center for abused women. Ka-Mer offers counseling in all Kurdish dialects, as well as legal and medical clinics, self-defense classes, shelter, and an employment service. The Diyarbakir group has already helped thousands of women. A few work on site at the Ka-Mer Kitchen, which has become a popular local restaurant. Following the best Western practice, men are not allowed into the women's center itself, which is housed upstairs in the same house.

Nebahat is waging a one-person campaign for Kurdish women's rights. On a good day, she can talk a village girl out of a bad marriage and a tribal chief out of an honor killing.

Ka-Mer was given a big boost in October 2000, when Nebahat won her case in Strasbourg. The court agreed with her on every point: that the killing of her husband violated Article 2 of the European Convention; that her own tortures violated Article 3; and that the threats she later endured violated her right to petition Strasbourg freely. None of these rulings broke new ground, but the *Akkoc* case is remarkable for the poetry of its justice. Nebahat took the $135,000 the court awarded her and plowed it into the cause of Kurdish women's rights.

Nebahat Akkoc is one of the few characters in this book who has belatedly achieved a measure of fame. In 2003, in recognition of Ka-Mer, *Time* magazine named her one of Europe's heroes. "Human rights is something referred to when violence occurs outside of homes," she told the *Turkish Daily News*. "Now we are trying to extend human rights into homes. We are working to make human rights valid for women." Having vindicated her own rights in the face of mortal risk, she is now trying to expand rights at the very edge of Europe and local social convention. That indeed makes Nebahat Akkoc a hero for a new Europe.

PART IV

Challenges for the Future

CHAPTER 14

The Chechen Challenge

*K*urdish cases began to dominate Strasbourg a few years after Turkey's full acceptance of European Court of Human Rights jurisdiction in 1990. Russia joined the Council of Europe in 1997, accompanied in the surrounding years by some twenty Eastern-bloc nations. It follows that the landmark challenges of the next few years will originate in the ex-Communist zone. The next two chapters examine what I believe to be the two greatest human rights crises in contemporary Europe, beginning with the Russian military's abuse of Chechen civilians.

The main gateway to Chechnya is Ingushetia, an obscure Russian republic perhaps best known to brokers of kidnap insurance. Traveling there is not easy. The first London travel agent I approached refused to help me, because the last clients it sent to the area had been decapitated. Insurers wanted a five-thousand-dollar premium to cover three days in the company of an armed guard. I found a reckless travel agent and took my chances without insurance. Too fearful to enter Chechnya proper, I relied on a local woman with a full set of gold teeth, who dodged gunfire to ferry my subjects across the border to Ingushetia, where I interviewed them at my hotel. One of the European plaintiffs invited me to her home in Grozny. "We have a Chechen saying," she said. "The devil is not as bad as he is painted." I demurred politely, keeping my thoughts to myself. What I was thinking is that, based on my reporting, the devil is even worse than painted.

Like the Kurds, the Chechens are mountain folk who have never been culturally absorbed by their neighbors and have spent much of their history rebelling. Both have employed terrorist tactics to provoke bloody and abusive counterinsurgencies on Strasbourg's watch. But while the Kurds represent one-fifth of Turkey's population, the Chechens make up less than 1 percent of Russia's population. If there is a common reason for the respective obsessions of Russia and Turkey with these small populations, it is not demographic but psychological. In the 1990s, the Kurds and Chechens each made the mistake of rebelling against a regional power with wounded pride, a power that had largely lost a great empire and was determined to preserve its remaining territory by any and all means. There followed a long and tragic stream of human rights violations. In the first resulting legal skirmishes, Strasbourg has shown the political courage needed to protect the Chechen people. As with Turkey, the court's Chechen challenge will be to enforce its will in a large, proud nation at the edge of Europe's cultural orbit.

The Wicked Chechen

Chechnya has always played an outsize role in Russian history and culture. Generations of Russian babies have cooed to the tune of a lullaby, with words by the poet Lermontov, on fighting the "wicked Chechen." Generations of infants in the Caucasus have dozed off to a ditty, cited in Tolstoy, on the complementary theme of bloody martyrdom. Not surprisingly, the history of Chechnya under the Russians is one of uprising, deportation, and death. The historian John B. Dunlop estimates that the Chechen population was reduced by half during the czarist campaigns in the Caucasus (1817–1864), and by a quarter or more under Stalin. A majority of the Chechens were exiled by Czar Nicholas to Turkey during the 1860s, only to return after the Russo-Ottoman war of the late 1870s. Virtually all the Chechens were deported to Central Asia in 1944, jammed into train cars with little or no food, only to return again after Stalin's death. Tolstoy and Solzhenitsyn, each in his time, marveled at the Chechens' defiance and resilience.

Tolstoy's novella *Hadji Murad* is an extended rumination on Czarist Russia's encounter with the Caucasus, based on the final days of the historical Chechen warrior Hadji Murad. At the story's end, when a Russian officer displays Hadji's decapitated head, one character memorably asks whether Russia's soldiers, having dispensed with the laws of war, were themselves reduced to bandits. "War? War indeed! Cut-throats and nothing else." If there were any doubt that Tolstoy himself was questioning the Caucasian war of his day, the great novelist tipped his hand in an unpublished draft of *Hadji*. In the draft, Tolstoy described this war as typical of "what always happens when a state, having large-scale military strength, enters into relations with primitive, small peoples." Inevitably, in such a situation, "the servants of large military states commit all sorts of villainy against small peoples, while maintaining that one cannot deal with them otherwise." This passage was perhaps too direct to make the final literary cut, but its wisdom would hold up well in any year's opinion columns.

During the Stalinist repression, Chechnya drew Solzhenitsyn's attention. Of all the Soviet exiles, he remarked in *The Gulag Archipelago*, the Chechens stood out for their ferocious independence. "There was one nation," he wrote,

> which would not give in, would not acquire the mental habits of submission—and not just individual rebels among them, but the whole nation to a man. These were the Chechens. . . . They had been treacherously snatched from their home, and from that day they believed in nothing. . . . The Chechens never sought to please, to ingratiate themselves with the bosses; their attitude was always haughty and indeed openly hostile. They treated the laws on universal education and the state curriculum with contempt, and to save them from corruption would not send their little girls to school, nor indeed all of their boys. . . . They were capable of rustling cattle, robbing a house, or sometimes simply taking what they wanted by force. As far as they were concerned, the local inhabitants, and those exiles who submitted so readily, belonged more or less to the same breed as the bosses. They respected only rebels.

The Chechens' antisocial bent earned them the respect of Russia's cranky dissident, even as he recognized that it prepared them poorly for life in a peaceful society.

In recent times, Chechnya and Russia have squared off in two bloody wars, from 1994 to 1996, and from 1999 to the present. Human Rights Watch has estimated the number of civilians to have "disappeared" during the current war to be between three and five thousand. Russian officials have taken advantage of the international antiterror climate and the limited involvement of foreign Islamists by labeling the Chechens "bandits and terrorists." The Law on the Suppression of Terrorism, adopted by Russia on July 25, 1998, gives the authorities broad, undefined search powers and entitles antiterror units to make arrests without limits on the length of detention. The trigger for the second Chechen war, in August 1999, was a mysterious series of deadly apartment bloc blasts in Russian cities, which were publicly blamed on Chechen terrorists.

From the start of the second war, Russian leaders set a tone of disdain for human life. "If we catch [rebel fighters] in the toilet," President Putin blustered, "we will rub them out in the outhouse." The Russian commander in the campaign, General Vladimir Shamanov, went a step further, saying that wives and children of bandits are equally bandits.

These attitudes trickled down into the ranks. Veterans of the Russian army's campaign in Chechnya, speaking anonymously to the *Los Angeles Times*, confessed to killing prisoners and civilians during mop-up, and explained their thinking. "There's no such thing as a Chechen civilian," one vet heard his commander say all the time. The very notion of law was scorned. "What kind of human rights can there be in wartime?" asked one ex-soldier. "What Geneva Conventions?" asked another. "In Russia these rules don't work." If any maxim was honored in Chechnya, it wasn't to be found in an international convention. One Russian vet who spoke to the *Los Angeles Times* formulated the operative law as follows: "Any war is a legitimized right granted by the government to one person to decide on the life and death of another person." Disturbingly, the men charged with investigating abuses seemed to share this view. If a Russian killed a Chechen, recalled an officer, it was as if the investigator's own son had killed a bandit. Strasbourg will be coping with the results of these attitudes for the next decade. Consider just two of the first tragedies to make their way up the legal transom.

The Convoy Bombing

During the first Chechen war, Medka Isayeva and her two children, Ilona and Said-Magomed, saw their Grozny flat destroyed. Between the wars, the Isayevs slowly rebuilt their lives and found a new flat in a suburb, near their cousin Zina Yusopova. In 1999, Ilona was sixteen and flourishing. In May, she graduated from technical school. In July she married her sweetheart, Rustam Khamidov. And in September she started at Grozny University, where she studied English and French. Ilona tried hard to look adult—she even wore glasses despite having perfect eyesight—but she gave her youth away by changing hairstyles every two months. In May she wore her hair in a straight bob. In the wedding photos her hair is curly and mid-length. At university her hair reached her shoulders.

A few weeks into the school term, war returned with a vengeance. On October 29, the day that Said-Magomed turned nine, the Russian authorities offered civilians safe passage to the Ingush border. Together with much of Grozny, the Isayevs took them up on the offer. They rented a white Rafiq minivan and hired a neighbor to drive. Thirteen extended family members piled in and joined a convoy that stretched for miles on the Baku-Moscow highway. After waiting most of the morning, the convoy was turned back by Russian soldiers at the border. The Isayevs' driver slowly headed back for Grozny, letting other cars pass.

At about midday, when the men would ordinarily be at mosque, two SU-25 bombers circled overhead at low altitude. As the warplanes swooped toward the Isayevs' section of the convoy, Zina remembers thinking that it must be their destiny to die. Asma Magomedova, who was Medka's daughter-in-law, sat by the front passenger door. Zina sat by the right-hand door in the second seat, with Said-Magomed squeezed between her and his mother. There was no door on Medka's side. The young couple, Ilona and Rustam, were sitting in the third seat, which had no side doors at all.

The first bomb struck several vehicles in front of them. "[We saw] an enormous cloud of char, dust, dirt, flying panels of a truck, shrapnel, rubbish, whatever," says Asma's son Aslambek. "Nothing hit our van, but we could see it all. People started to panic." There was a moment to react before the next bomb struck. Asma opened her door. Rustam shoved his wife Ilona one seat forward. Then Zina opened her door and, grasping for her shoe, stumbled out with Ilona and her brother, holding hands. Asma was sliced fatally in the thigh before she could move. Medka's children were killed instantly on the roadside. Zina and Medka were hit by shrapnel. Rustam jumped out through the rear window, screaming, "Mama, they killed my Ilona!" Medka could see that her daughter was dead, but she threw herself on Ilona's body in the road's shoulder, to protect it as the planes circled round. Rustam's mother recalls Medka "with eyes as if she were looking into an abyss, waiting for a rocket to hit her because she saw that her children had died. The girl lay there without a head."

Legally, the convoy bombing case is fascinating because it serves up the question of killing civilians in warfare. The European Court of Human Rights narrowly dodged this question after NATO's 1999 bombing campaign in the Balkans. In *Bankovic v. Denmark* (2001), NATO's seventeen European members were sued by the families of Serbian civilians who died in NATO's bombing of a Belgrade television station. The snag was that Serbia had not yet signed the European Convention, and the court will only consider violations committed within territory controlled by a member state. The Belgrade applicants argued that NATO nations exercised effective control of Serbia from the air. But the court didn't buy it. Under *Bankovic*, Strasbourg won't judge a bombing unless it takes place within a Council of Europe state. This holding has also let Strasbourg avoid challenges to the

UK bombing of Iraq. But Chechnya is another matter. In Chechnya, it wouldn't be so simple to use procedure to dodge political fallout.

A Second Tragedy: The Staropromyslovski Massacre

The Akayev family also saw their home destroyed during the first Chechen war, of 1994–1995. They spent the three years between the wars painstakingly rebuilding their home and trying not to offend anyone carrying a gun. But they were hit from both sides, literally. On one occasion Adlan Akayev had a tooth broken by an overenthusiastic Russian soldier at a security checkpoint; on another occasion, he was bludgeoned by a Chechen fighter at school. Surviving relatives recall the second incident in some detail.

Adlan was a professor and chair of the physics department at the Grozny Teaching Institute. He had given a bad grade to a student who was a rebel fighter. The student warned that a price would be paid if the mark were not changed. Adlan refused to budge. Soon afterward he was hit over the head from behind with a rifle, presumably by the student or one of his friends. Adlan was one of the few Chechens on the faculty and prided himself on his propriety. Unlike other professors, he refused to accept bribes from students seeking higher grades. Members of the Akayev family considered themselves to be from the party of peace. They started with a low opinion of both soldiers and rebels, and neither incident affected their opinion.

When the second Chechen war broke out, the women in Adlan's family fled Grozny. Adlan stayed behind to care for the rebuilt property. Also staying behind were a few members of the neighboring households, the Goigovs and Khasiyevs. Lida Khasiyeva, fifty-seven, worked as a cook at a kindergarten and raised her sons, Anzor and Rizvan Taimaskhanov, herself. Anzor was finishing college, and Rizvan was just starting. These three families had the misfortune of living in a finger-shaped section of northwest Grozny known as Staropromyslovski.

The Russian army came under deadly sniper fire as it advanced through Grozny in December 1999 and January 2000. On December 6, the Russian military dropped leaflets instructing civilians: "Those who remain will be viewed as terrorists and bandits and will be destroyed. . . . Everyone who does not leave the city will be destroyed." This ultimatum was formally retracted after international outcry, but many soldiers hewed to its spirit. According to the nonprofit groups Memorial and Human Rights Watch, at least thirty-eight civilians were massacred over the course of a few weeks, during the Russian mop-up in Staropromyslovski.

On January 19, Adlan's elderly neighbor Mariam Goigova was wounded by shrapnel. Three of the younger men—Mariam's son Magomet, Lida's son Rizvan, and Lida's brother Khamid—loaded Mariam into a wheelbarrow and ventured out in search of medical care. The next day, Mariam's daughter Petimat found her mother lying dead in the wheelbarrow a few blocks away, shot through the head. According to witnesses, the three men had disappeared in the company of Russian soldiers. Petimat kissed her mother's cheek and, with help, wheeled her body five kilometers to the city's edge.

On January 25, Magomet Khasiyev, who had been hiding in Ingushetia, found Adlan's body in the backyard of the Khasiyev home, together with the bodies of his sister Lida and his nephew Anzor. All three had been wearing white armbands to signal that they were civilians, and yet their bodies were mutilated. Lida was stabbed nineteen times, and her arms and legs were broken. Anzor was shot and stabbed, and his jaw broken. Adlan was shot from the back through his skull, heart, and abdomen, the bullets piercing the black wool sweater that he liked to wear around the house. His university ID card was in his shirt pocket. The left side of his face was bruised and his collarbone broken, suggesting that he had again been beaten with the butt of a rifle.

In mid-February, the bodies of the three men last seen wheeling Mariam Goigova turned up in a nearby garage. Moltgan Khasiyeva was fetched to identify her brother Khamid's body. She told Human Rights Watch, "Khamid's face was unrecognizable, his brain had leaked out and half of his face was smashed. I recognized him by his mouth and chin. His fingers were cut by a knife up to the bone." Magomet Goigov's body was pocked with thirteen bullets and his right ear had been sliced off. Rizvan had been shot about thirty times in the chest, as well as stabbed in the face and chest.

The Legal Fallout

These tragedies generated two of more than a hundred Chechen applications filed in Strasbourg. They were among the first trio of Chechen cases ruled admissible by the European Court of Human Rights in March 2003 and decided February 2005. The court picked one set of massacre complaints and two sets of bombing complaints. Based on the

Staropromyslovski massacre, the court admitted the complaints by Roza Akayeva and Magomet Khasiyev for the loss of their brothers. Based on the civilian convoy bombing, the court admitted the complaint by Medka Isayeva and Zina Yusopova for the loss of Medka's children. As the third case from Chechnya, the court picked a civilian bombing claim by Zara Isayeva (no relation to Medka), who lost a son and three nieces on February 4, 2000, when the family minivan was hit trying to escape the village of Katyr-Yurt during a battle.

Broadly, the court found in all three cases that Russia had violated the right to life guaranteed in Article 2 of the European Convention, both by killing the applicants' relatives and by failing to undertake a proper investigation. In reaching this conclusion, the court relied on the presumptions developed in Kurdish case law, placing the burden on the state to explain deaths occurring during detention. In addition, the court found that Russia had violated its Article 13 obligation to provide an effective remedy for legal violations. The court found it unnecessary to decide whether Russia was systematic in its abuses.

In the convoy bombing case, the court found no evidence to support Russia's contentions that the pilots had been under attack or at risk of attack, or that the pilots launched their missiles at isolated trucks, or that Chechen fighters were preventing civilians from taking advantage of the evacuation corridor that the Russian authorities had offered to the population. Rather, the court found that Russian pilots fired powerful weapons in a situation where they knew or should have known that civilians were at high risk. In doing so, they violated the state's obligations under Article 2 of the European Convention to use force in a manner strictly proportionate to the achievement of the state's aim, with the operation carefully planned and controlled to minimize the risk of death to civilians. In Tolstoy's terms, the court deemed the Russian pilots to be cutthroats rather than warriors.

The Chechen rulings should be broadly applicable. Although the court found it noteworthy that Russia had not invoked legislation governing the use of force, it is not clear why this fact has any relevance. After all, the court's right-to-life standards broadly resemble international norms on the use of force in a properly declared armed conflict. Under the Geneva Protocols of 1977, a nation is obligated at all times to distinguish between civilians and combatants; to do everything feasible to verify that civilians are not targeted; and to refrain from an attack that may be expected to cause collateral civilian damage disproportionate to the definite, concrete, and direct military advantage anticipated. While the court did not invoke humanitarian legal standards of civilian inviolability, it applied the same general rule of proportionality.

It now falls to the Council of Europe to enforce change in the face of Russia's political resistance. Chechnya thus presents the same dilemma as Turkish Kurdistan, but in more extreme form. Russia has greater strategic power and independence than Turkey. Yet, in the case of Russia, Europe lacks its strongest lever. Turkish reform was driven by Turkey's hopes of entering the European Union (see chapter 12). Russia has no aspirations to join the EU, although it does value its European reputation and trade privileges.

Human rights leaders had no illusions when Russia and its neighbors entered the European Convention system during the 1990s. Some argued that Strasbourg was swallowing problems too big to solve and that its authority would diminish when, inevitably, enforcement faltered. Others argued that the Eastern bloc desperately needed human rights and that change, even if incremental, could best be effected within the system. It's a perennial argument, and one only history can resolve.

The European Court of Human Rights has shown resolve in its initial dealings with Russia. In *Kalashnikov v. Russia* (2002), the court held that the severe overcrowding and health crisis in Russia's jails exposed the applicant to inhuman treatment. After the court shone a light on the problem, prison funding increased, and (as a result of broad criminal reform) overcrowding eased. In *Gusinskiy v. Russia* (2004), the court broke new legal ground, even as it directly challenged President Vladimir Putin's illiberal consolidation of power. By pressuring the mogul Vladimir Gusinskiy to relinquish control of his media empire to the state, the court held, Russia violated European Convention Article 18c and abused its criminal process for political or commercial ends. This judgment's timing—on the eve of the Russian criminal trial of the Yukos Oil Company moguls Mikhail Khodorkovsky and Platon Lebedev—suggests that Strasbourg may have intended to send Russia a cautionary message about another abusive prosecution. Applications have also been filed in Strasbourg by Khodorkovsky and Lebedev, who were later convicted of fraud and tax evasion, and by Yukos Oil Company, which was compelled by massive demands for back taxes to sell its principal assets. As an initial matter, in October 2007, the court ruled that Russia had violated Lebedev's pretrial rights by prolonging proceedings and interfering with his representation.

The court has also confronted Russia aggressively for its conduct in the breakaway sliver of Moldova that dubs itself Transdniestria. After local fact-finding hearings, the court in *Ilascu v. Moldova and Russia* (2004) held Russia liable for the persecution of four political dissidents by "Transdniestrian" authorities that were supported by Russia. The court directed that the three dissidents remaining in detention be freed, and it awarded each of the applicants 190,000 euros in compensation, an unprecedented sum in a detention case.

Most recently, the court took a hard line with Russia on disappearances in Chechnya. In *Yandiyev v. Russia* (2006), the court affirmed that a young Chechen man had been extrajudicially executed after a Russian general was caught on CNN ordering him shot. This promises to be the first in a long case line on Chechen disappearances. The Council of Europe's legislature once got tough with Russia too—but it backed down in a hurry. As a protest over Chechnya, the Parliamentary Assembly voted on April 6, 2000, to suspend the voting rights of Russia's delegation. The Assembly recommended that the Committee of Ministers suspend Russia from the Council of Europe outright. A month later, the Committee of Ministers declined, citing a supposed commitment by Russia to investigate human rights abuses in Chechnya. The Assembly restored full voting rights to Russia in January 2001, after a partial withdrawal of troops. Nothing, of course, had changed in Chechnya. In a 2003 report to the Assembly, the rapporteur Rudolf Bindig lamented that the Chechens "have a right not just to our pity but to our protection." Unfortunately, only the court may be up to the task of protection.

Bindig's report on Chechen suffering would have looked broadly familiar to Tolstoy or Solzhenitsyn. As in Tolstoy's day, it's not clear who is the warrior and who is the cutthroat, or, to update the terminology, who is the warrior and who is the terrorist. Drawing that distinction is the goal of much international law. At its core, the Chechen challenge to Strasbourg is to impose law on a lawless war. Russia's willingness to abide by the court's judgments and to embrace law will test whether it truly belongs in Europe.

CHAPTER 15

The Roma Challenge

School desegregation was the issue that kick-started the golden age of American rights jurisprudence, with the 1954 decision of *Brown v. Board of Education*. In Europe, the rights of equality seemed to be last on the agenda. Discrimination was finally pushed to the fore by a group of Czech Roma children, who filed a desegregation action based on statistics that would make a Selma school superintendent blush. Their case languished for so many years that it aroused suspicions (including those raised in the hardcover edition of this book) that it would be remembered as the *Brown v. Board of Education* that wasn't. But in November 2007 the Strasbourg tribunal found its voice, and showed itself to be the true successor of America's Warren Court.

The African Americans of Europe

Like Africans in the New World, the Roma in the Romanian region of Wallachia were enslaved outright for centuries. The experience of that particular Roma community was extreme, but through much of Europe, the status of today's Roma resembles that of blacks in America before the civil rights movement. Stereotyped as criminals, they must contend with police brutality and, in some cases, state-condoned mob violence. Trapped in the region's most depressed economies, they face discrimination in jobs and housing—and segregation in schools.

The former Czechoslovakia presents a microcosm of the Roma experience because, culturally, it straddles Eastern and Western Europe. In the industrialized Czech lands, the Roma followed the pattern of their brethren in the West, wandering from town to town, serving as horse dealers, fortune tellers, folk doctors, beggars, and petty thieves. Rural Slovakia fit the sedentary pattern of Eastern Europe, where the mass of Roma have always lived. In Romania, Bulgaria, Hungary, and Slovakia, the Roma exceed

5 percent of the population. Despite preconceptions formed in Western Europe, most Roma have been settled for centuries. They carved out places in the semi-agrarian economy as grooms, smiths, musicians, soldiers, servants, and washerwomen.

Several times in history, the process of sedentarization was accelerated by cruel state policies. In the mid-eighteenth century, the Habsburg empire banned the Romani language and music, and in some cases removed children from Roma homes. During the Holocaust, the Nazis exterminated 90 percent of the Roma who traditionally occupied the Czech lands of Moravia and Bohemia. After the war, Czechs expelled the ethnic Germans who dominated their industrial belt, known as the Sudetenland, and Roma from Slovakia were relocated to man the factories. In 1958, taking its cue from Stalin, the Czechoslovak state cracked down on the few nomads who remained. In some instances, officials took the wheels off the Roma's wagons and shot their horses.

The practice of sending Roma children to special schools, notably in Czechoslovakia and Hungary, also dates to Communist times. In 1979, the dissident group Charter 77, associated with Vaclav Havel, issued a prescient report on the Czechoslovak Roma. It denounced both the tracking of Roma into special schools and the treatment of Roma in the basic schools: "Everything, from the pictures in their spelling-primers to the entirety of the curriculum, continually forces upon them the idea that they are a foreign, inferior race without a language, without a past and without a face." A decade early, Charter 77 foresaw that the Roma situation would deteriorate with modernization of the economy: "The demand for unskilled labour will then fall, threatening the Roma with massive unemployment which will expose this ruthlessly urbanised minority to extreme pressures, and fuse their social ostracism and material oppression with a new ethnic consciousness, all the stronger the more cruelly it is today suppressed."

Sure enough, when Communism fell, the factories of the former Sudetenland closed, and the Czech Republic inherited a large population of unemployed Roma with roots in Slovakia. Today's Czech Roma are thus the product of multiple displacements. From the Czech perspective, the gypsies in their midst aren't even "our gypsies." The Czech Roma cluster in places like Ostrava, a gray Moravian town near the Polish border that's big enough to qualify as the Czech Republic's third city, although its empty squares give it the feel of a Communist backwater.

Researchers sent to Ostrava in 1999 by the European Roma Rights Center, a Budapest-based group funded by George Soros, found the town's anti-Roma prejudice to be overt and pervasive. While traveling with Roma colleagues, English activist Deborah Winterbourne was routinely cursed and spat at, and once even kicked. Winterbourne felt compelled to stop taking Czech language lessons because her tutor launched into an anti-Roma tirade. The manager at her hotel asked her not to bring Roma friends. On one occasion, Winterbourne walked into a restaurant in Ostrava with four Roma colleagues, and each tried to order a cappucino. The Roma researchers were asked to produce their passports and told to leave. When Deborah protested, a waiter told her that the restaurant didn't serve Roma. The Roma Rights Center threatened a lawsuit against the restaurant, which led to a settlement.

"I felt like a civil rights worker in the Deep South," Winterbourne says. "In Ostrava I never met one person who wasn't racist."

What the researchers found in the schools smacked even more of Selma in 1954. Though they comprise only about 5 percent of the Ostrava school population, Roma children dominated the special schools. Indeed, in Ostrava, Roma children were twenty-seven times more likely than non-Roma children to be placed in special schools. Nationally, Roma children were fifteen times more likely to be tracked in schools for the retarded. To give a sense of perspective, a U.S. government study referred to the situation in New York City, where blacks are more than twice as likely as whites to be referred for special education, as a "wide discrepancy."

Winterbourne and her friends found that Roma parents are routinely pressured and manipulated into transferring their children for little reason, without full informed consent. A typical argument encountered by Roma parents is: "Your child will go there sooner or later so let's just do it now." A social worker outside Prague reported a case where a teacher instructed her class to shun a Roma classmate. "Don't talk to him; he's a Gypsy," she said. "He won't be here for long." Those Roma who do remain in basic schools are apt to be called "black face" and "black swine." In one extreme case, in spring 1999, a basic school received a note threatening a bombing unless it removed its remaining Roma children.

Based on these findings, the European Roma Rights Center filed a school desegregation suit in 1999 in the Czech courts, on behalf of eighteen Roma children from Ostrava. Sadly, the activists encountered hostility to their cause even from the liberal professions. They ran through seven or eight local lawyers before they found one (in Prague) willing to take the case and stick with it. No teacher would testify. The initial remarks made by Czech officials in the press would have caused a scandal had they been made about African Americans. In 1999, a senior policymaker for the Czech Education Ministry, Milos Kusy, told *The Boston Globe*: "They know the special school is better for them. When they don't go to special schools, they fall behind. When they go to normal school, they don't go to school. They make problems throughout Prague and throughout the country. When Romany children go to special schools, the criminal problem is not so high."

In their official court responses, the Czech authorities argued that the educational tracking system, based on IQ testing levels, is transparent and always subject to parental approval. It also argued that Ostrava is atypical, because of its depressed socioeconomic conditions. In October 1999, the Ostrava children lost in the Czech Supreme Court. The court reasoned that its role was to adjudicate individual cases, and not to pass judgment on "the whole social, cultural or social context" through statistics and expert opinion.

As foreign criticism mounted, the Czech government announced a variety of policy initiatives. In 2004 it formally abolished "special schools," and proposed to move special school students into special classes in mainstream schools. But Roma advocates found the Czech reforms inadequate (while praising the desegregation plans and anti-discrimination laws embraced by Bulgaria and Hungary). As the suit in Strasbourg stretched on, little had changed on the ground for the Roma schoolchildren of Ostrava.

The Children of Ostrava

When I visited in 2002, Josef and Marcela M. lived with their son, J. M., across from a steel factory that spewed thick fumes into their living room. J. M. was a handsome and amiable boy with a small gold ring in his ear and a loose cough that seems unlikely to improve. He had enjoyed his early years at a mainstream basic school. J. M.'s teacher at the beginning of third grade told his mother that he was the second-best student in the class. Then that teacher got into a car crash. The new third-grade teacher, who was an older woman, treated him differently. The non-Roma children were sometimes given fairy-tale picture stamps as rewards for good behavior. The new teacher told J. M., "Even if you stood on your head, I wouldn't give you these stamps." J. M., who at the time lived near a chemical factory, missed weeks of school in spring 1998 because of a flare-up of his chronic bronchitis. J. M.'s non-Roma classmates wouldn't let him copy their lessons. On his return, the teacher immediately quizzed him on the material he hadn't learned, about Czech wars of the fourteenth and fifteenth century. The teacher recommended psychological testing for J. M. The psychologist admitted that J. M. was bright but school administrators still recommended that J. M be transferred, because of his absences. He began his next school year at a special school. J. M. was so out of place there that he sometimes did substitute teaching. Within a few months he found himself in the sixth grade at special school. In autumn 2000, he was put back in the fourth grade of the regular school. He'd lost a full year. The teachers at his new school have accused him of stealing snacks and tried to transfer him to a different basic school. J. M.'s mother, Marcela, says that this is a standard technique for getting rid of Roma kids.

The special students I interviewed complained that their schools didn't take education seriously. Sometimes three grades were taught in one room. The school day was short, and, given any excuse, the teachers let the pupils watch videos or listen to music. The students said they weren't expected to fully know the Czech alphabet until fourth grade. Ironically, any non-Roma kids in the class tended to be genuinely slow. In a cruel inversion of Czech society, the Roma children taunted the non-Roma and made them sit in the back of the class. The truly special were sometimes switched from "special schools" into truly special schools, known as "specialized schools."

The special students I interviewed complained that they were tracked into absurdly narrow secondary school courses. Many boys become brick-layer's helpers, wheeling wheelbarrows for the boys training to be brick-layers. Many girls become cook's helpers, peeling potatoes for the girls training to be cooks. At home Renata K. cooked a mean dish of meat pan-cakes with mushroom sauce, but her teacher wouldn't let her into the student kitchen. "You will never be a cook," the teacher told her. "You will always be a helper." Renata's younger sister H. K., who was a plaintiff in Strasbourg, chimed in: "I want to be a sweetmaker, not a sweetmaker's helper." No doubt she speaks for many Roma children. But when Milan K. tried to resist placing his younger daughter in a special school, he said, an administrator threatened to cut off their social benefits. Milan never knowingly gave permission, but H. K. entered special school.

The Ostrava adults voiced only despair. Like many of the plaintiffs' parents, Milan P. is himself the product of a special school. A diminutive man who complains of ulcers and backaches, he had only worked six months since the fall of Communism. Milan's prize possession was an eight-speed Peugeot bicycle, which he used as his main means of transport. "I am disappointed in the world," he said. "If I go there or I go there they tell me, 'You have a black face—get out of here.' If I drive a nice bicycle, they tell me I'm a thief." Milan, his wife, and their four teenage children lived in a one-room apartment without gas or hot water, sharing three beds among them. "Maybe if I went to basic school, I'd have had more chances," Milan said, "but maybe I'd have been denied anyway."

The children themselves held out hope. Because of his lost school year, J. M. told me, he'd be too old to attend secondary school when he graduated. "It's pretty unfair," he said. "I would have liked to show that Roma people can get somewhere." J. M and his father Josef watched the university graduation ceremonies on television and listened, virtually in vain, for Roma names. "It's a big sham," Josef said of Czech Roma education. "We hope our lawsuit brings change."

The Roma in Strasbourg

The Ostrava children applied to Strasbourg in April 2000, claiming discrimination in education, and racial discrimination so severe as to amount to degrading treatment. By way of remedies, the complaint sought an injunction integrating the Ostrava schools within three years, and the establishment of a fund to pay for the compensatory education for Czech Roma. In its comments on admissibility, the European Roma Rights Center cited a new study showing that the vast majority of Roma children assigned to special Czech schools are not mentally retarded. It accused the Czech state, in arguing that "education still carries no significant value for most Roma families," of harboring a "blame the victim" mentality.

In an amicus brief, the London-based human rights group Interights urged the European court to adopt the indirect discrimination standards first elucidated in the U.S. Supreme Court decision of *Griggs v. Duke Power Co.* (1971). Under *Griggs*, the plaintiff may establish a preliminary case of discrimination by pointing to a general policy with a disproportionate impact—even if it can't prove racist intent. Then the defendant must justify its policy. Such a test is vital to making equality meaningful, because racism is a subjective state of mind. Racism can rarely be proved unless a court is willing to put the burden of proof on the state.

The American-born *Griggs* test has been widely adopted: by the European Court of Justice, the UN treaty bodies, and the Inter-American Court of Human Rights, as well as by the national courts of Australia, the United Kingdom, Canada, and South Africa. But in an irony that is often overlooked, the U.S. Supreme Court long ago confined the *Griggs* test to statutory law. As far back as 1976, *Washington v. Davis* clarified that, under U.S. *constitutional* law, proof of intent is required to establish discrimination.

The Roma lawyers' arguments initially fell on deaf ears. In February 2006 a panel of the European court sharply rejected the Ostrava claims by a vote of six to one. In ruling that statistics alone could not prove racism, the panel seemed to adopt the tough constitutional standard of the U.S. Supreme Court over the plaintiff-friendly *Griggs* test.

Beyond invoking the court's traditional deference on matters of education, the panel expressed an extraordinarily narrow conception of the judicial role. "[L]ike the Czech Constitutional Court," wrote the panel, "it is not [this court's] task to assess the overall social context." Many theorists would argue that it is precisely a constitutional court's task to assess overall social context, and that the obligation falls with special weight on a higher-level constitutional court if the lower-level constitutional court has abdicated that role. In 1954, the U.S. Supreme Court didn't look to the Kansas Supreme Court for guidance on the scope of its power.

When it came to racism, the Strasbourg court even trailed some national courts. On July 22, 2005, the Sofia District Court found that the overconcentration of Roma students in an inferior Bulgarian grade school amounted to segregation. Apparently unafraid to look at social context, the Bulgarian court concluded that "the negative consequences for society resulting from the existing situation are tremendous." Roma advocates began to suspect that their best hope lay outside Strasbourg.

James Goldston of the Open Society Justice Initiative, who represented the Ostrava children, openly worried that Strasbourg had abdicated its role as a protector of minority rights. Perhaps the court was reflecting the social mores of the former Communist nations that joined the Council of Europe after the fall of the Berlin Wall. Or perhaps the court was overwhelmed by its caseload crisis—a victim of its own success—and was prioritizing systemic efficiency over individual justice.

Equality versus Administration

Strasbourg's initially timid judicial record on Roma desegregation was mirrored by a timid record on equality generally. Under Article 14 of the European Convention on Human Rights, the right against discrimination is not freestanding; it can only be invoked in combination with other rights, such as the right to life or the right to education. This gap was highlighted as early as spring 1990 by longtime ECHR president Rolv Ryssdal, at an international colloquy in Lund, Sweden. "The European Convention on Human Rights as it stands now," he said, "is not capable of addressing the problem of minorities in its entirety. There is a chink—a gap—in the Council of Europe's human rights armor which should be repaired, especially if the Council wishes to furnish concrete assistance to those parts of Europe where minorities exist." Ryssdal specifically had in mind the nations of Eastern Europe, which were expected to join the Council of Europe imminently, and did. The right to equality was, in the words of Ryssdal's successor Luzius Wildhaber, a "second-class guarantee."

On November 4, 2000, on the fiftieth anniversary of the European Convention's signing, the Council of Europe proposed to create a free-standing right against discrimination. A claim for educational bias, like *D. H.*, could always be brought because the Convention guarantees the right to education. The proposed Protocol 12 would allow claims in areas where the Convention has no freestanding right—for instance, discrimination in housing, employment, or social services. But is the Council of Europe willing to open the floodgates to such claims? Apparently not. Protocol 12 technically came into force in April 2005—but three years later it remained unratified by thirty Council of Europe nations, including the large states of Britain, France, Germany, and Italy. Until Protocol 12 is more fully embraced, discrimination in housing and employment is likelier to be redressed under the European Union's progressive "Race Directive," and the harmonizing legislation that was adopted by EU member states in 2003.

Believers in human rights are left to wonder whether the caseload crisis has displaced racism on the Council of Europe's agenda. While that question remains open, the council's judicial arm has finally answered its doubters.

Redemption

When the European court accepted *D. H. v. Czech Republic* for rehearing before a grand chamber, the *New York Times* encouraged it to "seize the opportunity . . . and reverse a decision that has anchored European race relations today well behind where America was in 1954." With no qualms about undertaking a broad social inquiry, the grand chamber grabbed the moment.

On November 13, 2007, by a vote of thirteen to four, the court reversed its initial ruling, and held that the Czech state had discriminated against Roma children by "quasi-automatically" tracking them into schools for the mentally retarded. In a significant philosophical shift, the court undertook the duty of protecting the "disadvantaged and vulnerable." In a significant legal shift, it accepted that claimants may rely on statistics to make a preliminary showing of discrimination, and compel the state to justify its policy.

Ironically, *D. H. v. Czech Republic* leaves the U.S. Supreme Court isolated in its cramped views on discrimination. Today, Europe is the unquestioned leader in a global dialogue on civil rights in which the United States is only a marginal participant. Strasbourg's new discrimination standards bring it into line with the law of the European Community and the UN, to which the grand chamber devoted twelve pages of citations. Sadly, the only U.S. case cited was *Griggs*, a ruling constitutionally orphaned in its home nation almost from the start. The U.S. Supreme Court has spent the past generation retreating from the promise of desegregation—a trend that culminated in June 2007 with the rejection of progressive school plans in Louisville and Seattle.

Back in the 1970s, it was U.S. law that inspired British and Irish barristers to transform the European Convention into a force for social change. One leading early advocate was Anthony Lester. In the "East African Asians" case of 1973, Lester used U.S. precedents to persuade Strasbourg to rebuke Britain for denying entry to Indians with UK citizenship after they were expelled from East Africa. Now a member of the House of Lords, Lester has carried on the good fight as a barrister for the Roma children, while the flame of the Warren Court flickers only dimly in its home nation.

"The [*D. H.*] decision underscores the growing divergence between the United States and the rest of the world in the field of equality rights," says James Goldston, a former U.S. prosecutor who collaborated with Lord Lester on the Ostrava case. "Since *Griggs* was decided in 1971, the U.S. Supreme Court has, on the whole, narrowed the scope of protection against racial discrimination, while courts in other countries—including, now most prominently, the ECHR—have steadily broadened it."

But if *D. H. v. Czech Republic* is remembered for one thing, it will be for accepting a broad mandate of social justice—and laying to rest fears that the Strasbourg court had lost its reformist drive. "This judgment is a most welcome affirmation," says Goldston, "that the Strasbourg court remains a dynamic model of progressive rights enforcement and interpretation."

Justice Harlan Fiske Stone first voiced the philosophy, in a footnote to *U.S. v. Carolene Products* (1938), that it is a constitutional court's ultimate duty to protect the politically vulnerable—or as he put it, "discrete and insular minorities." It fell to the Warren Court to give that philosophy life, sixteen years later, in *Brown v. Board of Education*. In an intriguing parallel, Judge Siep Martens first issued a call for the European court to pursue social justice in his 1990 dissent to *Cossey v. U.K.*, when he dubbed the court the "last resort protector of oppressed individuals." It took seventeen years for the European court—under President Jean-Paul Costa and *D. H.* presiding judge Nicolas Bratza—to undertake the protection of the "disadvantaged and vulnerable." In addition to grounding its mission in historical persecution, as did *Brown*, the European court invoked the contemporary ideal of diversity. Thus the grand chamber identified an emerging European consensus that recognizes an obligation to protect minorities, both for their sakes and "to preserve a cultural diversity of value to the whole community."

As America knows well, the real trick is to translate bold judicial action into lasting social change. The *D. H.* ruling simply ignored the claimants' sweeping request for injunctive relief or a compensatory fund. The effect of declaring Czech special schools in violation of the European Convention is unclear, for the court acknowledged that the Czech Republic already abolished special schools in 2004. At the same time, the effectiveness of that reform is highly debatable, and the grand chamber noted the persistence of Roma school segregation throughout Central and Eastern Europe. So although *D. H.* may not technically compel further Czech action, it will surely help civil society to push educational reform in Prague and elsewhere. Where nonprofits are disappointed with the progress in Roma desegregation, they may bring new cases armed with powerful new law. The same holds true for other realms of discrimination (especially where Protocol 12 has been ratified), and other European minorities. The big beneficiaries of *D. H.* will be, to borrow the court's words, Europe's most "disadvantaged and vulnerable." That means the Roma to the east, and the Muslims to the west.

The U.S. Supreme Court fulfilled its historic role in 1954 by decreeing equality for America's most persecuted group. In 2007, the European Court of Human Rights settled any doubt that, in its protection of despised minorities, it is the Warren Court's rightful heir. Sadly, vindication came too late for the Ostrava children to retrieve their lost school years. But thanks to the *D. H.* ruling, the next generation of Roma children may follow their dreams. The day may not be distant when lawyers of Roma origin sit on the European Court of Human Rights.

PART V

Concluding Thoughts

CHAPTER 16

A Constitutional Identity for Europe

*T*he stories in this book may be read for their human drama. Individually, they tell us something about Muslims in France, Kurds in Turkey, gays in Britain, and so forth. The larger question is: do they say anything about Europe as a whole?

Universal human rights became European human rights because when the idea came along after World War II, the universe wasn't ready—but Europe was. The United Nations embraced lofty rhetoric in the Universal Declaration of Human Rights of 1948. Elegant as that document may be, it is merely aspirational. The UN lacked the unity to agree upon a practical, enforceable treaty. The United States, among others, vetoed the creation of a right to individual petition. The Council of Europe, which signed the European Convention on Human Rights two years later, was the broadest grouping with the political will needed to create a practical regime of supranational law. As the Convention's preamble stated, it was the aim of "European countries which are like-minded and have a common heritage of political traditions, ideals, freedom and the rule of law, to take the first steps for the collective enforcement of certain of the Rights stated in the Universal Declaration."

A 1949 pamphlet by the European Movement made the same point more explicitly: "It is difficult to see how [the Universal Declaration] can produce any practical results so long as the United Nations include totalitarian states. . . . However, what may not as yet be feasible on a world-wide scale is both possible and necessary within the more limited and more homogeneous circle of the European democracies." The European Convention had the advantage of being immediately doable.

The German philosopher Jurgen Habermas, in much of his work, calls on the inhabitants of Europe to will into being a "constitutional identity." By constitutional identity, he means an ethical-political self-understanding evolved in the public sphere—especially in the media. The jurisprudence of the European Court of Human Rights might be seen as an answer to Habermas's call. And in its own small way, so might this book. Assembled here are the identity-forming vignettes that should have been written by a corps of reporters in Strasbourg over the past twenty-five years. If a European constitutional fabric can be woven, then surely it will be woven out of stories like these.

Some leading figures in Strasbourg have been explicit about the project of binding the continent. In "The Coming of Age of the European Convention on Human Rights," published in the inaugural issue of the *European Human Rights Law Review* (1996), the Norwegian judge Rolv Ryssdal, then president of the court, declared the Convention "the single most important legal and political common denominator of the States of the continent of Europe." The scholar Guy Haarscher has similarly argued that the distinctive articulation of rights by Strasbourg is helping to create a new "soul" for Europe. Henry Schermers, a longtime European jurist from the Netherlands, has confessed, "One really feels European when listening to the pleading of a Swedish lawyer before the Commission invoking the Marckx case . . . and referring to further developments in Belgium and the Netherlands. The Convention and its organs not only create a body of European law, but they also open the eyes of lawyers to developments in other parts of Europe. And gradually they bring the national legal systems closer together." Unfortunately for the European project, it's unclear whether such abstractions resonate outside the chambers of Strasbourg, the think tanks of Brussels, and the classrooms devoted to their study. The French and Dutch electorates, in rejecting the EU draft constitution and charter of rights in 2004, expressed a blanket Euro-skepticism, with no distinction drawn between the EU and the Council of Europe.

A Thin European Identity

A few years ago, Habermas debated the possibility of a European constitution with Dieter Grimm, a leading Continental legal thinker who then sat on the German Constitutional Court. Although the two differed about the future (Grimm is a Euro-skeptic), they agreed that Europe now lacks the common identity that must undergird a constitution.

The best measure of continental awareness comes from surveys by the European Union. According to one Eurobarometer poll, only 38 percent of EU residents agree that there is a European cultural identity shared by all Europeans. (This number might be even skimpier if similar surveys were taken in the broader grouping of the Council of Europe.) Fifty-two percent of EU residents view themselves as European, but the vast majority of those list their European identity as second to their national identity. In other words, they see themselves as "Italian and European" or "Irish and European." According to another Eurobarometer poll, only 43 percent of the public perceive the EU as beneficial. It seems that for most Europeans, "Europeanness" is a supplementary identity at best.

European elites tell a very different story, with 90 percent of top decision makers regarding the EU as beneficial. A regional identity is nothing new for Europe's scholarly class, which has mingled for hundreds of years. In the Middle Ages, Christian orders dispatched monks from Spain to Poland, from Germany to Spain, and from France to Ireland and Cyprus. There were times in the sixteenth century when more than 40 percent of students at Krakow University were foreign, and more than six thousand Germans studied in Padua. Today, a much broader educated class ignores borders during an extended youth of travel and education. But is regional consciousness among the elite a sufficient basis for a constitutional identity?

Voltaire claimed that the "peoples of Europe share humane principles which are not found in other parts of the world." Social scientists who have surveyed world values would beg to differ. The sociologists Jos Becker and Johan Verweij conclude that, given the variations within Europe, one cannot speak of a European culture. Consider a few extreme contrasts. A Frenchman is eight times less likely than an Irishman to attend church weekly, and five times likelier than Icelanders to view marriage as outdated. A Turk is six times less likely than a Russian to be divorced, ten times likelier than a Dutchman to be a homophobe, and twelve times likelier than an Icelander to disapprove of single mothers. It's true that most of Western Europe shows a pattern of "individualism, a certain resistance to conformism, some measure of indifference to working hard, and a secularized way of thinking." Far from being unique to Europe, however, this pattern fits highly educated groups everywhere.

"Do you feel European?" I put the same question to every European Court plaintiff I met. Surprisingly, even those who might be cast as "Euroheroes" do not identify as European patriots. They simply fought for their causes by whatever means were at hand. At bottom, the only thing these people have in common is that they're frustrated lawyers.

The marginalized Roma applicants, like the mother of the Ostrava schoolchild N.C., laughed at my question. "We're not Czech," she said, "so how can we be European?" The downtrodden Chechens understood the question pragmatically. "Russia is clearly not a part of Europe now," said Medka Isayeva. "It would be a good thing for us if they became more a part of Europe."

The most nationalistic answers, predictably, came from the Britons. Both Jeff Dudgeon and Duncan Lustig-Prean felt disappointed that they needed to petition Europe for gay justice, because they feel proud of Britain's own rights tradition.

For others, a European identity was not universal enough. The Jehovah's Witnesses expressed solidarity with their brethren around the world. The Lopez-Ostras replied that environmental concerns transcend borders. The Marckxes, who in their current lives run a Web site on pet-friendly travel, professed devotion to the virtual community of dog-lovers around the world.

The most Eurocentric applicant is, not surprisingly, the most elite. Peter Michael Lingens, who reached the pinnacle of the Austrian media world and is a scion of leading families in Vienna and the Ruhr, has retired with his wife, a lawyer, to the Spanish Costa del Sol. "We hate borders," he says, "and we're glad they're falling." He boasts that his school-age son speaks English like an Englishman, Spanish like a Spaniard, and German like an Austrian. But Lingens is the exception that proves the rule.

A Modern European Mythology

The preeminent British scholar of nationalism, Anthony D. Smith, argues persuasively that regional identity is formed by the same process as national identity. Myth and symbol, Smith stresses, are the key to winning the hearts and minds of ordinary people. At the same time, he cautions, any new pan-European rituals must respect the continuing hold of national loyalties on the masses. Smith writes, "If a European political community is created that will have a *popular* resonance, then we may be sure that it will be founded on the basis of a common European cultural heritage by a pan-European nationalist movement that is able to forge common European myths, symbols, values, and memories out of this common heritage in such a way that they do not compete with still powerful and vigorous national cultures." In short, the "emergence of a "European super-nation" must await "a sense of specifically 'European' heritage and . . . mythology."

Outside of human rights law, the list of Europe-wide rituals is short—and not very serious. The Eurovision Song Contest grew out of the San Remo Song Festival, which was designed to foster postwar European unity. Modern devotees may be surprised to learn that the contest's rulebook encourages the use of each country's native language, folk dress, and instruments. Today's Eurovision features young dancers in spandex reciting remarkably uniform pop love songs in accented English over a synthesizer beat. Imagine the kitschiest American kitsch translated into thirty-six languages and back. This is not to say that Eurovision is either unpopular or boring. It draws an audience in the hundreds of millions. And the British commentators openly mock the show, in a mesmerizing postmodern counterpoint to the Boy Scout earnestness of the local hosts. Watching Eurovision has become a can't-miss ritual for many members of the gay community, who treat it as a communal joke.

Perhaps a more promising model for European identity is the Ryder Cup golf tournament. The Ryder Cup was reorganized in 1979 to pit European golfers as a team against American golfers, because, when the tournament was organized on the basis of national teams, the Americans were too dominant. (As in sports, so in foreign affairs.) Somewhat to their surprise, European golf fans of all plaids find themselves cheering in unison: "Eu—rope, Eu—rope."

The euro currency is also a common symbol of sorts, within the twelve-nation euro-zone. Recognizing that European pride can never entirely supplant the local, an ad campaign for the launch of the euro cleverly accentuated Europe's diversity. "Imagine what you could buy for 100 Euros," exhorted one ad, ". . . a box at the Vienna Opera House . . . a ticket to the Moulin Rouge in Paris." "Imagine what you could buy for 10 Euros," exhorted a second ad, ". . . three pints of Guinness in a central Dublin pub . . . two shots of vodka in a Helsinki bar." This series strikes the right note. It honors the individuality of the local while emphasizing traits that set Europe apart. Europeans care more about high culture than Americans, and, as any expat could tell you, they drink a lot more.

But human rights law would be far the most satisfying basis for a communal identity. Americans are raised to revere cases like *Brown v. Board of Education* and *New York Times v. Sullivan* as central pieces of the civic culture. Clarence Gideon, who established the indigent right to counsel in the case of *Gideon v. Wainwright*, has become an American folk hero, thanks to the book *Gideon's Trumpet* by journalist Anthony Lewis, and the movie version starring Henry Fonda. By all rights, *Lingens v. Austria* ought to be as famous in Europe as *New York Times v. Sullivan* is in America. Inspiring figures like Zeki Aksoy and P. J. McClean ought to become rallying symbols for European sentiment. The case law of the European Court of Human Rights is a veritable mythology in waiting.

Strasbourg, moreover, is the perfect site to forge a European identity. Founded as a Roman fort on the Rhine River, it is the main city of Alsace, the meeting point of French and German cultures. The Strasbourg Oath of Alliance, signed in 842 by Charlemagne's grandsons, Lewis the German and Charles the Bald, is the oldest text written in both the Romance and Teutonic languages. Gutenberg is widely thought to have invented the printing press while living in Strasbourg, in 1440. The town soon became a European printing capital, a center of humanism and Reformation, and, to quote the historian Fernand Braudel, part of a "glittering archipelago" of market towns in the continental economy centered on Venice. Then, for four hundred years, the region passed bloodily back and forth between France and Germany. A plaque in the town square calls Strasbourg "a city which, more than any other, has been the victim of the stupidity of the nations of Europe which thought they could solve their problems by waging war." The physical home of the European Court of Human Rghts, the Palais des Droits de l'Homme, was designed in the early 1990s by the modernist architect Sir Richard Rogers, best known for Paris's Pompidou Centre and London's Millennium Dome. The two cylinders housing the courtrooms are clad in steel and unified by a glass atrium, symbolizing the court's accessibility to the common man.

Which "Supreme Court" Will Be Supreme?

If the case law reviewed in this book forms a mythology for Europe, who is its legal guardian? That is not an easy question. The relationship between Europe's two "supreme courts" is so confusing that even a leading treatise, *Comparative Constitutional Law*, confuses the two.

The EU itself is not a member of the Council of Europe. The EU's European Court of Justice takes the position that, while the EU is bound by the European Convention, it is not bound by the interpretations of the European Court of Human Rights. For its part, the ECHR is prepared to hold a state liable for observing EU law. But—because EU law affords an equivalent level of respect for fundamental rights—the ECHR will presume a state action under EU law to be justified unless it is shown to be manifestly deficient. See *Bosphorus Airways v. Ireland* (2005).

Collision has largely been avoided so far. On the relatively rare occasions when the ECJ deals with fundamental rights, it tends to agree with the ECHR. There are two notable exceptions, both relating to white-collar crime.

Strasbourg is more apt than the EU courts to perceive a government raid on a business office as a right-to-privacy issue. Compare *Niemietz v. Germany* (1992), which found that the search of a lawyer's office in support of a criminal investigation violated the lawyer's Article 8 privacy rights, with *Hoechst AG v. Commission* (European Court of Justice 1989), finding that a dawn raid by the EU anti-cartel unit did not violate Article 8 of the European Convention.

Strasbourg also interprets European Convention Article 6 in a way that is more protective of business defendants. It suggests that the right against self-incrimination may be used by corporations to protect against civil discovery demands, and not merely to bar the use of a defendant's confession, which is the position of the EU courts. Compare *Saunders v. United Kingdom* (1996) *and Funke v. France* (1993) with *Orkem v. Commission* (ECJ 1989).

For the moment, these inconsistent case lines coexist. In the long run, they cannot. The issue was nearly forced in *Senator Lines GmbH v. Austria*, when the European Company Lawyers' Association asked the ECHR to declare the EU in violation of the European Convention in its aggressive conduct of cartel investigations. But the issue became moot after the EU courts overruled the fine against Senator Lines, and the ECHR declined to admit the case. The question remains: which is really supreme—the EU court or the ECHR?

Because the EU sometimes regulates things like equality, the EU court sometimes poaches on human rights turf. These incursions are increasing as the EU's directives get more ambitious. In the summer of 2003, a directive extended EU equality law to cover discrimination on the basis of race, religion, and sexual orientation. And conflicts will proliferate if the EU ever gives force to its proposed Charter of Fundamental Rights. In the long run, one court or the other must emerge as supreme on questions of fundamental rights, whether through formal structural change or through informal assertions of judicial power.

The EU's accession to the Strasbourg convention is a top priority for the ECHR. Surprisingly, the proposal is very much in the realm of possibility. In the Laeken Declaration of December 15, 2001, the EU invited its constitutional convention to consider whether the EU should accede to the European Convention. The draft European constitution explicitly states that the EU has legal personality, thus clarifying that it has the power to sign a treaty. Meanwhile, Protocol 14 of the European Convention, which opened for signature in May 2004, states that the EU "may accede to this Convention." It seems unlikely for an institution to surrender power voluntarily, but there's a history of that happening in Europe. Perhaps the "Eurocrats" of Brussels and Luxembourg feel they have chewed off enough and are happy to leave the values discourse to Strasbourg. In any event, whichever court emerges as the supreme arbiter of "Euro-rights," it must build upon the cases discussed in this book.

Europe's Missing Bards

No court can fulfill its mythmaking function unless it is amplified by the media; Homer needs his troubadours. Both Habermas and Justice Grimm blame the lack of a European identity, above all, on the absence of regional media coverage. In Grimm's words, "A search for European media, whether in print or broadcast, would be completely fruitless. . . . [N]ational media . . . [can]not create any European public." In a similar spirit, Habermas wrote, "[T]here can be no European federal state worthy of the name of a democratic Europe unless a Europe-wide, integrated public sphere develops." This has long been conventional wisdom in Brussels. A 1984 EU policy report put the problem succinctly: "European unification will only be achieved if Europeans want it. Europeans will only want it if there is such a thing as European identity. A European identity will only develop if Europeans are adequately informed. At present, information via the mass media is controlled at the national level."

In fairness, a search today for Europe-wide media would not be utterly fruitless. In the few years since the Grimm-Habermas debate, several leading American publications have developed impressive European editions, among them *Time, Newsweek, Business Week*, and the *Wall Street Journal*. Although it at first seems curious, it makes sense that American editors, as outsiders, more readily conceive of Europe as a whole than do Scottish or Flemish editors. Only time will tell whether this outsider perspective is distorted or, as in the case of Tocqueville, acute. For now, these American-European titles appeal mainly to expatriates and other business elites.

It's true that the business press, led by London's *Financial Times*, covers Brussels thoroughly. Business papers probably serve the Habermasian function of building a supranational sense of self. But they reach only the educated elite. Even in the *Financial Times*, coverage of Strasbourg is spotty and lacks a broad perspective. That leaves Strasbourg to the whims of the national, and usually nationalistic, media. The tabloids are entertainingly hostile.

Europhobia is especially evident in London. Consider the news coverage when the euro currency hit the streets. In a spoof entitled "How Europe Read the Historic News," the British magazine *Private Eye* compared the cheery Continental banners—"Bonjour a L'euro!" "Buon Giorno Euro!" "Guten Morgen Euro!"—with a British headline that focused on the sex life of actress Elizabeth Hurley. The actual coverage was just as comic. The *Daily Telegraph* ran a squib under the caption "Euro can trigger allergic reaction," warning that, because of their nickel content, the euro coins might be "poisonous." When Britain debated the incorporation of the European Convention into its domestic law, the *Daily Mail* ran an editorial under the head "A new Tyranny of Human Rights?" In the lead, it conjured the fanciful image of a judge ordering a schoolmaster to pay damages for banning gay sex among children. But it is Strasbourg's case line on Northern Ireland that has most sorely provoked Little Britain. After the *McCann* judgment, which held Britain liable for shooting IRA operatives during a terrorist attack in Gibraltar, a London tabloid published the telephone number of the European Court of Human Rights, and Strasbourg was deluged with calls. Typical headlines by the *Daily Mail* in the wake of Northern Irish decisions include "Britain Defeated" and "Another Surrender to Europe." After a victory by IRA families in 2001, the London tabloid *The Express* editorialized that the European Court of Human Rights supports terrorists bent on destroying British society, even as it strips Britain of its sovereign rights. The tabloids usually make a point of lamenting the cession of British choices to "remote foreign judges."

A similar pattern may be seen elsewhere in Europe among nationalist newspapers and politicians. After Strasbourg compelled Romania to pay significant compensation for seized property, the Romanian prime minister said mockingly that he didn't realize the court served as a real estate agent. After the court rebuked France for police torture in the *Selmouni* decision in 1999, Interior Minister Jean-Pierre Chevenement stated, "The judgments of the European Court of Human Rights do not concern French judges, who remain the masters of their own decisions." After Strasbourg found that a Dutch court should not have convicted bank robbers based on anonymous testimony, the right-wing newspaper *De Telegraaf* ran a headline: "Gangsters Set Free by Euro-court." The Turkish foreign ministry reacted to its first setback in Strasbourg, in September 1996, by stating that Ankara would "carry on its continuing struggle against separatist terrorism." At about the same time, the chief state security prosecutor of Diyarbakir told a visiting mission from the Lawyers Committee for Human Rights: "I have my own objectives and if the European Convention conflicts with them it must take second place." Entrenched state interests and tabloid media unite to create the false impression that, if Europe is united by anything, it's united by Europhobia.

To this observer, that seems a shame. The case law of the European Court of Human Rights is an unmined source of self-understanding in a region that seemingly craves self-understanding. It's a system of myth in search of an audience. The nineteenth-century Italian nationalist Massimo d'Azeglio once said, "We have made Italy; Now we must make Italians." By the same token, those who have made Europe must make Europeans. It would not be appropriate for me, as an outsider, to dictate the use to be made of the stories gathered in this book. What can safely be said is that— if the idea of Europe is to thrive—Europe's native media and mass opinion must evolve.

CHAPTER 17

Human Rights in Europe and America

*T*he field of European human rights was pioneered by a handful of lawyers who studied American law during the civil rights era. The grand irony is that they brought home the innovations of the Warren Court, only to find a generation later that they bear the torch of civil liberties alone.

The barristers David Pannick and Lord Anthony Lester have aptly called the European Court of Human Rights before 1966 "a sleeping beauty." The crucial event that year was the United Kingdom's acceptance of the right of individuals to petition Strasbourg. Individual plaintiffs are a driving force for change in law, because state plaintiffs, as repeat players and guardians of the establishment, are inherently cautious. In the United Kingdom, the power of individual chutzpah was harnessed to a large, talented, and imaginative army of attorneys. Crucially, the UK recognized the right of individual petition at a moment when its lawyers were soaked in the liberating currents of American legal culture. If the court was a sleeping beauty, it was roused by English and Irish barristers who were self-consciously influenced by the American civil rights movement.

In 1968, Lester, who had studied at Yale Law School, enlisted the help of Yale's Professor Charles Black, in what's known as the "East African Asians case." The case was brought on behalf of Indian families that were kicked out of Kenya, Tanzania, and Uganda after independence and were then, despite holding British citizenship, barred by legislation from migrating to Britain. In 1973, Lester and Black persuaded the European Commission on Human Rights that, in extreme cases, racism could amount to inhuman and degrading treatment in violation of European Convention Article 3. In support, they cited a raft of American landmarks, including *Trop v. Dulles* and the dissent in *Plessy v. Ferguson*.

Also in 1968, a Chicago lawyer named James C. Heaney brought the earliest Strasbourg cases against Britain for its conduct in Northern Ireland. Fast on Heaney's heels was an Irish/American team led by barrister Kevin Boyle of Belfast, who, like Lester, had studied at Yale Law School. In filing *Donnelly v. United Kingdom* (1972), Boyle teamed up with Professors Hurst Hannum and Frank Newman, both then of the University of California at Berkeley's Boalt Hall School of Law. Although all of the early Irish applications were ruled inadmissible, they paved the way for breakthrough in the case of the "hooded men," recounted in chapter 11.

The later campaign of Irish feminists for abortion information was expressly patterned on American precedents. So was the quest for religious freedom by Jehovah's Witnesses in Greece. And so is the incipient Roma crusade against police brutality and school segregation in Central Europe. In all three of these instances, there are strong organizational links between the European advocates and their American models.

To be sure, European law is less absolute than American law in many aspects of First Amendment freedom. Europe doesn't protect hate speech, and it sometimes allows prior restraints on publication. Strasbourg generally upholds neutral laws affecting religion, like laws that forbid headscarves, or laws that force students to march in militaristic parades. Most misguidedly, the European Court of Human Rights, in its vigilance to protect democracy, has tried to quell an authentic movement for Islamic democracy in Turkey.

Today, however, American progressives often gaze at European law with envy. Consider some of the practical differences reviewed in this book. Europe was twenty years ahead in legalizing gay sex. On gays in the military, Europe is still a generation ahead. In Europe, there's a constitutional right to a healthy environment; and there are constitutional limits on deportation. In Europe, a state may not limit public information on abortion. Europe bans judicial corporal punishment while placing sharp limits on educational beatings and loose limits on parental beatings. Europe imposes positive obligations on the state to protect the vulnerable against private violence. Europe has eliminated the death penalty and, where possible, refuses to enable American executions. Perhaps most importantly, Europe brooks no exception to the ban on torture. Strasbourg has long struggled to strike a balance between antiterror and civil rights. Its rulings on detention and torture, especially psychological torture, deserve study as the United States gropes for the war on terror's limits.

The European court's greatest achievement has no U.S. analogue. Since 1996, Strasbourg has documented Turkish atrocities against the Kurds, refined its legal standards on torture, detention, disappearances, extrajudicial execution, and village destruction, and—with a big assist from the EU—done its best to enforce them. If it can muster the political will and tenacity, Strasbourg faces a similar task in Russian Chechnya. These case lines best embody the noble postwar vision of Strasbourg as Europe's conscience. Yes, there is an analogous project in the Western Hemisphere; it's called the Inter-American Court of Human Rights, and its rulings on Guatemala inspired the Kurds. But the United States never joined the Inter-American system, to the detriment of both. Until now, the United States has largely abstained from the enterprise of international human rights law.

The United States and the World

Lawrence v. Texas was a bit of a coming-out party for the Supreme Court's internationalists. The U.S. Supreme Court had conspicuously ignored the European Court of Human Rights in its 1986 decision on gay sex, *Bowers v. Hardwick*. But when *Lawrence* overruled *Bowers* in 2003 and agreed that anti-sodomy laws violate basic rights, it cited the European court prominently. Indeed, the reference to *Dudgeon v. United Kingdom* was so prominent that the sodomy decision reignited a debate over the place of American law in the world.

Within a few months of the second American sodomy case, two justices gave extracurricular speeches on the theme of internationalism. "No institution of government can afford to ignore the rest of the world," argued Sandra Day O'Connor. "Our 'island' or 'lone ranger' mentality is beginning to change," observed Ruth Bader Ginsburg. "Our Justices . . . are becoming more open to comparative and international law perspectives. The term that just ended may be a milestone in that regard."

Justices Antonin Scalia and Clarence Thomas impolitely disagree. Justice Thomas wrote in his 2003 sodomy dissent that the Supreme Court "should not impose foreign moods, fads, or fashions on Americans." In a decision earlier that term, Justice Scalia scorned as irrelevant the views of "the so-called 'world community,'" "whose notions of justice are (thankfully) not always those of our people." The supposed American ideal for which Scalia gave thanks was the acceptability of executing the mentally retarded. Fortunately, he, too, wrote in dissent.

Soon after *Lawrence v. Texas*, the conservative polemicist Thomas Sowell echoed these sentiments on the *Wall Street Journal*'s editorial page under the headline "Who Needs Europe?" He gently suggested, "Those who think of Europe as being in the vanguard of new ideas need to at least consider the possibility that history may yet record that Europe was where the degeneration of Western civilization began." I am prepared to consider the possibility. However, Sowell mainly cited French foreign policy. He didn't explain how this could possibly disqualify the European Court of Human Rights from meriting consideration on the legalization of sodomy.

The more serious critics of legal internationalism, like the scholar and judge Richard Posner, merely make the weak point that foreign law ought not be binding in a national system. But Posner is knocking down a straw man. No one says that European law is authoritative everywhere, not even the scholar who is nominally paired with Posner in debate. The real divide is between those who are open to foreign influence and those who are close-minded. Even Chief Justice William Rehnquist (who dissented in *Lawrence v. Texas*) conceded in a 1999 speech: "It's time the U.S. courts began looking to the decisions of other constitutional courts."

In her book *A New World Order*, the political theorist Anne-Marie Slaughter of Princeton University identifies and celebrates an emerging global jurisprudence. The European Court of Human Rights is at the center of a web of national and international courts that increasingly engage in dialogue on common problems with potentially common solutions.

An excellent example is the diffusion of European principles on corporal and capital punishment (chapter 10). In 1988 the Supreme Court of Zimbabwe cited *Tyrer v. United Kingdom* in holding corporal punishment to be unconstitutional, and recent years have seen similar rulings by the supreme courts in South Africa, Namibia, and Israel. In 1993 the Zimbabwe court cited *Soering v. United Kingdom* in holding that an extended wait on death row is inhuman and degrading. The same conclusion was reached that year by the Judicial Committee of the Privy Council, which serves as the court of last resort for many former British colonies. Hundreds of death row prisoners in Jamaica, Trinidad, and Mauritius were saved as a result. In 1995 the South African Constitutional Court cited *Soering* in ruling the death penalty outright unconstitutional. In 2001, faced with two Canadians wanted in the United States for murder, Canada's supreme court generally adopted the *Soering* approach, barring extradition unless the United States gives assurances that it will not seek the death penalty.

In countless other instances, the European Court of Human Rights influences national courts indirectly, through its influence on other international tribunals. In particular, the European court's decisions are routinely cited by the Inter-American Court of Human Rights, based in Costa Rica; the African Commission on Human Rights, based in The Gambia; and the Human Rights Committee in Geneva, which issues nonbinding opinions under the United Nations human rights accords.

European law is by far the most developed system of case law based on a human rights convention. That makes it indispensable both in the development of other conventions and in the development of national systems of constitutional law that look to international conventions for guidance. In the world outside the United States, the judicial discourse on rights is slowly converging.

The United States resists direct influence by European law because it has a preexisting rights tradition, with distinct intellectual pathways. The United States resists indirect influence because, unlike other major powers, it has failed to ratify its region's human rights convention, and several major UN accords. Nonetheless, confident judges should look to all authorities that grapple with similar problems. To the extent that the U.S. Supreme Court closes itself to human rights law, it will increasingly be playing legal baseball to the rest of the world's football.

"Soft power" describes the ability to exert influence on other nations through the power of example rather than coercion. The phrase is often used in the abstract, but soft power is wielded through institutions, and as the political theorist Joseph Nye has noted, a human rights court is a prime example. To a significant extent, the observation that Europe leads the United States in soft power is a tribute to the European Court of Human Rights.

SOURCES

Where possible, the author relied heavily on personal interviews with the principal actors (who are listed at the beginning of the source list for each chapter) and on the case law. A searchable database of European Court of Human Rights judgments and European Commission on Human Rights reports may be found on the court's Web site at http://www.echr.coe.int/ECHR/EN/Header/Case-Law/HUDOC/HUDOC+database/.

Introduction

Sydney D. Bailey, *United Europe: A Short History of the Idea* (National News-letter, London, 1947).

Thomas Buergenthal, *International Human Rights in a Nutshell*, 2nd ed. (West, 1995).

Antonio Cassese, "The Impact of the European Convention on Human Rights on the International Criminal Tribunal for the former Yugoslavia," in *Protecting Human Rights: The European Perspective*, ed. Paul Mahoney et al. (Carl Heymanns Verlag, 2000).

Andrea Coomber, "Judicial Independence: Law and Practice of Appointments to the European Court of Human Rights," 2003 *European Human Rights Law Review* 486.

Marie-Benedicte Dembour, "'Finishing Off' Cases: The Radical Solution to the Problem of the Expanding EctHR Caseload," 2002 *European Human Rights Law Review* 604.

European Movement and The Council of Europe (Hutchinson and Co. Ltd., 1949).

D. J. Harris, Michael O'Boyle, and Colin Warbrick, *Law of the European Convention on Human Rights*, 2nd ed. (Butterworths, 1995).

Matthew Happold, "Letting States Get Away with Murder," *New Law Journal* 1323 (September 14, 2001).

Denys Hay, *Europe: The Emergence of an Idea* (University of Edinburgh Press, 1957).

Laurence R. Helfer and Anne-Marie Slaughter, "Toward a Theory of Effective Supranational Adjudication," 107 *Yale Law Journal* 273 (November 1997).

Vikki C. Jackson and Mark Tushnet, *Comparative Constitutional Law* (Foundation Press, 1999), 171.

Mark W. Janis, Richard S. Kay, and Anthony W. Bradley, *European Human Rights Law: Text and Materials*, 2nd ed., (Oxford University Press, 2000).

Toby King, "Ensuring Human Rights Review of Inter-governmental Acts in Europe," 25 *European Law Review* 79 (February 2000).

H. Lauterpacht, *An International Bill of the Rights of Man* (Columbia University Press, 1945).

Philip Leach, *Taking a Case to the European Court of Human Rights* (Blackstone Press, 2001).

Anthony Lester, "U.K. Acceptance of the Strasbourg Jurisdiction: What Really Went on in Whitehall in 1965," 1998 *Public Law* 237.

Anthony Lester and David Pannick, *Human Rights Law and Practice* (Butterworths 1999).

Paul Mahoney, "New Challenges for the European Court of Human Rights Resulting from the Expanding Case Load and Membership, 21 *Penn State International Law Review* 101 (Fall 2002).

John Mortimer, "Rumpole and the Rights of Man," in *Rumpole and the Angel of Death* (Viking, 1995).

Michael O'Boyle, "Reflections on the Effectiveness of the European System for the Protection of Human Rights," in *The U.N. Human Rights Treaty System: Universality at the Crossroads*, ed. Anne F. Bayefsky (Kluwer Law International, 2001).

Andrew Reding, "Europe Overtakes U.S. on Frontiers of Human Rights Law," Pacific News Service (January 17, 2000).

Karen Reid, *A Practitioner's Guide to the European Convention on Human Rights* (Sweet & Maxwell, 1998).

A. H. Robertson and J. G. Merrills, *Human Rights in Europe: A Study of the European Convention on Human Rights,* 3rd ed. (Manchester University Press, 1993), chapter 1.

Rolv Ryssdall, "Opinion: The Coming of Age of the European Convention on Human Rights," 1996 *European Human Rights Law Review* 18.

Pietro Sardaro, "*Jus Non Dicere* for Allegations of Serious Violations of Human Rights: Questionable Trends in the Recent Case Law of the Strasbourg Court," 2003 *European Human Rights Law Review* 601.

Henry G. Schermers, "Election of Judges to the European Court of Human Rights," 23 *European Law Review* 568 (December 1998).

A. W. Brian Simpson, *Human Rights and the End of Empire: Britain and the Genesis of the European Convention* (Oxford University Press, 2001).

Keir Starmer, *European Human Rights Law: The Human Rights Act 1998 and the European Convention on Human Rights* (Legal Action Group, 1999).

Adam Tomkins, "Civil Liberties in the Council of Europe: A Critical Survey," in *European Civil Liberties and the European Convention on Human Rights: A Comparative Study*, ed. Conor Gearty (Martinus Nijhoff, 1997), 1.

Christian Tomuschat, "Quo Vadis, Argentoratum? The Success Story of the European Convention on Human Rights and a few Dark Stains," 13 *Human Rights Law Journal* 401 (1992).

Pieter Van Dijk and G. J. H. Van Hoof, *Theory and Practice of the European Convention on Human Rights* (Kluwer, 1998).

H. G. Wells, *The Rights of Man: or What Are We Fighting For* (Penguin Books, 1940).

Kevin Wilson and Jan van der Dussen, eds., *The History of the Idea of Europe* (Routledge, 1993).

Michael Wintle, "Cultural Identity in Europe: Shared Experience," in *Culture and Identity in Europe: Perceptions of Divergence and Unity in Past and Present*, ed. Michael Wintle (Avebury, 1996), 9.

Michael Wintle, "Europe's Image: Visual Representations of Europe from the Earliest Times to the Twentieth Century," in *Culture and Identity in Europe*, 52.

Henry G. Schermers, "A European Supreme Court," in *Protecting Human Rights*, ed. Mahoney et al., 1271.

Dean Spielmann, "Human Rights Case Law in the Strasbourg and Luxembourg Courts: Conflicts, Inconsistencies, and Complementarities," in *The EU and Human Rights*, ed. Philip Alston (Oxford University Press, 1999).

John Wadham and Tazeen Said, "What Price the Right of Individual Petition: Report of the Evaluation Group to the Committee of Ministers on the European Court of Human Rights," 2002 *European Human Rights Law Review* 169.

Luzius Wildhaber, "A constitutional future for the European Court of Human Rights?" 23 *Human Rights Law Journal* 161 (October 30, 2002).

Luzius Wildhaber, "The Coordination of the Protection of Fundamental Rights in Europe" (September 8, 2005), available on www.echr.coe.int.

Lord Harry Woolf, et al., *Review of the Working Methods of the European Court of Human Rights* (December 2005), available on www.echr.coe.int.

*F*or assessments of the ECHR, see Buergenthal, *International Human Rights in a Nutshell* ("the most advanced and effective of those [human rights systems] currently in existence"); Cassese, "The impact of the European Convention on Human Rights on the International Criminal Tribunal for the former Yugoslavia" ("no other human rights treaty can claim the level of influence"); Helfer and Slaughter, "Toward a Theory of Effective Supranational Adjudication" ("as effective, for the most part, as national court rulings"); Janis, Kay, and Bradley, *European Human Rights Law* ("world's most successful system of international law for the protection of human rights"); O'Boyle, "Reflections on the Effectiveness of the European System for the Protection of Human Rights" ("without a doubt the world's most developed regional treaty system for the protection of human rights"); Reding, "Europe Overtakes U.S. on Frontiers of Human Rights Law" ("The Supreme Court is being upstaged in its traditional role as the world's most powerful and innovative legal body."); Robertson and Merrills, *Human Rights in Europe* ("certainly the most fully developed and the best observed [human rights treaty in the world]"); Ryssdall, "Opinion: The Coming of Age of the European Convention on Human Rights" ("the single most important legal and political common denominator of the States of the continent of Europe");

Simpson, *Human Rights and the End of Empire* ("pre-eminent system of international human rights protection which exists anywhere in the world"); Tomkins, "Civil Liberties in the Council of Europe" ("the most comprehensive international legal order for the protection of human rights the world has yet seen").

Chapter 1

Interviews with Alexandra Marckx, Paula Marckx, and Leonora Van Look in Antwerp, Belgium, autumn 2001.

Gisela Bock, *Women in European History* (Blackwell, 2002).

Owen Chadwick, *The Secularization of the European Mind in the Nineteenth Century* (Cambridge University Press, 1975), 3.

Nicolas Bratza, "The Implications of the Human Rights Act 1998 for Commercial Practice," 2000 *European Human Rights Law Review* 1.

Maurits Dolmans et al., Request for intervention on behalf of the European Company Lawyers Association, Case 56672/00 DSR, *Senator Lines v. Austria and others*, on file with the author.

Edward J. Eberle, "Human Dignity, Privacy, and Personality in German and American Constitutional Law," 1997 *Utah Law Review* 963.

K. D. Ewing and C. A. Gearty, "Rocky Foundations for Labour's New Rights," 1997 *European Human Rights Law Review* 146.

Ian Forrester, "Modernization of EC Competition Law," 23 *Fordham International Law Journal* 1028, 1067–1088 (April 2000).

Jack Goody, *The European Family: An Historico-Anthropological Essay* (Blackwell, 2000).

Gerda A. Kleijkamp, *Family Life and Family Interests: A Comparative Study on the Influence of Human Rights on Dutch Family Law and the Influence of the United States Constitution on American Family Law* (Kluwer Law International, 1999).

Donald P. Kommers, "Human Dignity and Personhood," in *The Constitutional Jurisprudence of the Federal Republic of Germany* (Duke University Press, 1988).

Sarah Lyall, "To More Europeans, Love Doesn't Mean Marriage," *International Herald Tribune*, March 25, 2002.

Clare McGlynn, "Families and the European Union Charter of Fundamental Rights: Progressive Change or Entrenching The Status Quo?" 26 *European Law Review* 582 (2001).

Isabel Madruga Torremocha, "Lone Parenthood and Social Policies for Lone-parent Families in Europe," in *Family Life and Family Policies in Europe*, ed. Franz-Xaver Kaufmann et al. (Oxford University Press, 2002).

Marc Salzberg, "The Marckx Case: The Impact on European Jurisprudence of the European Court of Human Rights," 13 *Denver Journal of International Law & Policy* 283 (1984).

Michael Smyth, *Business and the Human Rights Act* (Jordan, 2000).

Luzius Wildhaber, "The Right to Respect for Family Life: New Case-Law on Art. 8 of the European Convention on Human Rights," in *The Modern World of Human Rights: Essays in Honor of Thomas Buergenthal*, ed. Antonio A. Cancado Trindade (Inter-American Institute of Human Rights, 1996).

Howard Charles Yourow, *The Margin of Appreciation Doctrine in the Dynamics of European Human Rights Jurisprudence* (Martinus Nijhoff, 1995).
Martha T. Zingo and Kevin E. Early, *Nameless Persons: Legal Discrimination Against Non-marital Children in the United States* (Praeger, 1994).

Chapter 2

Interviews with Deirdre Dowling, Maeve Geraghty, and Bonnie Maher in Dublin, Ireland, February 2003.
Michael D. Goldhaber, "Europe's *Roe v. Wade?*" *The American Lawyer* (November 2007).
Liz Heffernan, ed., *Human Rights: A European Perspective* (Round Hall Press, 1994).
Machteld Nijsten, *Abortion and Constitutional Law: A Comparative European-American Study* (European University Institute, 1990).
Ruth Riddick, *Making Choices: The Abortion Experience of Irish Women* (Northern Ireland Abortion Law Reform Association, 1988).
Ruth Riddick, "Tragedy in Kerry Ten Years On," *Irish Times*, February 4, 1994, 16.
Bill Rolston and Anna Eggert, eds., *Abortion in the New Europe: A Comparative Handbook* (Greenwood Press, 1994).
Ailbhe Smyth, ed., *The Abortion Papers: Ireland* (Attic Press, 1992).

Chapters 3 and 4

Interviews with Jeffrey Dudgeon in Belfast, Northern Ireland, autumn 2001; interview with Richard Kennedy in London, England, autumn 2001; interview with Duncan Lustig-Prean in Brighton, England, autumn 2001.
"Fine Military Service of Gay Personnel," http://news.bbc.co.uk, September 27, 1999.
Edmund Hall, *We Can't Even March Straight* (Vintage, 2000).
Lawrence R. Helfer, "Sexual Orientation and the European Court of Human Rights: New Activism or Cautious Incrementalism," *International Civil Liberties Report* 11 (2001).
Richard Kamm, "European Court of Human Rights Overturns British Ban on Gays in the Military," 7 *Human Rights Brief* 18 (Spring 2000).
Joyce Murdoch and Deb Price, *Courting Justice: Gay Men and Lesbians v. the Supreme Court* (Basic Books, 2001).
Raymond A. Psonak, "'Don't Ask, Don't Tell, Don't Discharge,' at Least in Europe: A Comparison of the Policies on Homosexuals in the Military in the United States and Europe After Grady v. United Kingdom," 33 *Connecticut Law Review* 337 (Fall 2000).
Rhona K. M. Smith, "International Decision," 94 *American Journal International Law* 382 (April 2000).
James D. Willets, "Using International Law to Vindicate the Civil Rights of Gays and Lesbians in United States Courts, 27 *Columbia Human Rights Law Review* 33 (Fall 1995).
Robert Wintemute, *Sexual Orientation and Human Rights: The United States Constitution, the European Convention, and the Canadian Charter* (Clarendon Press, 1995).

Chapter 5

Interviews with Ana-Maria Gómez López, Maria Gómcz López, Cristina López Ostra, Gregoria López Ostra, and Jose-Luis Mazón Costa in Lorca, Spain, July 2002.

Michael R. Anderson, "Human Rights Approaches to Environmental Protection: An Overview," in *Human Rights Approaches to Environmental Protection*, ed. Alan E. Boyle and Michael R. Anderson (Clarendon Press, 1996).

Patricia Birnie and Alan Boyle, eds., *International Law and the Environment*, 2nd. ed. (Oxford University Press, 2002).

R. R. Churchill, "Environmental Rights in Existing Human Rights Treaties*,"* in *Human Rights Approaches to Environmental Protectio*n, ed. Boyle and Anderson.

Kate Cook, "Environmental Rights as Human Rights," 2002 *European Human Rights Law Review* 196.

Phillippe Cullet, "Definition of an Environmental Right in a Human Rights Context," 1995 *Netherlands Quarterly on Human Rights* 25.

Richard Desgagne, "Integrating Environmental Values into the European Convention on Human Rights," 89 *American Journal International Law* 263 (April 1995).

S. Douglas-Scott, "Environmental Rights in the European Union—Participatory Democracy or Democratic Deficit?" in *Human Rights Approaches to Environmental Protection*, ed. Boyle and Anderson.

Sionaidh Douglas-Scott, "Environmental Rights: Taking the Environment Seriously," in *Understanding Human Rights*, ed. Conor Gearty and Adam Tomkins (Pinter Press, 1996).

"European Court of Human Rights Finds Violation in Siting of Treatment Plant," 17 *International Environment Reporter* 1043 (December 14, 1994).

Bruce Ledewitz, "Establishing a Federal Constitutional Right to a Healthy Environment in Us and in Our Posterity," 68 *Mississippi Law Journal* 565 (Winter 1998).

Sarah Lyall, "Under Noisy Skies, Britons Assert a Right to Sleep," *New York Times*, October 14, 2001.

"Rage against the Flying of the Night," *Financial Times*, October 21, 2000.

Philippe Sands, "Human Rights, Environment and the *López Ostra* Case: Context and Consequences," 1996 *European Human Rights Law Review* 597.

Dinah Shelton, "Environmental Rights," in *People's Rights*, ed. Philip Alston (Oxford University Press, 2001).

"Spanish Woman Wins Environmental Nuisance Case Under Human Rights Convention," *Environment Watch Western Europe*, January 6, 1995.

Chapter 6

Interviews with Jacques Debray and Ali Mehemi in Lyons, France, July 2002.

Nina Bernstein, "When a Metrocard Led Far out of Town: Post-9/11, Even Evading Subway Fares Can Raise the Prospect of Deportation," *New York Times*, October 11, 2004.

Ryszard Cholewinski, "Strasbourg's 'Hidden Agenda'?: The Protection of Second-Generation Migrants from Expulsion under Article 8 of the European Convention on Human Rights," 3 *Netherlands Quarterly of Human Rights* 287 (1994).

Blanca Villa Costa, "The Quest for a Consistent Set of Rules Governing the Status of non-Community Nationals," in *The EU and Human Rights*, ed. Philip Alston (Oxford University Press, 1999).

Adrian Favell, "Exposing the Nation-state's True Colours," London *Times Higher Education Supplement*, May 3, 2002.

Adrian Favell, *Philosophies of Integration: Immigration and the Idea of Citizenship in France and Britain*, 2nd ed. (Palgrave, 2001).

Joel S. Fetzer, *Public Attitudes toward Immigration in the United States, France, and Germany* (Cambridge University Press, 2000).

Kees Groenendijk, "Long-term Immigrants and the Council of Europe," 1 *European Journal of Migration and Law* 275 (1999).

Alec G. Hargreaves, *Immigration, "Race" and Ethnicity in Contemporary France* (Routledge, 1995).

James F. Hollifield, "Immigration and the Politics of Rights: The French Case in Comparative Perspective," *in Immigration and Welfare: Challenging the Borders of the Welfare State*, ed. Michael Bommes and Andrew Geddes (Routledge, 2000).

Colin Harvey, "Promoting Insecurity: Public Order, Expulsion and the European Convention on Human Rights," in *Security of Residence and Expulsion: Protection of Aliens in Europe*, ed. Elspeth Guild and Paul Minderhoud (Kluwer Law International, 2001).

Rey Koslowski, *Migrants and Citizens: Demographic Change in the European State System* (Cornell University Press, 2000).

Remy Leveau, "The Political Culture of the 'Beurs,'" in *Islam in Europe: The Politics of Religion and Community*, ed. Steven Vertovec and Ceri Peach (St. Martin's Press, 1997).

Anthony Lewis, "The Mills of Cruelty," *New York Times*, December 14, 1999.

Anthony Lewis, "Serving Family Values," *New York Times*, April 8, 1999.

Jean Eric Malabre, "Security of Residence and Expulsion: Protection of Aliens in Europe: The French Experience," in *Security of Residence and Expulsion: Protection of Aliens in Europe*, ed. Guild and Minderhoud .

P. Van Dijk, "Protection of 'Integrated' Aliens Against Explusion under the European Convention on Human Rights, 1 *European Journal of Migration and Law* 293 (1999).

Colin Warbrick, "The Structure of Article 8," 1998 *European Human Rights Law Review* 32.

Luzius Wildhaber, "Precedent in the European Court of Human Rights," in *Protecting Human Rights: The European Perspective*, ed. Paul Mahoney et al., (Carl Heymanns Verlag, 2000).

Chapter 7

Interviews with Panos Bitsaxis, Gail Kokkinakis Kanavakis, and Thanasis Reppas in Athens, Greece, June 2002; interviews with Janus Kokkinakis, Manolis Kokkinakis, and Pericles Yannouris in Sitia, Greece, June 2002.

Takis Michas, *Unholy Alliance: Greece and Milosevic's Serbia* (Texas A&M University Press, 2002).

Charalambos K. Papastathis, "The Hellenic Republic and the Prevailing Religion," 1996 *BYU Law Review* 815.

Shawn Francis Peters, *Judging Jehovah's Witnesses: Religious Persecution and the Dawn of the Rights Revolution* (University Press of Kansas, 2000).

Nicos C. Alivizatos, "The Constitutional Treatment of Religious Minorities in Greece," in *Melange en L'honneur de Nicolas Valticos: Droit et Justice*, ed. René-Jean Dupuy (Editions A. Pedone, 1999).

David H. Close, *Greece Since 1945: Politics, Economy and Society* (Longman, 2002).

Peter Cumper, "The Public Manifestations of Religion or Belief: Challenges for a Multi-faith Society in the Twenty-first Century," in *Law and Religion: Current Legal Issues 2001*, ed. Richard O'Dair and Andrew Lewis (Oxford University Press, 2001).

Keturah A. Dunne, "Addressing Religious Intolerance in Europe: The Limited Application of Article 9 of the European Convention of Human Rights and Fundamental Freedoms," 30 *California Western International Law Journal* 117 (Fall 1999).

Carolyn Evans, *Freedom of Religion under the European Convention on Human Rights* (Oxford University Press, 2002).

Will Fuhrmann, "Perspectives on Religious Freedom from the Vantage Point of the European Court of Human Rights," 2000 *BYU Law Review* 829.

Howard Gilbert, "The Slow Development of the Right to Military Service under the European Convention on Human Rights," 2001 *European Human Rights Law Review* 554.

T. Jeremy Gunn, "Adjudicating Rights of Conscience Under the European Convention on Human Rights," in *Religious Human Rights in Global Perspective: Legal Perspectives*, ed. Johan D. van der Vyver and John Witte Jr. (Martinus Nijhoff, 1996).

Andrew Holden, *Jehovah's Witnesses: Portrait of a Contemporary Religious Movement* (Routledge, 2002).

"Jehovah's Witnesses are Being Kept under Close Watch," *Eleftherotypia*, December 14, 1994.

Dahlia Lithwick, "Who's That Knocking on My Door? No Surprise, It's Those Darn Jehovah's Witnesses," http://www.slate.com, February 26, 2002.

Javier Martinez-Torron, "The European Court of Human Rights and Religion," in *Law and Religion: Current Legal Issues 2001*, ed. O'Dair and Lewis.

Javier Martinez-Torron and Rafael Navarro-Valls, "The Protection of Religious Freedom in the System of the European Convention on Human Rights," in *Helsinki Monitor Quarterly on Security and Cooperation in Europe, Special Issue: Freedom of Religion or Belief* (Netherlands Helsinki Committee, 1999).

Sebastian Poulter, "The Rights of Ethnic, Religious and Linguistic Minorities," 1997 *European Human Rights Law Review* 254.

Stephanos Stavros, "Freedom of Religion and Claims for Exemption from Generally Applicable Neutral Laws: Lessons from Across the Pond?" 1997 *European Human Rights Law Review* 607.

Chapter 8

Interview with Peter Michael Lingens in Andalucia, Spain, July 2002; interview with Gerhard Oberschlick in Vienna, Austria, July 2002.

Case-Law Concerning Article 10 of the European Convention on Human Rights: Forty Years of Case-Law (Directorate of Human Rights, Strasbourg, 1999).

Bonnie Docherty, "Defamation Law: Positive Jurisprudence," 13 *Harvard Human Rights Journal* 263 (Spring 2000).

David Elder, "Freedom of Expression and the Law of Defamation: The American Approach to the Problems Raised by the *Lingens* Case," 35 *International Constitutional Law Quarterly* 891 (1986).

Tony Judt, "The Past is Another Country: Myth and Memory in Postwar Europe," *Daedalus* 121, no. 4 (Fall 1992): 83.

Gunter Bischof and Anton Pelinka, eds., *Austrian Historical Memory & National Identity* (Transaction Publishers, 1997).

Gordon Brook-Shepherd, *The Austrians: A Thousand-year Odyssey* (HarperCollins, 1996).

Ella Lingens-Reiner, *Prisoners of Fear* (Victor Gollancz, 1948).

Peten Michael Lingens, "Reconciliation with the Nazis—But in What Way?" *Profil*, November 1970 (English translation).

Andrew Nicol, Gavin Millar, and Andrew Sharland, *Media Law & Human Rights* (Blackstone Press, 2001).

Gerhard Oberschlick, "P.S.: 'Trottel' instead of Nazi," *Forum*, March 19, 1991 (English translation).

Michael O'Boyle, "Blasphemy and Freedom of Expression: Recent Developments Before the European Court of Human Rights," in *Mainly Human Rights: Studies in Honour of J. J. Cremona*, ed. Salvino Busuttil (Fondation Internationale Malte, 1999).

Anton Pelinka, *Austria: Out of the Shadow of the Past* (Westview Press, 1998).

Martti Ahtisaari, Jochen Frowein, and Marcelino Oreja, *Report* [on Austria's Human Rights Record] (European Court of Human Rights, September 8, 2000).

H. Pierre Secher, *Bruno Kreisky: Chancellor of Austria* (Dorrance, 1993).

Luzius Wildhaber, "The Right to Offend, Shock or Disturb?—Aspects of Freedom of Expression under the European Convention on Human Rights," 36 *Irish Jurist* 17 (2001).

Simon Wiesenthal, "Kreisky's Brown Harvest," in *Justice Not Vengeance* (Weidenfeld and Nicolson, 1989).

Robert S. Wistrich, "The Kreisky Phenomenon: A Reassessment," in *Austrians and Jews in the Twentieth Century*, ed. Robert S. Wistrich (St. Martin's Press, 1992).

Ruth Wodak and Anton Pelinka, eds., *The Haider Phenomenon in Austria* (Transaction, 2002).

Chapter 9

Interviews with Sevket Kazan and Seref Malkogbeye in Ankara, Turkey, July 2003.

Ibrahim Abdulla Al-Marzouqi, *Human Rights in Islamic Law* (Morgan, 2000).

Mashood A. Baderin, "Establishing Areas of Common Ground between Islamic Law and International Human Rights," *International Journal of Human Rights* 5, no. 2 (Summer 2001): 72.

Mohamed Berween, "The Fundamental Human Rights: An Islamic Perspective," *International Journal of Human Rights* 6, no. 1 (Spring 2002): 61.

Grace Davie, *Religion in Modern Europe: A Memory Mutates* (Oxford University Press, 2002).

Noah Feldman, *After Jihad: America and the Struggle for Islamic Democracy* (Farrar, Straus and Giroux, 2003).

Graham E. Fuller, *The Future of Political Islam* (Palgrave Macmillan, 2003).

Graham E. Fuller, "Turkey's Strategic Model: Myths and Realities," *Washington Quarterly* (Summer 2004), 51.

T. Jeremy Gunn, "Fearful Symbols: The Islamic Headscarf and the European Court of Human Rights" (draft of July 4, 2005), available on www.strasbourgconfer ence.org.

Stathis N. Kalyvas, *The Rise of Christian Democracy in Europe* (Cornell University Press, 1996).

Robert D. Kaplan, "At the Gates of Brussels," *Atlantic Monthly*, December 2004, 44.

Christian Moe, "Refah Revisited: Strasbourg's Construction of Islam" (draft prepared in advance of conference, June 3–4, 2005), available on www.strasbourgcon ference.org.

Alistair Mowbray, "The Role of the European Court of Human Rights in the Promotion of Democracy," 1999 *European Human Rights Law Review* 703.

Ben Olbourne, "Case Analysis: Refah Partisi (The Welfare Party) v Turkey," 2003 *European Human Rights Law Review* 437.

David Remnick, "The Experiment: Will Turkey Be the Model for Islamic Democracy?" *The New Yorker*, November 18, 2002, 50.

Andrew Wheatcroft, *Infidels: The Conflict between Christendom and Islam, 638–2002* (Viking, 2003).

Stephen Wheatley, "Democracy in International Law: A European Perspective," 51 *International & Comparative Law Quarterly* 235 (April 2002).

Chapter 10

Interview with Iain Campbell in Bishopbriggs, Scotland, August 2002.

Jeremy Black, *Eighteenth Century Europe, 1700–1789* (Macmillan, 1992), 332–338.

Andrew Clapham, *Human Rights in the Private Sphere* (Clarendon Press, 1993).

Terence Copley, *Black Tom: Arnold of Rugby: The Myth and the Man* (Continuum, 2002).

Jean Overton Fuller, *Swinburne: A Critical Biography* (Chatto and Windus, 1968).

Colin Farrell, "Birching in the Isle of Man, 1945 to 1976," http://www.corpun.com.

Colin Farrell, "The Cane and the Tawse in Scottish Schools," http://www.corpun.com.

Peter Gay, *The Cultivation of Hatred* (W. W. Norton, 1993).

Thomas Hughes, *Tom Brown's Schooldays* (Oxford World's Classics, 1989).

Francesca Klug, *Values for a Godless Age* (Penguin Books, 2000), 141.

Anthony Lewis, *Gideon's Trumpet* (Vintage Books, 1964), 239.

Michael H. Reggio, "History of the Death Penalty," in *Society's Final Solution: A History and Discussion of the Death Penalty*, ed. Laura E. Randa (University Press of America, 1997).

William A. Schabas, *The Abolition of the Death Penalty in International Law*, 3rd. ed. (Cambridge University Press, 2002).

Jens Soering, *Mortal Thoughts*, http://lucy.ukc.ac.uk/Soering (1985).

Society of Teachers opposed to Physical Punishment, *Corporal Punishment in the Schools—The Unacceptable Face of British Education* (offprint, January 1981).

Chapter 11

Interview with Annie McClean and Paddy Joe McClean in Beragh, Ireland, summer 2003.

Jonathan Alter, "Time to Think About Torture," *Newsweek*, November 5, 2001, p. 45.

Cesare Beccaria, "Treatise on Crimes and Punishments (1766)," in *The Human Rights Reader: Major Political Writings, Essays, Speeches, and Documents From the Bible to the Present*, ed. Micheline R. Ishay (Routledge, 1997), 119.

Mark Bowden, "The Dark Art of Interrogation," *Atlantic Monthly*, October 2003.

Antonio Cassese, *Inhuman States: Imprisonment, Detention and Torture in Europe Today* (Polity Press, 1996).

John Conroy, *Unspeakable Acts, Ordinary People: The Dynamics of Torture* (Vision Paperbacks, 2001).

Alan M. Dershowitz, *Why Terrorism Works: Understanding the Threat, Responding to the Challenge* (Yale University Press, 2002).

Edwin Dobb, "Should John Walker Lindh Go Free? On the Rights of the Detained," *Harper's Monthly*, May 1, 2002.

Malcolm D. Evans and Rod Morgan, *Preventing Torture: A Study of the European Conventio for the Prevention of Torture and Inhuman or Degrading Treatment or Punishment* (Oxford University Press, 1998).

Denis Faul and Raymond Murray, *The Hooded Men: British Torture in Ireland* (privately printed, 1974).

Peter Gay, *The Enlightenment: An Interpretation: The Science of Freedom* (W. W. Norton, 1969).

Andrew Grice, "Blunkett Says UK Will Stay in Human Rights Convention," *The Independent*, February 5, 2003.

Hendrik Hertzberg, "Comment: Terror and Torture," *The New Yorker* March 24, 2003, 29.

Eric Hobsbawm, "Barbarism: A User's Guide," in *On History* (Weidenfeld and Nicolson, 1997).

Home Office and Northern Ireland Office, "Enquiry into Alleged Brutality against Detainees in Northern Ireland (Compton Committee); Correspondence between Sir E. Compton and Cardinal Conway," UK Public Records Office CJ 4 109 (August–November 1971).

Human Rights Watch, *Descriptions of Techniques Allegedly Authorized by the CIA* (November 21, 2005).

Human Rights Watch, *"Stress and Duress" Techniques Used Worldwide* (June 1, 2004).

Michael Ignatieff, "The Torture Wars," *New Republic*, April 22, 2002, 40.

Douglas Jehl, "Qaeda-Iraq Link U.S. Cited is Tied to Coercion Claim," *New York Times*, December 9, 2005.

Douglas Jehl and David Johnston, "Rule Change Lets C.I.A. Freely Send Suspects Abroad," *New York Times*, March 6, 2005.

Hugh Jordan, "State of Torture: Smuggled Note out of Army Barracks Made Ted Heath Shut Down Beating Sessions," *Sunday World*, July 29, 2001, 4.

John H. Langbein, *Torture and the Law of Proof* (University of Chicago Press, 1976).

Paddy Joe McClean, "Degrading Detention Didn't Work Here and It Won't Work in Cuba," *Belfast Telegraph*, January 18, 2002.

John McGuffin, *The Guinea Pigs* (Penguin Books, 1974).

John McGuffin, *The Guinea Pigs*, 2nd ed. (Minuteman Press, 1981).

Mitchell B. Merback, *The Thief, the Cross and the Wheel: Pain and the Spectacle of Punishment in Medieval and Renaissance Europe* (University of Chicago Press, 1998).

Lord Parker of Waddington, "Report of the Committee of Privy Counsellors Appointed to Consider Authorised Procedures for the Interrogation of Persons Suspected of Terrorism (Her Majesty's Stationery Office, March 1972).

John T. Parry, "Escalation and Necessity: Defining Torture at Home and Abroad," in *Torture: A Collection*, ed. Sanford Levinson (Oxford University Press, 2004), 145.

Dana Priest, "CIA Holds Terror Suspects in Secret Prisons," *Washington Post*, November 2, 2005.

Dana Priest and Barton Gellman, "U.S. Decries Abuse but Defends Interrogations; 'Stress and Duress' Tactics Used on Terrorism Suspects Held in Secret Overseas Facilities," *Washington Post,* December 26, 2002.

Adam Shatz, "The Torture of Algiers," *New York Review of Books*, November 21, 2002, 53.

Susan Sontag, "Looking at War: Photography's View of Devastation and Death," *The New Yorker*, December 9, 2002.

"Special Report: Torture: Ends, Means, and Barbarity," *The Economist*, January 11, 2003, 21.

Don Van Natta Jr., "A Dark Jail for Qaeda Suspects: Captives Are Deprived of Sleep and Sometimes Chilled," *International Herald Tribune*, March 10, 2003.

Colin Warbrick, "The Principles of the European Convention on Human Rights and the Response of States to Terrorism," 2002 *European Human Rights Law Review* 287.

Chapter 12

Interview with Serif Aksoy in Istanbul Turkey, July 2003; interviews with Yilmaz Ensaroglu, Husnu Ondul, and Mahmut Sakar in Ankara, Turkey, March 2002; interview with Sezgin Tanrikulu in Diyarbakir, Turkey, March 2002.

Evert Albert Alkema, "The European Convention as a Constitution and its Court as a Constitutional Court," in *Protecting Human Rights: The European Perspective*, ed. Paul Mahoney et al. (Carl Heymanns Verlag, 2000), 41, 62–63.

Aksoy v. Turkey, Verbatim Record of Hearing, on file with the author (April 26, 1996).

Amnesty International, *Failures at Fifty: Impunity for Torture and Ill-treatment in Europe on the 50th* Anniversary of European Convention on Human Rights (June 2000).

Amnesty International, *Torture in Turkey: Widespread and Systematic Torture Committed with Impunity* (December 2001).

Henri J. Barkey and Graham E. Fuller, *Turkey's Kurdish Question* (Rowman and Littlefield, 1998).

Carla Buckley, *Turkey and the European Convention on Human Rights: The Litigation Programme of the Kurdish Human Rights Project* (Pluto Press, 2001).

Council of Europe Parliamentary Assembly, Resolution 1297, "Implementation of decisions of the European Court of Human Rights by Turkey" (September 23, 2002).

Council of Europe Parliamentary Assembly Committee on Legal Affairs and Human Rights Doc. 9537 (Report), "Implementation of decisions of the European Court of Human Rights by Turkey" (September 5, 2002).

European Committee for the Prevention of Torture and Inhuman or Degrading Treatment or Punishment, "Report to the Turkish Government on the Visits to Turkey Carried Out by the European Committee for the Prevention of Torture and Inhuman or Degrading Treatment or Punishment" (December 13, 2001).

European Committee for the Prevention of Torture and Inhuman or Degrading Treatment or Punishment, "Public Statement on Turkey" (December 6, 1996).

European Committee for the Prevention of Torture and Inhuman or Degrading Treatment or Punishment, "Public Statement on Turkey" (December 15, 1992).

Federation Internationale des Droits de l'Homme, *Torture: Still a Routine Practice* (May 2003).

Oren Gross, "'Once More unto the Breach': The Systemic Failure of Applying the European Convention on Human Rights to Entrenched Emergencies," 23 *Yale Journal of International Law* 437 (Summer 1998).

Human Rights Watch, *Turkey: Alleged Cases of Torture in Ordu* (November 15, 2005).

Human Rights Watch, *Eradicating Torture in Turkey's Police Stations: Analysis and Recommendations* (September 2004).

Human Rights Watch, *Turkey: Enhanced Police Station Monitoring Will Prevent Torture* (April 22, 2005).

Human Rights Watch, *Turkey: Violations of the Right of Petition to the European Commission on Human Rights* (April 1996).

Sarah Joseph, "Denouement of the Deaths on the Rock: the Right to Life of Terrorists," 14 *Netherlands Quarterly of Human Rights* 5 (1996).

Menno T. Kamminga, "Is the European Convention on Human Rights Sufficiently Equipped to Cope with Gross and Systemic Violations?" 2 *Netherlands Quarterly of Human Rights* 153 (1994).

Stephen Kinzer, *Crescent & Star: Turkey Between Two Worlds* (Farrar, Straus and Giroux, 2001).

Stephen Kinzer, "Will Turkey Make It?" *New York Review of Books*, July 15, 2004, 51.

Kurdish Human Rights Project, *Turkey's Non-implementation of European Court Judgments* (September 2003).

Lawyers Committee for Human Rights, *Justice Undermined* (November 1996).

Andrew Mango, *Ataturk: The Biography of the Founder of Modern Turkey* (Overlook Press, 1999).

David McDowall, *A Modern History of the Kurds* (I. B. Tauris, 2000).

Fionnuala Ni Aolain, "Truth Telling, Accountability and the Right to Life in Northern Ireland," 2002 *European Human Rights Law Review* 572.

Winston P. Nagan and Lucie Atkins, "The International Law of Torture: From Universal Proscription to Effective Application and Enforcement," 14 *Harvard Human Rights Journal* 87 (Spring 2001).

Aisling Reidy, Francoise Hampson, and Kevin Boyle, "Gross Violations of Human Rights: Invoking the European Convention on Human Rights in the Case of Turkey," 15 *Netherlands Quarterly of Human Rights* 161 (June 1997).

Eric Rouleau, "Turkey's Dream of Democracy," *Foreign Affairs*, November– December 2000, 100 .

M. Sezgin Tanrikulu, "The Practice of a State of Emergency in Decisions by the European Court of Human Rights," *Toplum & Hukuk* 1, no. 1 (Foundation for Social and Legal Studies, Winter 2001) English translation.

Chapter 13

Interviews with Nebahat Akkoc, Meral Danis Bestas, and Nazmi Gur in Diyarbakir, Turkey, March 2002; interviews with Kerim Yildiz in London, England, winter 2002 and summer 2003.

Amnesty International, *Turkey: End Sexual Violence against Women in Custody!* (February 26, 2003).

Aydin v. Turkey, materials on file with the author:

Appendices 1–4 to the Applicant's Memorial (November 12, 1996).

"Rape at the Gendarmerie Station!" Kurdish Human Rights Project translation from unidentified Kurdish newspaper (January 8, 1996).

Mahmut Sakar, "Sexual Torture and Kurdish Women: A Sociological Study," report submitted to the European Court of Human Rights (May 4, 1994).

Verbatim Record of Hearing (January 22, 1997).

Kurdish Human Rights Project, *The State and Sexual Violence: Turkish Court Silences Female Advocate* (January 2003).

Project Legal Aid for Women Raped or Sexually Assaulted by State Security Forces, *Sexual Violence: Perpetrated by the State: A Documentation of Victim Stories* (DOZ Basim-Yayin Ltd., 2000).

Christine Strumpen-Darrie, "Rape: A Survey of Current International Jurisprudence," 7 *Human Rights Brief* 12 (Spring 2000).

Chapter 14

Interviews with Suryana Asueva, Marzet Imakaeva, Medka Isayeva, and Zara Isayeva in Nazran (Ingushetia), Russia, June 2003; interviews with Roza Akaeva, Svetlana Gannushkina, and Kirill Koroteev in Moscow, Russia, June 2003.

Amnesty International, *The Russian Federation: Denial of Justice* (Amnesty International Publications, 2002).

Vanora Bennett, *Crying Wolf: The Return of War to Chechnya* (Picador, 1998).

Bill Bowring, "Russia's Accession to the Council of Europe and Human Rights: Compliance or Cross-Purposes?" 1997 *European Human Rights Law Review* 628.

Bill Bowring, "Russia's Accession to the Council of Europe and Human Rights: Four Years On," 2000 *European Human Rights Law Review* 362.

John B. Dunlop, *Russia Confronts Chechnya: Roots of a Separatist Conflict* (Cambridge University Press, 1998).

Human Rights Watch, *Civilian Killings in the Staropromyslovski District of Grozny,* (February 2000).

Human Rights Watch, *Worse Than a War: "Disappearances" in Chechnya Constitute a Crime against Humanity* (March 2005).

Isayeva v. Russian Federation, materials on file with the author:
  Applicants' Observations on the Merits of the Case
  Response of Applicants to Observations of the Russian Federation

Isaeva, Yusopova, and Bazaeva v. Russian Federation, materials on file with the author:
  Applicants' Observations on the Merits of the Case
  Response of Applicants to Observations of the Russian Federation

Khasiev and Akaeva v. Russian Federation, materials on file with the author:
  Applicants' Observations on the Merits of the Case
  Response of Applicants to Observations of the Russian Federation
  Statement of Petimat Goigova

Andrew Jack, *Inside Putin's Russia* (Granta Books, 2004).

Mark Janis, "Russia and the 'Legality' of Strasbourg Law," *European Journal of International Law* 8, no. 1, www.ejil.org/journal/Vol8/No1/ art5.html.

Andre Liebich, "Janus at Strasbourg: The Council of Europe between East and West," *Helsinki Monitor* (1999), 7.

Anatol Lieven, *Chechnya: Tombstone of Russian Power* (Yale University Press, 1998).

Matthew Lippmann, "Aerial Attacks on Civilians and the Humanitarian Law of War: Technology and Terror from World War I to Afghanistan," 33 *California Western International Law Journal* (Fall 2002).

Anna Politkovskaya, *A Dirty War: A Russian Reporter in Chechnya* (Harvill, 2001).

Maura Reynolds, "War Has No Rules for Russian Forces Fighting in Chechnya," *Los Angeles Times,* September 17, 2000.

William A. Schabas, "Theoretical and International Framework :Punishment of Non-state Actors in Non-international Armed Conflict, 26 *Fordham International Law Journal* 907 (April 2003).

Anne-Marie Slaughter and William Burke-White, "An International Constitutional Moment," 43 *Harvard International Law Journal* 1 (Winter 2002).

Leo Tolstoy, *Hadji Murad, in Great Short Works of Leo Tolstoy* (Harper Perennial, 1967).

Chapter 15

Interviews with N.C. and mother, H.K. and father, D.M. and mother, J.M. and parents, M.P. and father, Markus Pape, and Z.V. and mother in Ostrava, Czech Republic,

June 2002; interview with Deborah Winterbourne in London, England, November 2002; interviews with James Goldston in New York City, autumn 2004 and winter 2006.

Edwin Busuttil, "The Case Law of the Commission as Regards Non-discrimination: Article 14 of the Convention," in *The Birth of European Human Rights Law*, ed. Michele de Salvia and Mark E. Villiger (Nomos Verlagsgesellschaft, 1998).

David M. Crowe, *A History of the Gypsies of Eastern Europe and Russia* (I. B. Tauris, 1995).

David Crowe and John Kolsti, eds., *The Gypsies of Eastern Europe* (M. E. Sharpe, 1991).

Isabel Fonseca, *The Gypsies and their Journey* (Vintage, 1996).

Angus Fraser, *The Gypsies* (Blackwell, 1992).

James A. Goldston, "Roma Rights, Roma Wrongs," *Foreign Affairs*, March–April 2002, 144.

Will Guy, ed., *Between Past and Future: The Roma of Central and Eastern Europe* (University of Hertfordshire Press, 2001).

D. H. and Others v. The Czech Republic, materials on file with the author:
  Resolution of Constitutional Court (October 20, 1999).
  Application of the Plaintiffs (April 18, 2000).
  Observations of the Government on Admissibility and Merits of the Application (March 15, 2004).
  An Outline of the Main Issues at the Core of the Instant Case and a Summary of the Applicants' Written Comments on the Admissibility and the Merits (June 1, 2004).
  Interights Amicus Brief (June 11, 2004).

European Roma Rights Centre, *A Special Remedy: Roma and Schools for the Mentally Handicapped in the Czech Republic*, Country Report Series, no. 8 (June 1999).

European Roma Rights Centre, *Desegregation Court Victory* (October 26, 2005).

European Roma Rights Centre, *Stigmata: Segregated Schooling of Roma in Central and Eastern Europe* (May 2004).

European Roma Rights Centre, "What Is Roma Rights?" *Roma Rights* no. 1 (2004).

Charlotte McCafferty, "General Prohibition of Discrimination: The New Protocol to the Human Rights Convention," *Human Rights* 20 (March 2002).

Eric Mose, "New Rights for the New Court?" in *Protecting Human Rights: The European Perspective*, ed. Paul Mahoney et al. (Carl Heymanns Verlag, 2000), 943.

Susan Rona and Linda E. Lee, *School Success for Roma Children: Step by Step Special Schools Initiative, Interim Report* (Open Society Institute, December 2001).

Rolv Ryssdal, "Final Report," in *Rights of Persons Deprived of their Liberty: Equality and Non-discrimination, Proceedings of the 7th International Colloquy on the European Convention on Human Rights, 30 May–2 June 1990* (Council of Europe, 1994).

Rolv Ryssdal, "Speeches at the Opening and Closing Sessions," 7th International Colloquy on the European Convention on Human Rights (30 May–2 June 1990), on file at the Library of the European Court of Human Rights.

Erika B. Schlager, "European Court Rules in Critical Czech Desegregation Case: Equal," *Helsinki Commission Digest* no. 1 (February 21, 2006): 39.

Michael Stewart, *The Time of the Gypsies* (Westview Press, 1997).

Luzius Wildhaber, "Protection Against Discrimination under the European Convention on Human Rights—A Second-Class Guarantee?" (amended text of an address delivered at the Riga [Latvia] Graduate School of Law, March 8, 2001), on file at the Library of the European Court of Human Rights).

Chapter 16

"A New Tyranny of Human Rights?" *London Daily Mirror*, March 30, 2000.

"Another Surrender to Europe," *London Daily Mail*, December 27, 1995.

Timothy Garton Ash, "Is Britain European?" *Prospect,* January 25, 2001.

Sheena Ashford and Noel Timms, *What Europe Thinks: A Study of Western European Values* (Dartmouth Publishing Group, 1992).

Vian Bakir, "An Identity for Europe? The Role of the Media," in *Culture and Identity in Europe: Perceptions of Divergence and Unity in Past and Present,* ed. Michael Wintle (Avebury, 1996), 177.

Robert Bartlett, *The Making of Europe: Conquest, Colonization and Cultural Change, 950–1350* (Penguin Books, 1994).

Jos Becker and Johan Verweij, "Is There a European Superego?" in *The European Challenge: Essays on Culture, Values and Policy in a Changing Continent,* ed. K. Paling and V. Veldheer (Vuga, 1998).

Fernand Braudel, *Civilization and Capitalism, 15th–18th Century,* 3 vols. (HarperCollins, 1985).

C. Delisle Burns, *The First Europe: A Study of the Establishment of Medieval Christendom, A.D. 400–800* (George Allen and Unwin Ltd., 1947).

A. S. Byatt, "What Is a European? *New York Times Magazine*, October 13, 2002, 46.

Christopher Clarey, "Can Golf Really Create Europeans?" *International Herald Tribune*, October 5–6, 2002, 23.

Alan Clark, "Why Do They Hate Britain?" *London Daily Mail*, September 28, 1995.

Jean-Baptiste Doroselle, *Europe: A History of Its Peoples* (Viking, 1990).

Mark Dowdney and Sheree Dodd, "Euro Pullout Threat at Shoot-to-kill Rap: Britain Threatens to Quit European Court of Human Rights After Being Condemned over Gibraltar Killings," *London Daily Mirror*, September 28, 1995.

Peter Ester et al., *The Individualizing Society: Value Change in Europe and North America* (Tilburg University Press, 1993).

"Extradition and Death Row," *Manchester Guardian Weekly*, July 16, 1989.

Dieter Grimm, "Does Europe Need a Constitution?" in *The Question of Europe*, ed. Peter Gowan and Perry Anderson (Verso, 1997), 239.

Robert J. Guttman, ed., *Europe in the New Century: Visions of an Emerging Superpower* (Lynne Rienner, 2001).

Guy Haarscher, "Europe's Soul: Freedom and Rights," in *A Soul for Europe*, vol. 1, *A Reader*, ed. Furio Cerutti and Enno Rudolph (Peeters Leuven, 2001), 95.

Jurgen Habermas, "Further Reflections on the Public Sphere," in *Habermas and the Public Sphere*, ed. Craig Calhoun (MIT Press, 1992).

Jurgen Habermas, "Kant's Idea of Perpetual Peace, with the Benefit of Two Hundred Years' Hindsight," in *Perpetual Peace: Essays on Kant's Cosmopolitan Idea*, ed. James Bohman and Matthias Lutz-Bachmann (MIT Press, 1997).

Jurgen Habermas, "Reply to Grimm," in *The Question of Europe*, ed. Peter Gowan and Perry Anderson (Verso, 1997), 259.

E. J. Hobsbawm, *Nations and Nationalism Since 1780: Programme, Myth, Reality* (Cambridge University Press, 1990).

Eric Hobsbawm, "Mass Producing Traditions: Europe, 1870–1914" in *The Invention of Tradition*, ed. Eric Hobsbawm and Terence Ranger (Cambridge University Press, 1983), 263.

How Europeans See Themselves: Looking through the Mirror with Public Opinion Surveys (European Commission, 2001).

Ronald Inglehart et al., *Human Values and Beliefs: A Cross-Cultural Sourcebook: Political, Religious, Sexual, and Economic Norms in 43 Societies: Findings from the 1990–93 World Values Survey* (University of Michigan Press, 1998).

Milan Kundera, *The Art of the Novel* (Faber and Faber, 1988), 127–128.

"La condamnation de la France pour 'torture' embarrasse le gouvernement," *Le Monde*, July 30, 1999.

John Laughland, "British Law Should Not Be Undermined by these Euro Outsiders; Human Rights Ruling Destroys Our Freedom," *The Express*, May 7, 2001.

John Laughland, "European Court of Human Rights: The Creeping Revolution," *The Mail on Sunday* (February 13, 2000).

Charles Leben, "Is there a European Approach to Human Rights?" in *The EU and Human Rights*, ed. Philip Alston (Oxford University Press, 1999).

Frank I. Michelman, "Morality, Identity and 'Constitutional Patriotism,'" 76 *Denver University Law Review* 1009 (1999).

Hugh Muir, "Tory Anger as Europe Backs Caned Boy," *Daily Telegraph*, September 10, 1996.

Roy Mulholland, "British Home Secretary's Week of Embarrassing Court Reverses," Agence France-Presse, November 16, 1996.

Joshua Rozenberg and Peter Foster, "Fury as European Court Awards 10,000 Pounds to IRA Men's Families," *Daily Telegraph*, May 5, 2001.

H. G. Schermers, *The European Commission of Human Rights from the Inside: Some Thoughts on Human Rights in Western Europe* (Hull University Press, 1990).

Anthony D. Smith, *National Identity* (University of Nevada Press, 1991).

Andrew Sparrow and Stephen Oldfield, "40,000 Pound Present for IRA Families," *London Daily Mail*, December 27, 1995.

Chapter 17

Robert Blackburn and Jorg Polakiewicz, *Fundamental Rights in Europe: The ECHR and Its Member States, 1950–2000* (Oxford University Press, 2001).

Kevin Boyle, Tom Hadden, and Paddy Hillyard, *Law and State: The Case of Northern Ireland* (Martin Robertson, 1975).

Antonio Cassese, "The Impact of the European Convention on Human Rights on the International Criminal Tribunal for the former Yugoslavia," in *Protecting Human*

Rights: The European Perspective, ed. Paul Mahoney et al. (Carl Heymanns Verlag, 2000), 213.

Council of Europe, "Execution of Judgments of the European Court," http://www.coe.int/T/E/Human_rights/execution/.

Mary Ann Glendon, *Rights Talk: The Impoverishment of Political Discourse* (Free Press, 1991), 148.

Global Initiative to End All Corporal Punishment for Children, "Key Judgments," http://www.endcorporalpunishment.org/pages/hrlaw/judgments.html.

Vikki Jackson, "Could I Interest You in Some Foreign Laws? Yes Please, I'd Love to Talk to You," *Legal Affairs* 40 (July/August 2004).

Anthony Lester, "The Overseas Trade in the American Bill of Rights," 88 *Columbia Law Review* 537 (April 1988).

Anthony Lester, "Thirty Years On: The East African Asians Case Revisited," 2002 *Public Law* 52.

Anthony Lester and David Pannick, *Human Rights Law and Practice* (Butterworths, 1999), chapter 1.

Richard B. Lillich, "Here and There: The Constitution and International Human Rights," 83 *American Journal of International Law* 851 (October 1989).

Joseph S. Nye Jr., "The Power We Must Not Squander," *New York Times*, January 3, 2000.

Joseph S. Nye Jr., *Soft Power: The Means to Success in World Politics* (Public Affairs, 2004).

Richard Posner, "Could I Interest You in Some Foreign Laws? No Thanks, We Already Have Our Own Laws" *Legal Affairs* 43 (July–August 2004).

G. Ress, "The Effects of Judgments and Decisions in Domestic Law," in *The European System for the Protection of Human Rights*, ed. R. St. J. Macdonald et al. (Martinus Nijhoff, 1993).

Javier H. Rubinstein, "Global Litigation: International law's New Importance in the U.S.; The Supreme Court's Latest Term Provides the Most Recent Example," *National Law Journal*, September 15, 2003.

Anne-Marie Slaughter, *A New World Order* (Princeton University Press, 2004), 80–81.

Anne-Marie Slaughter, "Judicial Globalization," 40 *Virginia Journal of International Law* 1103 (Summer 2000).

Thomas Sowell, "Who Needs Europe?" *Wall Street Journal*, August 25, 2003.

Henry J. Steiner and Philip Alston, eds., *International Human Rights in Context: Law, Politics, Morals*, 2nd ed. (Oxford University Press, 2000).

Eva Steiner, "France," in *European Civil Liberties and the European Convention on Human Rights: A Comparative Study*, ed. C. A. Gearty (Martinus Nijhoff, 1997), 267.

Tim Wu, "Foreign Exchange: Should the Supreme Court Care What Other Countries Think?" *http://www.slate.com*, April 9, 2004.

INDEX

About the Author

Michael D. Goldhaber is a Senior International Correspondent at *The American Lawyer* magazine, where he previously served as Chief European Correspondent. Mr. Goldhaber is a graduate of Columbia Journalism School (1997), Yale Law School (1993), and Harvard College (summa cum laude, 1990). He writes widely on legal affairs, with a focus on human rights and international arbitration.